D0271411

Armed
Services
and
Society

Armed
Services
and
Society

Martin
Edmonds

1988
Leicester University Press

First published in 1988 by
Leicester University Press

Copyright © Leicester University Press 1988

Designed by Geoffrey Wadsley
Filmset in Linotron 101 Plantin
Printed and bound in Great Britain by
Biddles Ltd, Guildford and King's Lynn

British Library Cataloguing in Publication Data
Edmonds, Martin, 1939–
Armed services and society.
1. Society. Role of military forces
I. Title
306'.27

ISBN 0–7185–1266–9

Contents

Preface

This volume on armed services and society was written with three objectives in mind: the first, and most important, was to provide a text for undergraduate and postgraduate students on the relationship between society on the one hand, and one of its most powerful, symbolic, permanent and distinctive institutions on the other. The second, recognizing that all societies almost bar none have armed forces (even Andorra has two men to fire the state ceremonial canon!), was to offer a comprehensive guide to identifying the more pertinent questions about the subject, and to serve as a helpful introduction to more fruitful ways in which reasonably authoritative – or at least convincing – answers might be found. To this end, it seeks not only to give a fair and accurate summary of the contributions of other scholars, but also to offer some novel approaches of my own, approaches that many of my students have found useful and have used to good effect. The third objective was to try and convey something of the fascination, excitement and variety that the subject holds for those who think of giving it their attention.

But more than all this, I have also tried to convey something of the relevance and, moreover, the importance of the subject. As Chapter 1 demonstrates, it is not just an interdisciplinary study of comparative government, contemporary sociology, modern political history, organizational behaviour, constitutional law, or science and technology policy all rolled into one. It is a subject that goes most of the way towards an understanding of why individual states consistently spend up to a quarter, and often up to a half, of their public resources on their armed services; why, collectively, almost a quarter of the world's gross national product (GNP) is spent on the capacity to wage war; why there have, at the last count, been over 170 wars in the last 40 years; why over 70 of the world's states are directly governed by armed servicemen; and, finally, why the capability to destroy the world is left in the custody of armed servicemen, even if the authority (but not the ability) to decide on their actual use is left to others. None of these important and, I would suggest, basic questions about today's world can be satisfactorily addressed without a comprehensive background knowledge of the relationship between armed services and society.

The book has been structured as logically as possible. This proved a more problematical task than I had originally thought, in part because of the range and complexity of the subject and in part because there was all too frequently a tendency to repetition. Indeed, parts of Chapter 4 in my original scheme (which addressed what I judged to be salient variables affecting armed services and society relationships) became repeated in Chapters 5 and 6, in which I developed novel frameworks for analysis. Had these variables not been salient, the credibility of my frameworks would have been very suspect. Reluctantly, I excised Chapter 4 completely, and rewrote Chapters 5 and 6 so that salient variables, such as national security and legitimacy, assumed a more central part in the discussion. Theories of civil–military relations, my original Chapter 5 moved forward to become Chapter 4.

I owe an explanation for the exclusion of footnotes. Although influenced by the passing observation of a Manchester colleague many years ago that the value of any academic work is inversely proportional to the number of footnotes, I felt that the text should speak for itself. Where I use or refer to the contributions of others, which I do frequently, I decided that they should be where they properly belonged, that is in the text, and not lurking in the shadows of some endnote or footnote, or extended list of references at the back of the book. Nonetheless, I have included a bibliography with each chapter, so that readers will know where to go for further study. Since the book is predominantly about theory and method, rather than being a heavily documented case study, the scholarly necessity for source references was minimal.

Armed Services and Society was many years in preparation; 21 years, in fact. Such a length of time might raise a few eyebrows, but it does not represent yet another author driving his publisher to the point of despair – though I freely confess to have taken advantage of my editor's patience and forbearance somewhat – but to the time that I first started teaching undergraduate special subject third-year and postgraduate Master's courses on civil–military relations (course 319) in the Politics Department at the University of Lancaster.

During that time 178 students have studied the subject with me, and in their separate and collective ways have helped me to expand and improve my knowledge and understanding of this ever-changing, rich, absorbing and highly relevant subject. Without their intellectual curiosity in security matters, genuine fascination for armed forces and the services, and a sincere concern for a proper and balanced relationship between society and the military, my own appreciation would have been so much the poorer. Indeed, the courses upon which this volume is based were structured in such a way as to raise what I judged to be the important questions, and to introduce my students to the theories, models and approaches to the subject that would give them the opportunity – for many their very first chance – to do their own substantive piece of research.

In this way we created a synergistic relationship: I pointed the way and provided the necessary tools; my students reciprocated with impressive initiative, astonishing determination and enthusiasm, and a level of scholarly integrity of the very highest order. Their consistently high results confirmed that. I was never let down or disappointed, and have been left a legacy of those many years, not only in the weighty form of 178 15,000-word dissertations on subjects ranging from Chinese war lords to Columbian military coups, First World War poetry to opposition to the Vietnam War, and Women in Armed Forces to the German *Reichswehr*, but also in the knowledge that many have continued with their interest in the subject on graduating, either out of intellectual interest or professionally, as teachers and lecturers. They have given me many fulfilling years and many warm memories. It is to them all that this volume is dedicated – the only way I have been able to show my profound gratitude.

But thanks are also due to the many others who have, directly or indirectly, made the course and, therefore, this volume possible. My first acknowledgment must go to Sammy Finer, my professor at UCNS (Keele University) whose course 'Man on Horseback' (itself later a book) in my second undergraduate year inspired my interest in armed services and politics. Even so, it would never have occurred to me to devise and develop my own course on the subject had not Philip Reynolds invited me to introduce it when I arrived at Lancaster in 1966. To him, and then to Peter Campbell (the course's first external examiner who permitted and went on to encourage me to employ the compulsory dissertation option as an integral part of course teaching when many were opposed to the idea as being too 'radical' and administratively inconvenient), I owe another early debt of gratitude.

In 1974 I was given the rare opportunity by the Ministry of Defence (MoD) under its Lectureship in Higher Defence Studies Scheme to develop further the subject of civil–military relations. This was a privileged appointment inasmuch as it accorded me the resources to purchase materials and books, and supported my endeavours to give my students access to some firsthand knowledge of the subject of their study and inquiry. To Professor Peter Nailor, who appointed me to that post, and successive MoD administrative staff with whom I had the benefit of working for 14 years, not least the late Julian Armitage-Smith, Trevor Cliffe, Clive Ponting and Gloria Franklin, and their executive staffs, I also record my thanks. Although coming somewhat after the event, this volume at least finally reveals something of what I was doing under their sponsorship, if not exactly in their name.

One irreplaceable asset that the Defence Lectureship Scheme afforded me was secretarial assistance. For 14 years I was privileged to have the support of four very dedicated people. Their commitment to the course, my students and my endeavours was beyond mere call of duty. I was privileged to have it, and it was support that I deeply valued. Each in her own distinctive, personal way, prepared many books, articles, chapters, and, of course, notes on civil–military relations, defence studies and strategy, and cared for and organized a burgeoning library of documents, mimeographical papers, articles, journals, press cuttings and miscellaneous ephemera that I compulsively collected all the time.

To those who helped in this capacity when I started, Kathleen Lord and Hazel Walker, and those with me under the Defence Lectureship Scheme, Jackie Townson, Lesley Hoyle, Valerie Robinson and Lynda Crabtree, and to Susan Parkinson, ever there in an emergency, I want to take this opportunity to say that all they have done has not been taken for granted; and if this volume does anything it says a big 'thank you' for putting up with me over the years. But of Lynda Crabtree special mention must be made: it was upon her shoulders that the burden of converting my scrawl into a manuscript fell, a task that she accepted with quite remarkable equanimity and executed with great skill.

Over the years, most of my students have suggested changes in structure, content, emphasis or interpretation – and I am notorious for changing my mind or contradicting myself. I cannot list all 178 names, and it would be invidious to single out any one person or group of people. I would like to think they know who they are anyway. But a number of academic colleagues have discussed with me aspects of my teaching of the subject and this is reflected in the book. They deserve mention: Roger Beaumont, Lucien Mandeville, Wilfred von Bredow, Richard Little, Michael Dillon, Michael Elliott-Bateman, 'Bayo Adekanye, Bob McKinlay, Cathy Downes, John Erikson, Catherine Kelleher and Roger Williams. Numerous external examiners also have contributed: Peter Campbell, the late Brian Chapman, Peter Nailor, Bill Tordoff, Gwyn Harries-Jenkins, Roy Jones and Jack Spence.

Two valued colleagues have given me direct help with the book itself: James Higgs and John Gooch. I am sorry to have put our friendship to the test, but admire their diplomacy in pointing out errors of fact or judgment and appreciate their advice. They must take no blame for any indiscretions contained herein. John Illingworth of the University of Lancaster Library for 21 years has helped me and all my students get material on civil–military relations from all around the world. I wish to thank him for his tireless efforts, individual help and professional dedication.

My thanks must go to Peter Boulton, Secretary to Leicester University Press, for his patience and understanding when the volume got into difficulty, his highly professional editorial staff, and the University Press Committee both for their invitation and their confidence that I could deliver something worthwhile. To my wife, Eve, and children, Matthew, Rebecca and Daniel, go my thanks for their empathy when things were not turning out as I had first intended. And finally, I should record that neither Porridge nor Digby were any help at all – except in so much as they kept me company through the early hours of many a morning when Chapter 4 proved beyond my intellectual powers to sort out.

Martin Edmonds

Reader in Political and Defence Studies,
Politics Department, University of Lancaster

December 1987

1

Introduction: Questions and Assumptions

This book sets out to show that the relationship of armed forces and society is extremely rewarding to study in its own right, and that it is relevant to a better understanding and appreciation of other areas of social and political inquiry. In other words, it is a subject that holds hidden promises and even surprises that should attract students and scholars from a wide variety of disciplines.

Why, then, study the relationship of armed forces and society? What are its benefits? Perhaps the best answer to these questions lies in the content of this book as a whole; for the moment, however, it must rest with a series of assertions, the justifications for which will become explicit later. The subject should appeal to those who have an interest in war, either as a subject of study for its own sake or as a focus of concerned moral and intellectual attention in today's nuclear age. But what is the connection between polemology – the study of war – and the relationship between armed forces and society? How can the latter improve and enlarge an understanding of the former?

With a little reflection, the connection should become obvious: war, society and the armed forces are inseparable and interrelated. War, a subject that has commanded the attention of most major thinkers and intellectuals throughout recorded history, may be defined as the use of violence, or physical coercion, by a state, a society or a group against another to achieve a desired objective. It is a physical means employed by one group or society against another and, as such, it is not, nor ever can be, independent of their internal affairs. A decision whether or not to resort to war, or to use violent means for whatever reason, rests to a high and significant degree on that society's own nature and values. Some societies or their governments have, over time, displayed a greater propensity than others to resort to violence to achieve their objectives, for any number of ideological, geopolitical and cultural reasons. Others, which might be considered more pacific in their

1

approaches to their relations with outside bodies, have demonstrated nonetheless a resolute determination to protect and defend themselves by physical means against real, or perceived, predators. In either case, whether for offence or defence, the organized use of force and violence against outsiders is the principal, if not exclusive, function of the armed forces of society, or, tcday, of the nation-state.

If a society, or nation-state, perceives that war is a possibility – and history shows conclusively that a state of peace cannot be taken for granted and that violent conflict is more a probability than a possibility at some time or other – then it acquires for itself armed forces. In the process, *ipso facto*, it gains possession of a structured and organized body of men and, thereby, a coercive capability which affords it the option to apply physical force as a means to achieve a wide range of desired objectives. It is frequently argued that in today's world of superpower confrontation, and because of the enormous costs involved, the possession of a military capability is a clear, if not the only, positive and quantifiable indication of a readiness to use physical force for political objectives. Assuming this to be the case, the very existence of armed forces within a society therefore alters the perceptions of the members of that society, not merely about other societies, but in particular about its own status and ability to take unilateral action within the international community. In simple terms, military capability spells power, and the possession of power alters attitudes, contributing sometimes to an unintentional but inexorable slide towards war between societies.

A society that acquires a military capability, either as a matter of prudence to defend itself against predators or as a necessary condition of maintaining and enforcing the rule of law internally, also builds for itself the option to use force as a means to achieve any number of political objectives. When a decision is taken to employ that armed force against outsiders, it is in effect a decision to go to war. The likelihood is also that the other party will, to the best of its ability, take reciprocal action to defend itself and its perceived vital interests. This is essentially the phenomenon known more commonly as the 'security dilemma', whereby military action taken by one society, or state, to defend itself and its interests becomes the *raison d'être* for others to do likewise. In other words, the existence of permanent armed forces, or the residual industrial and technological capability to acquire them at relatively short notice, in some form, becomes a self-fulfilling prophecy of conflict: sustained peace cannot be guaranteed while there are armed forces, and armed forces exist because of the possibility of conflict and war. The problem of putting an end to war and achieving perpetual

2

peace has not yet been solved; and despite some of the claims made for policies of deterrence and the constraints on military adventurism introduced by weapons of mass destruction, it is unlikely to be resolved with any acceptable guarantee in the foreseeable future. The outcome of all this – desirable or otherwise – is that armed forces will continue as a permanent and accepted feature of modern nation-states.

The relevance of the 'security dilemma' to the study of the relationship of armed forces to society lies in the influence that the existence of armed forces continues to have in shaping people's perceptions of the 'security dilemma' itself. Herein lies the 'Catch-22': the armed forces of any state are normally charged with the responsibility for the security and protection of the population against external threat; they have consequently an incentive to acquire and maintain as much military capability as possible, often expressed in terms of their planning on the basis of a 'worst case analysis'. The challenge is always to have an adequate and prepared capability (men and weapons) on call at relatively short notice to meet all anticipated contingencies. Prudence might suggest at face value that this is the best course to follow. Certainly, there is enough historical precedent to demonstrate that failure to do so invites opportunism on the part of others. Paradoxically, the more extensive these provisions become, the greater the threat they pose to other societies; correspondingly, the military response of those other societies also increases. The outcome, all things being equal, is one of no appreciable advantage by way of increased protection and security to either party over time, though both could likely have an additional economic and opportunity cost to bear. Furthermore this predicament has heralded what is customarily known as the 'arms race', a phenomenon that is often explained simply in terms of the 'action–reaction' hypothesis.

The self-evident consequence of the security dilemma and the arms race is that the immediate beneficiaries are the armed forces themselves. The security dilemma, in effect, ensures *ab initio* that those who serve in the ranks of the armed forces have a 'job for life', a particular status within society, and an immense potential economic, political and social influence. Only when war breaks out does the issue of job security, in a direct and brutal way, come into question; in this instance, a concomitant of military service is an acceptance of an 'unlimited liability' as a condition of employment. One advantage that a strategy of deterrence has given to the armed forces is job security with a diminished likelihood of actually having to fight in a war, and, frequently, a role that carries no greater physical danger than that facing civilians. Were deterrence to fail, the weapons of mass destruction that might possibly be used in the ensuing conflict make the traditional distinction between military and civilian less marked. The notion of the frontline of battle in war has long since disappeared – arguably since the introduction of the long-range bomber. Given, therefore, the partial interest of armed forces in the security dilemma (its continuation and, under some circumstances, its intensification), their relationship with society becomes an issue of vital importance. With such considerations as estimates of external threats and the determination of the appropriate long-term military and strategic responses, this military self-interest becomes especially relevant.

Awareness of the potential self-interest of armed forces in the maintenance of the structure of the present international system and the continuing security dilemma has increased over the past 40 years. Frequent references to a widening militarization of Western society and to the existence in the more economically advanced states of a phenomenon referred to as the 'military–industrial complex', reflect this awareness. Furthermore, public debates in Britain, Europe and elsewhere over the definition of the military threat to the West from the Soviet Union, particularly in respect of nuclear weapons and the logic of deterrence theory, indicate a widened public appreciation of the influence of armed forces on national security planning, science and technology policy, and public expenditure generally on defence. This public interest is stimulated by governments' increasing use of terms such as 'national security' and 'official secrets' to justify a wide range of executive action about which they are reluctant to provide information.

A first reason, therefore, why the relationship between armed forces and society should be studied is that it offers an insight, and, possibly, a significant causal explanation for the continuation, characteristics and intensity of the international security dilemma. And, as a consequence, it can simultaneously throw light on the maintenance of, and, more-over, acceleration in, the international arms race; the value nation states currently place upon high defence spending during times of peace; and the retention of trained equipped professional armed forces and reserves, all of whom are held at a constant and high state of readiness by so many of the world's governments. If we accept Clausewitz's dictum that 'state policy is the womb in which war develops', therefore, a full understanding and appreciation of the relationship between armed forces and society in both general and specific terms is a necessary condition of the proper and full understanding of the role of war in international relations.

The study or armed forces and society does not end just with its contribution to the wider study of war and international relations.

Arguably, its major and most important contribution is in respect of the study of domestic politics and comparative government. A glance at the current membership of the United Nations should reveal not merely the absolute increase in members since its inception in 1945, but, more significantly, the large number that are directly ruled by the military, or that are dependent indirectly upon military backing and support. Indeed, it is almost the case that civilian government, a condition taken for granted by the more advanced industrial Western states of Europe and North America, is the exception rather than the rule. This was a revelation first highlighted in Samuel Finer's pioneering, and now classic, study of the intervention of the military in politics, *The Man on Horseback* (1962). Addressing the question of why it was that armed forces intervened so frequently in the domestic politics of modern states, and invariably supplanted the civilian government with one of their own making, or introduced direct military rule, he soon came to the conclusion that this pattern of events was more often the norm. His observation immediately drew attention to the fundamental point about armed forces, namely, that even whilst ostensibly under civilian control, as provided for under constitutional legal provision, they represent a significant, and generally major, source of power. It is this power that also is to be found at the root of much political influence.

The problem, as Finer went some way to demonstrate, is considerably more complex. It is not simply a question of whether or not armed forces take over the functions of government, but the extent to which they have concerns, as any other interest articulation or pressure group, with a whole variety of national issues that extend far beyond immediate matters of defence, strategy and security. No matter how much it is considered preferable that issues of concern to armed forces should be separate and independent of civil affairs, experience and reality demonstrate that such a marked distinction is both inaccurate and distorting.

Leaving aside the interest that armed forces have in projecting their own views on and interpretations of *Weltanschauung*, the world and potential external threats, there are numerous other areas where they have intimate and positive interest. These inevitably involve them in the broader arena of domestic politics. For example, expenditure on defence, especially if it is high relative either to total public expenditure or to gross domestic product (GDP), adduces an influence to armed forces which is, if circumstances allow, open to wide political and economic exploitation. Areas such as scientific and technological research and development, industrial output, regional development, civil construction, communications, and so on, are of direct interest and concern to armed forces, as well as to the civil organizations more immediately involved. These areas may have security implications, but it need not necessarily be the case. Another example is that of education, not merely in its national purposes but also its relevance to military requirements. As Cynthia Enloe has pertinently pointed out in her study *Ethnic Soldiers*, the deliberate use of armed forces as a means of population control for political purposes (through conscription and relocation), has been a common feature in many a state, irrespective of its age, traditions, or wealth.

There is a strong propensity for the older, more mature, Western states to assume a high degree of professionalism within their armed forces, and to ascribe to them in law the clearly defined purpose of defending society against external attack. The idea of armed forces employed by the governments of these states for domestic political purposes is still seldom contemplated, except by those of a particular ideological persuasion. Seen from this perspective, armed forces are viewed no more and no less than as a state institution. As such, they are neither independent of the state itself, nor neutral in the sense that the constitutional provisions which define and delineate political power and authority within the state reflect, and are founded upon, a particular ideology. When the use of armed forces by governments is justified in terms of 'defending democracy', it is a particular view, or inter-pretation, of democracy that they have in mind. In the West, this is a brand of liberal democracy which, *inter alia*, holds the armed forces of the state to be subservient to civilian political authority at all times, and explains why great anxiety is generated when armed forces are felt to be acting in secret and without accountability.

Any group within society, from the extreme Left to the extreme Right of the political spectrum, that challenges not so much the policies of the government, but its authority as set out in the constitution, also challenges the very foundation upon which the armed forces of the state are based. The use of armed force by governments against such domestic political challenges has become an increasing phenomenon in recent years. Political extremism is certainly not new; there have been plenty of political revolutions in the past. But what have changed are the tactics that political groups have adopted and are using today, including terrorism and guerrilla warfare. The moral, political and material support which is afforded these highly active groups from external sources as a form of 'state sponsored terrorism' is also increasing, as is the inability of the domestic institutions usually responsible for the maintenance of domestic law and order (pre-dominantly the Police) to contend with, monitor, or control, the situation. Nevertheless, the militarization of the Police and their being armed with specialized equipment and weapons is an increasingly frequent phenomenon almost everywhere.

When armed forces become involved in internal conflicts, or are employed to intervene in such domestic political crises as industrial strikes, trade union demonstrations, separatist movements, or breakdowns in law and order orchestrated by extremist political groups, the relationship between them and society, particularly open ones, changes significantly. The use of armed forces in these domestic situations is on the increase, with a proliferation of both official and unofficial paramilitary organizations concerned with domestic security and order. For this reason the study of the relationship of armed forces and society immediately takes on a new dimension, and may become one of profound concern to students of politics, law, public administration and comparative government.

The scope of such studies, however, is not restricted to the politics of Western, liberal democratic states. One of the essential features of the study of armed forces is that, almost without exception, every state, and even primitive society, has possessed an organized armed force in one form or another. This means that the study of the relations between armed forces and society has an important anthropological and historical dimension, as well as a contemporary political, social and economic one. For analytical purposes, states are frequently typed and grouped according to one or other taxonomy: the more usual ones are identified according to the nature of their political systems, or to the extent of their economic development. For the student of politics, states tend to be divided for analytical purposes depending on whether or not they are, for example, 'liberal democratic', 'socialist', or 'fascist' according to the former; or 'emerging', 'underdeveloped' or 'less developed', on the strength of the latter. Irrespective of which typology is used, the simple fact remains that all states have armed forces in one or other form; this, then, offers clear scope for cross-national comparisons based on their armed forces, an approach which is not always so readily available when other political institutions are used, such as parties, legislatures and bureaucracies.

Cross-national comparisons based on differences and similarities between armed forces present one opportunity; another is to use the relationship between armed forces and society within different categories of states: for example, the role and function of armed forces in totalitarian states and their relationship with a single party system. Studies of this nature have tended to reveal that armed forces in communist and fascist states play a significant, and sometimes determining, role in domestic politics in addition to their immediate defence function. Then, they can also be studied in contrast with liberal or pluralist states.

Arguably, however, most work to date on the influence of armed forces in domestic politics has been directed at Third World, 'emerging', and 'less developed' states. There is one obvious reason for this: it is in these states, categorized by Finer in *The Man on Horseback* as being of 'low' or 'minimal' political culture, that armed forces have mostly intervened in the affairs of government. Their intervention has not just been the behaviour of a pressure, or interest articulation, group, operating on a day-to-day basis. More frequently than is the case in the more advanced and 'mature' states, they have acted politically, either to supplant the civilian government with another of which they approve, or to replace it with a military regime or junta made up of their own members. In such instances the armed forces invariably have had to suspend the state constitution in the first instance, and subsequently substitute an alternative of their own design.

These less developed states are the more obvious, and therefore the more frequent, subjects for the study of armed forces and society. Not only do the armed forces in such states tend to be more overtly politically active, but the study of politics within them cannot properly or satisfactorily be accomplished without their armed forces being given close attention. Significantly, it is in these states that the external role of armed forces is generally only of minor significance. But there is more to the study of armed forces in less developed states than merely *coups d'état* and military regimes. During the 1960s interest expanded: this was stimulated to a large degree, first, by a surge of altruism on the part of a United States administration which had a practical concern to provide financial and material aid to newly independent Third World states; secondly, there arose the academic challenge to provide for that administration, and for concerned American philanthropic foundations, prescriptions of priorities for the effective economic and political development of what came to be called the 'Third World'.

Doubtless there were ideological as well as purely philanthropic motives behind this largely American initiative. Nevertheless, one important conclusion among others emerged from their studies: the role and function of armed forces in underdeveloped and emergent countries as nationbuilders should not be underestimated. In much the same way as the US Army Corps of Engineers had played a significant role in the development and building of a communications infra-structure in the United States and had helped to push the frontier West whilst the rest of the US Army maintained some semblance of domestic order, so too did the armed forces contribute in a practical way to modernization in such states as Brazil, Indonesia and the sub-Saharan states of Africa. In the transition from traditional social, political and economic structures of these independent, Third World states, the armed forces have assumed a leading role, and have contributed markedly to the maintenance of stability during periods of sometimes political turbulence, economic difficulty and rapid social change. For students of development, as for those interested in international relations, strategic studies, comparative government and the history of warfare, the study of the relationship between armed forces and society offers rich dividends.

In recent years, a new area of study has opened up, for which a better understanding of the relationship between armed forces and society offers valuable and important insights. As a direct consequence of the Cold War confrontation between East and West after the Second World War, the realization of the decisive influence of science and technology on the outcome and, in particular, the effect of weapons of mass destruction upon strategic thinking, today's advanced industrial states have found it necessary to break with the traditions of the past and maintain, both at home and abroad, large, expensive and professional peacetime standing armed forces, ready and equipped with the latest weapons. Several consequences have followed from this phenomenon, not least of which are those noted above, including the international arms race, the increasing use of armed forces for internal security purposes, and the enlarged influence exercised by armed forces on the political, economic and social life of modern states.

The perceived imperative, however, to maintain vigilance in a hostile world of irreconcilable ideologies, and to deter aggression through denial or retribution, now places a high premium on pure and applied scientific research, applied technology and the development of novel weapons systems. Over the past 40 years the advanced industrial states in the main have found it necessary to allocate increasing proportions of their human, material and financial resources in pursuit of the acquisition of weapons of immense sophistication and destructive potential. The rationale has been, crudely, to maintain a 'state of equilibrium' – some would say in the special context of Russo–American relations a 'balance of terror' – with perceived adversaries. In the process, a vast industrial and scientific infrastructure has emerged within each state, which has close links with its armed forces.

Those who form part of this new infrastructure, and the organizations within it, have found themselves with considerable political influence, an influence that has a bearing not merely on government priorities generally, and military and strategic policies specifically, but more especially on the decisions about the priorities of future scientific research. Bearing in mind that the work of this immensely influential technical and scientific community is customarily done in secret, on the grounds that public knowledge of the content and details of its work would be prejudicial to the security of the state, its place within the pattern of relations between the armed forces and society is a constructive place to begin to study how the direction and thrust of scientific research priorities is determined today.

The study of the relationship of armed forces and society is not without theoretical interest either. Machiavelli stands out among many political theorists from his early recognition, based upon his own experience of the *condottieri* in the Italian city states during the sixteenth century, that the relationship between those with political authority and those with control over coercive force (the military) is fundamental to any prescription for a well-ordered and effectively governed state. Indeed, Machiavelli himself proffered sound advice to those in power when he suggested that the only successful way to retain political authority, even when they had popular support, was to keep a firm control over the armed forces. With the emergence of the nation-state, a phenomenon itself a product of military developments, Machiavelli's practical prescriptions were followed by the monarchs, princes and leaders of the day. One prudent course they took was to ensure, through legislation, an absolute monopolistic control over the manufacture of munitions and gunpowder. It is no coincidence, for example, to find that the oldest office in the British Army is that of the Master General of the Ordnance, or that the old arsenals in France were, and many still are, state-controlled.

Close analysis of all the major political theorists since the sixteenth century will reveal that either war, or the consequence of violent conflict, prompted their argued prescriptions for good (or better) government. It is also noteworthy that their prescriptions for better government always placed great emphasis on strict control of armed forces. Some saw this control being the *sine qua non* of democratic government and popular sovereignty; others felt it was necessary for effective government. The works of Marx and Engels were unequivocal about the armed forces of a state being not just *an*, but *the*, essential feature of capitalism and imperialism; they saw the relationship between armed forces and the state, and the nature of the political system, as being synonymous. This perspective enabled Engels to note that students of politics who wished to find out where power and influence really lay in society, should look *first* at the armed forces. This was a point of view echoed almost a century later by Chairman Mao Tse-tung when leading his guerrilla campaign against the Chinese Nationalist government forces; he also recognized that, as political power came from the barrel of a gun, the critical question was always who controlled the gun.

The effect of physical coercion, and therefore by association of armed forces as its organized instrument, on the course of history has never been fully analysed. Some scholars, however, have attached significant importance to it: Robert Nisbet, for example, in his *Social Philosophers*, attributed the breakdown of kinship (*Gemeinschaft*) societies and the emergence of structured, hierarchical societies (*Gesellschaft*) to a combination of armed conflict and the necessary creation of organized armed forces. Stanislav Andreski went one stage further: in his study, *Military Organisation and Society*, he argued from the premise that the physical struggle for power, wealth and status has been omnipresent over time and that this has been the dominant motivating force behind human behaviour. For him, therefore, armed forces have been largely responsible for all significant changes in the historical development of human society.

In sum, there are very sound reasons indeed why the relationship between armed forces and society should be studied: ignorance, or a lack of understanding, of the relationship would leave a large and significant gap in the study of international relations, strategy, comparative government, public policy and administration, development and political theory. Furthermore, from a broader sociological, anthropological and historical perspective, study of the relationship has yet more to offer to our understanding of primitive societies, to questions of social culture, militarism and power elites. And yet the study of armed forces and society is not just of value as a means of gaining better insight into the workings of the world's societies and their political machinations; it can well stand as a subject worthy of study in its own right. Instead of being merely useful to improve understanding of other subjects, the study of armed forces and society justifiably stands as a single focus of concern; indeed, all other subjects and disciplines can contribute to an improvement of our understanding of what that relationship is, and how it came about. Reduced to its simplest terms, the study of a nation at war is synonymous with the study of armed forces and society: since the history of the twentieth century is largely one of total wars, and we live today in a state of global confrontation with the future of mankind potentially at stake, this extreme view is not as extravagant, or indulgent, as it may at first appear.

11

This is the sentiment behind the approach that has been adopted in this volume. It is assumed here that the armed forces of states have been a major factor in influencing the course of political, social and economic events, not just in today's world but over time. More often than not, it has been the major and dominant factor. The relationship between armed forces and society is of central concern both for purposes of description and explanation, and should be comprehensively and thoroughly studied. If this is successfully done, then the returns by way of insights into many other dimensions of the study of politics, sociology, social and political theory, and anthropology, are immense. Wherever armed forces are to be found and on whatever scale, there the interest and focus of this volume are to be found.

From this discussion of the reasons why relationships between armed forces and society should be studied, it can be concluded that the subject is eclectic and multidisciplinary. It draws analytical approaches from, and feeds back into, numerous disciplines. This is both its challenge and its fascination. The immediate problem now is how to address the subject, and to identify what questions should best be asked. This problem is in itself challenge enough; and the content of much of this volume is directed at posing both the most pertinent questions and finding suitable, if not satisfactory answers.

There are several good reasons for this approach, the more evident of which should already have become apparent from what has been noted above: first, armed forces have existed for as long as there have been men and women living in social groups. There is, in other words, a long history of challenging relationships between armed forces and society, and no one relationship can apply to all instances; it is for ever changing according to circumstances. Second, the concern here is not with one society or state, but with all societies and states. The teaching of social science emphasizes the uniqueness of each individual, each society and each state. No one person, society or state is exactly like another, for all their superficial similarities. The logical conclusion, therefore, is that each society or state, its armed forces, and the relationship between them, should be studied *sui generis*, at whatever moment in time. Such an approach, however, would immediately deprive the subject of its richness, analytic power and explanatory potential, particularly in its ability to draw comparisons and contrasts between different societies, and between different armed forces at different or similar points in time. The ultimate challenge, therefore, is to find or to formulate an overarching theory, and to design some analytical model, by which those factors, that are either contingent or necessary to the relationship between armed forces and society, can be identified, and their impact explained and assessed.

Civil–military relations – the relationship of armed forces and society – as a field of study is relatively new. Its emergence and expansion, like most subjects of inquiry, is a product of its social and political relevance on the one hand, and the development of new theories and analytical approaches within academic disciplines on the other. With regard to the former, the cost of today's armed forces, their permanence in large numbers, and the continued threat of war and violent conflict has ensured its being a focus of investigation, interest and concern. The latter is a direct consequence, first, of the emergence post-Second World War and rapid expansion of the social sciences and, second, the recognition that so much of what fundamentally affects society can only be understood from an interdisciplinary perspective.

The approach to the study of armed forces and society today cannot benefit greatly from looking at scholarly works written before the Second World War. Even then, not much of great analytical value was accomplished until the middle to late 1950s. This is not to say that scholars and analysts were not interested either in armed forces or in their complex relationship with society. There are numerous works before this time, mostly by historians, which examine in detail the interaction of the military and society, but these were written almost exclusively from a decision making perspective between military and political elites in time of war or international crisis. The focus then was on the pattern of argument and influence within a narrow, but powerful and exclusive, circle over decisions on how, when, and where wars might be declared and subsequently fought. No great concern outside political theory was given to the wider issue of the place of armed forces within society, except among a few German sociologists, and some from Durkheim's school of sociology in France. In Britain, the one notable exception was Herbert Spencer.

The impetus after the Second World War to the development of the study of civil–military relations was the coming together of three largely separate developments. The first was the Second World War itself and the immense intellectual effort that was put into understanding both why it had started, and why the outcome was not as intended. Within this, there were the subsidiary questions of the nature of the relationship between the Nazi Party and the Army in Germany; the issues raised over the political and military command and control over the Allied forces during the war; and the rediscovery of Clausewitz and the interrelationship of military means and political objectives, not only with regard to the future of Germany, but also after the Japanese surrender; the implications of strategic bombing; and the nuclear weapon. Each helped to focus attention on the military dimension of political and social life.

A second impetus was the development, principally in the United States, of the academic study of the social sciences. Although the intellectual study of society had existed for more than half a century before, it had not expanded in any systematic, extensive, or comprehensive way until after the Second World War. Indeed, even in the United States, universities and colleges were slow to adopt the study of sociology until well into the 1950s. Then, the major impetus came from a desire to understand better the United States itself; this came as a consequence of the depression, Roosevelt's New Deal policies, and the social, economic and political changes that occurred after the Second World War. With the acceptance of sociology as a legitimate and potentially fruitful field of study, a number of prominent scholars turned their attention to the study of the military as a social organism; among them the names of Morris Janowitz and S. Stouffer were to become prominent. Indeed, the experience of the American armed forces in war was to offer a fruitful field of sociological inquiry, and one which enabled the development of new approaches and methodologies.

As with every general statement that verges on the categorical, there is always an exception that disproves the rule. In this case, it would be grossly misleading not to mention Harold Lasswell, arguably one of the greatest names in the field of Western political science. Lasswell's most productive and imaginative period was in the late 1930s when he addressed the question why it was that the Weimar Republic had failed and Nazism had taken root. Following on earlier work on the power of propaganda in mobilizing the masses, Lasswell noted the link between the domestic and the international environments, particularly with regard to what was, and was not, acceptable to the majority of the population. This, in turn, became synthesized in a short article entitled 'The garrison–state hypothesis' published in 1941, a hypothesis that was to be revived with immense relevance and pertinence 21 years later with only minor modifications. In it, Lasswell warned of the general drift in the world towards a situation where decision making power within states would accrue to the 'specialists in violence', by which he meant more specifically the Police, the armed forces, and a small inner elite group of ideologues.

Although the study of society and social organisms expanded rapidly during the 1950s, specific interest in the military and its relations with society was not fully kindled until the late 1950s. To a marked extent, this interest can be closely linked to the publication of three books, each

14

published within two years of one another. The first was C. Wright Mills's *The Power Elite*. It was an attempt to provide a synthesis of the earlier elite theories of Marx, Mosca and Pareto, by concentrating on the major institutions of society, and the economic, political and social contexts within which they operated. On examining the USA and its various elites, Mills discovered a concentration of power and influence that was the product of what he referred to as an 'institutional landscape'. This, he discovered, was dominated by a coalition of the executive branch of government, the big industrial corporations and the military, brought together by a coalescence of common interests. In articulating this view, Mills was not just challenging the accepted belief among many Americans that pluralism and liberalism as a political prescription afforded the best protection of democracy and freedom; he also laid the foundation for the concept which later became known as the 'military–industrial complex'. His book helped significantly to create a greater public awareness of the extent of the centralization of decision making power and the concentration of influence within the United States.

It was indeed the realization that these post-Second World War developments presented a challenge to the fundamental principles underlying the American Constitution that largely prompted the other two books. Arguably the most widely read, if not influential, was Samuel Huntington's *The Soldier and the State*, published in 1957. Although presented as a theory of civil–military relations, its original intention was to put to the test the extent to which the democratic principles of the Founding Fathers had been undermined and compromised by the maintenance of a large, professional standing continental army within the North American continent and serving overseas. Traditionally, Americans had been raised to believe that standing armies were a threat to democracy; that, at least, had been the experience of the colonialists under British rule in the seventeenth and eighteenth centuries, for which reason the architects of the American Constitution had prescribed that no national army should be raised or maintained except in time of real and imminent threat. On the cessation of hostilities, the national army would be demobilized and disbanded. Whilst this had largely happened after the First World War, the difficulties over the future of Germany after the Second World War leading to overt confrontation with the Soviet Union, the containment of communism, and the era of the Cold War had determined that a break with this tradition was necessary. Huntington's examination of the implication of this break for democracy in the United States, whilst reassuring in his conclusions for Americans, nonetheless highlighted the importance of adequate political control over the armed forces in any state, and the need for healthy, open and stable civil–military relationships.

The third book, *The Professional Soldier* by Morris Janowitz, also addressed the basic question that was concerning more and more Americans at the time: were the four branches of the American armed forces becoming a threat to American democracy? Adopting a sociological approach, Janowitz focused less upon the relationship between the armed forces and American society, and more upon the armed forces as social organisms. By analysing the armed services themselves, their ideology, traditions, and organizational 'realities', Janowitz was able to demonstrate that they had changed in more ways than simply becoming a permanent, standing institution of the state. He concluded that they had collectively become a form of constabulary with more concern for their professional responsibilities, and in the officer corps for their narrow individual and collective career aspirations, than for any political motive inimical to the American Constitution.

The effect of these three books cannot, nor should they be, under-estimated. Theoretically, sociologically and politically they opened the door not only to a wide array of studies of the military and its relations with society, but also to a close examination of the political and social structures of states and of the exercise of power within them. Not that they were necessarily correct in their analysis or conclusions at the time or later, but the hallmark of all classical works is their pioneering contribution, and the extent to which they raise more questions than they answer, and the opportunities they open up for later scholarship.

Had there not been a kernel of truth in what these writers were saying about the perceived or real significance of the military in modern society, the field of civil–military relations would not have developed and expanded as a field of study to the extent or at the rate that it did. A number of developments within the United States and else-where contributed to this development, not least being President Eisenhower's televised farewell address on 17 January 1961, in which he warned the nation to guard against the acquisition of unwarranted influence by the military–industrial and scientific complex, and never to let the weight of this apparent common interest endanger the country's democratic process, or the liberties of the individual. The increasingly unpopular war in South-East Asia throughout the 1960s, high annual defence budgets over that decade, an accelerating and public arms race with the Soviet Union, and the maintenance of American forces throughout the world have, since, ensured that military considerations have remained high on the agenda of academics and commentators as well as politicians and the public in the United States ever since.

Without question it is the Americans who have taken the lead in the development of civil–military relations as a field of study. They have expressed the most profound concern with the tendency towards the militarization not just of their own society, but also that of other states. Nonetheless, academics from elsewhere have followed their lead and example, examining civil–military relations in their own states and beyond. With almost half the nations of the world governed by the military or their proxies, there has been no dearth of opportunity or of subject matter. Furthermore, as other subject areas have expanded, such as international relations, strategic studies, development studies and so on, so concern with civil–military relationships has also increased.

Reflecting and stimulating this expansion has been the important contribution of an international body – a fellowship – of scholars, military officers, *fonctionnaires*, civil servants, journalists and so on under the Inter-University Seminar on Armed Forces and Society. First founded by Morris Janowitz in the middle 1960s it has pioneered and sponsored the study of the relationship between the armed forces and society; its Journal, *Armed Forces and Society*, founded in 1976, has a high reputation for scholarship and is perhaps the best indicator of the intellectual stature of the field in its own right.

To summarize, the field of civil–military relations has become accepted as a subject of significance and importance. It is, furthermore, a subject that has become established with its own parameters and body of theory. Its reward is that it can stand both on its own as a subject in its own right, and as an approach to enlighten understanding in other fields of inquiry as well. The 'military factor' in its social, economic and political manifestations is, today, pervasive in all societies to a degree that is not always fully appreciated. If, by the time the end of this volume is reached, that degree is better appreciated, then my objective has been achieved.

All this, however, still begs the important question: how should the relationship between the armed forces – that is to say the military – and society be studied? What is the most fruitful way of structuring this volume? All that has already been intimated above is that the subject demands an interdisciplinary approach; it is concerned as much with the contemporary world as with the past, and its empirical base is as wide as there are armed forces as organizations, societies and events involving the military. Some organizing set of concepts and ideas is needed in order to analyse and make sense of this jungle (or should it be mountain?) of data, issues, problems and times.

The clue how to address this task lies in the traditional but effective approach of reverting to 'basic principles'. As Kurt Lang observed in his bibliographical review of military institutions and the study of war, the subject, civil–military relations, only has meaning if there is a clear differentiation between what is 'military' in an institutional sense, and the more encompassing civil, social order. Returning to basic principles, therefore, it would be prudent, if not expedient, to devote the next chapter to an examination of armed forces (the military *per se*) to establish what it is that distinguishes and differentiates them from other social organizations and state institutions. My approach will be to look first at the armed forces in the abstract, considering them in general, almost universal terms. They will be examined from a Manichaean standpoint – that is to say they will be seen first as an extreme at one end of a spectrum, at the other end of which is the archetypal 'civilian' institution. The purpose of this approach is to put to the test the proposition, first, that there is an imperative which dictates the dominant characteristics of *all* armed forces irrespective of the society they serve; and, second, that relatively little impinges on these dominant characteristics.

Conceptually, Chapter 2 views armed forces as being exclusive, functionally unique, distanced from society, and impervious to outside influences. From this perspective, relations between the parent society and its armed forces are, therefore, prescribed by their respective institutional boundaries, and are seen as an interaction of two, largely discrete entities which are legally and institutionally separate. This view must be seen in contrast with Chapter 3, which adopts the approach that the military is not separate from society, but an integral part of it. It considers that no distinction can usefully be made between armed forces and the society they serve; that is to say, the dominant characteristics of armed forces are assumed to be similar to, derived from, and indistinguishable from the parent society. When talking about the armed forces in this context, the society at large is the dominant variable. In effect, institutional boundaries between the armed forces and society are of secondary importance. Both are permeated. In some one party states, for example, it is unhelpful to differentiate between the party and state institutions where power or influence is concerned; the same principle applies generally to the societally based approach to civil–military relationships.

Both Chapters 2 and 3 are deliberately artificial constructs, and offer diametrically opposed approaches. They are two extreme points of view, but serve one important analytical purpose: they help to identify and isolate the salient variables within armed forces and society that bear on the pattern of relationships between them. Which of these variables, their combination and their weight will help in understanding the relationship between the armed forces of any particular state with the parent society at any point in time is the challenge facing the remainder of the book.

Chapter 4 looks at the more important theories of civil–military relations that have been developed over the past 20 years. Many of these theories, and the variables to which several of the authors attributed particular importance, or salience, provide the basis for Chapter 5, particularly those which were concerned more with the intervention of armed services in the role of governing, than in the wider context of armed services in society. Chapter 5, in fact, addresses the issue of armed services intervention in government, since it is that sphere of their 'extra-curricular' activity which has been given most prominence. It is the military's naked use of coercive power for political ends, and is the one that most attracts disapprobation, even in those instances where the military is seen as a revolutionary force. The chapter, however, takes issue with the conventional interpretation of what constitutes 'intervention', arguing that it gives to one sphere of military political activity – the tip of the iceberg, so to speak, too much importance. A model of military involvement is offered as an alternative, leading to a tentative hypothesis as to why the military get involved, and how.

Chapter 6 offers a novel overarching theory of civil–military relations, in the advanced industrial states on the one hand and the less developed countries on the other. The objective here is to identify the major issues in civil–military relations with which each group of states is confronted today; it does not attempt to analyse in any depth or detail any one or number of civil–military problems. Chapters 7 and 8 draw on the preceding two chapters and consider a number of core issues in the relationship between armed services and society which should give concern. The selected topics are conscientious objection to military service, public accountability (treated together in Chapter 7), and the military industrial complex and central organizations of defence, in Chapter 8. The final chapter addresses the problems of the relationships of armed forces and society in Third World states.

The postscript is a brief recapitulation, with an exhortation to those who have found the book interesting or relevant, to accept the challenge to inquire into armed services and their relationship with society. 'Go to it!' Delve into this rich and diverse field which has stimulated me, and many others, for so long. The rewards are rich and numerous.

2
Armed Services: The Organizational Dimension

Throughout Chapter 1, reference was made only to 'armed forces'. The title of this book, however, is 'Armed *Services* and Society'. This was entirely intentional; the term 'armed forces' is much more familiar to most people than 'armed services' and an abrupt change at the outset seemed undesirable. Even the general subject matter of this book is usually known by a different term – either as 'civil–military relations' or as 'armed forces and society'; therefore it seemed preferable at the outset to use these more common terms before embarking on a more precise discussion of how to refer to the subject matter. An explanation for the change of title, nevertheless, is clearly warranted. In the first instance, the decision to substitute 'armed services' for military was dictated largely by semantic considerations, and not just for its own sake. The term 'military' has been so widely used and has assumed so many different meanings, that it has virtually lost both its conceptual and its analytical utility. Over time, it has become imprecise and at best merely differentiates, by way of contrast, something that is not 'civil'.

If there were reasonable doubts about the utility of the term 'military', then obviously a better alternative had to be found. A number immediately offered themselves, such as 'armed forces', 'armed services', 'armies', and 'soldiers'. To determine which of these was the most suitable for a clear and rigorous understanding of the subject area of civil–military relations, the term 'military' itself needed first to be analysed. The normal process of refining concepts is to differentiate those elements necessary to its definition from those which are merely contingent: necessary elements are those which, if absent, would alter significantly the meaning of a word, term, or concept completely. Elements which are contingent tend merely to give them context and colour, and generally only figure as a consequence of common, everyday use and familiarity. The approach is similar to that found in the science of classification (taxonomy), where the objective is

20

the establishment of a set of principles with which to be able to differentiate one species or phenomenon from others, and from it, therefore, to construct a typology.

If, then, the question is posed, 'who, or what, are (or is) the military?', the answer cannot readily be found simply from common usage. The term has tended to be used generically and its meaning altered according to the context in which it is used. Compare, for example, the phrases 'the military in Sparta', 'world military expenditures', and 'military ranks': the military in Sparta certainly is not the same phenomenon as today's standing armies; world military expenditures encompass more than just the cost of armies; and 'military ranks' normally refers to army ranks, as opposed to those of navies, air forces or, even, the police. According to context, time and function, so the term 'military' assumes different meanings; it is for this reason that a more precise and universally acceptable one needs to be found.

Fundamentally, the search is for a *stipulative* concept; that is to say, a word with an attendant definition that serves the analytical, descriptive, and prescriptive purposes of this volume. A first step might be to explore whether or not the term 'military' means the same as 'armed forces'. So far, the latter has been used but without definition, relying on people's general idea of what the term means, which has been sufficient, so far, to put across the general line of argument. At this juncture, this is no longer adequate. 'Armed forces' was preferred initially over 'military' because it was more general, and therefore more relevant for a broad, wide-ranging discussion. It is normally employed to refer to any group, organization, or body of individuals that is structured in such a way as effectively to apply coercive means to achieve specific objectives. Such entities encompass a whole spectrum of standing military units of the state at one extreme, to street corner gangs at the other, with irregular, guerrilla-type groups and paramilitary organizations somewhere in between. Only the relative frequency with which the term tends to be associated with the armed services of the state enables it to assume institutional and constitutional/legal connotations. But with the prevalence, today, of the use of physical, violent and coercive means to prosecute and pursue political objectives, it has become preferable, if not necessary, to seek an alternative term, which is more specifically related to the organized coercive institutions of the state.

It was, therefore, advantageous to explore whether or not the term 'armed services' might be more suitable for the identification and analysis of the relationship between society at large and those institutions of the state charged with the principal responsibility of securing its protection against an external, or foreign, coercive threat. A first question was whether or not the word 'military' meant the same as 'armed services'? The answer had to be negative, since the latter, according to convention and legal terminology, refers to standing, permanent, trained, state organizations which have clearly defined duties and responsibilities, involving the application of coercive means to achieve political ends; the word 'military' is much too general to meet this requirement. Indeed, the word 'military', like the term 'armed forces', has been widely used to identify and describe groups that are neither permanent, nor of the state, as in such instances as, the 'military' arm of a national liberation movement or a criminal gang. Furthermore, the word 'military' is frequently used to cover all branches of the armed services – Army, Navy, Air Force, marines, strategic rocket forces, home service forces, border guards, and so on – whilst at other times it is used exclusively as a synonym for the Army. If the intention of this book is to focus on relations between the military as an institution charged with responsibilities for the physical protection of both the state from coercive threat or attack, and society, a term offering greater precision is required. The term 'armed services' would appear to meet this requirement as it provides greater precision.

If the concept of 'armed services', superficially at least, offers a more promising framework and, therefore, more analytical precision, the problem still remains to define, stipulatively, what the term 'armed services' means. In recent years, the terms 'military' and 'armed services' have had attached to them the notion of 'specialists – or managers – in the application in violence'. As a necessary condition, this definition is no more accurate a description of 'armed services' than it is of the 'military'; the obvious point is that neither is *exclusively* concerned with the specialist application or management of violence. Many other groups and organizations also manifest this characteristic, ranging from the Police, to security guards, to gangs and, even, certain categories of sporting societies and clubs. Simply to define armed services by their function, therefore, only invites overlap with other groups in society; further refinement, consequently, is therefore needed.

One of the most evident manifestations of armed services is their appearance; it is through their distinctive uniform and insignia that most people – civilians – differentiate them from other organizations. Whilst there may be sound functional and practical reasons for uniforms, both for those who serve in armed services and, more-over, for society at large, attire and symbols are only a contingent consideration. For example, armed services are not the only organizations to use exclusively distinctive attire. Furthermore, the uniforms normally associated with men and women who serve in the armed services are widely and even frequently worn by civilians as everyday practical wear. There is moreover an element that finds them sartorially attractive. Conversely, given the nature of modern terrorism and internal warfare, armed servicemen and women, often when on duty, are frequently required to wear civilian clothes as a matter of expedience as well as policy. In addition, there is an increasing number of civilian organizations adopting uniforms and working clothes which are scarcely distinguishable from those of the armed services; and, not infrequently, identical. Today's armed services do not necessarily any longer stand out in the crowd, from which the conclusion has to be drawn that the association of organizational function with outward, public appearance, whilst often distinctive in the case of armed services and prescribed in agreements and the international laws designed to govern and limit the conduct of war, is not a necessary condition of a definition of the term. Nevertheless, it is a useful starting point and gives discussion of armed services both colour and context.

It is one thing to be a specialist in violence; it is quite another to be a specialist in the *management* of violence. The point here is that a distinction must be drawn between, on the one hand, an individual or group that is, simply, violent and destructive in an uncontrolled and random manner, and, on the other, a specialism in the application of violent means in a controlled, deliberate, purposeful and constrained way. Further, there is the implicit distinction between individual behaviour and that of an organization in respect of the specialist use of violence. The armed services of a state are, without question, the specialists in the application of violence, but a violence that is either used as a threat or applied through an established, legally recognized organization that is both managed and controlled by a superior state authority. A further implication is the emphasis on the management of organized violence, rather than on the violence itself or the purposes for which it is employed. It is absolutely essential in any discussion of armed services to recognize that the ends for which they exist should not be confused with the means they employ.

'Armed services', as distinct from the term 'armed forces', carries a further important condition. 'Armed forces' is a term that can, and invariably does, also apply to *all* organized groups that have a specialism in the managed application of violence; what differentiates it from 'armed services' is that the latter applies specifically and exclusively to those institutions and organizations that belong to the state. Often the two are treated as if they were synonymous, and are used interchangeably. Stipulatively, 'armed services', as used here, refers only to those state organizations concerned with the managed application of violence to achieve the ends of state policy. This condition carries with it a further connotation, which is again necessary, namely the notion of legality.

As state organizations forming part of the official apparatus, and serving through the appropriate authority the public at large, the armed services are established by law. Normally, their existence is based on constitutional provisions that define the extent of their authority and sphere of competence and, on occasion, international legal provisions. The legal basis of armed services should not be confused, however, with their legitimacy. The two concepts should, ideally, be coexistent, but this has not always proved to have been the case in recent times. Legitimate or not, the armed services of states are always legal until, at least, the constitution which provides for their existence and defines their powers and responsibilities is changed. This is not to say, however, that the duties and responsibilities that armed services are required to assume, and the tasks they are ordered by the civil authorities to perform, have necessarily to be legal. All that the concept establishes is that the existence of armed services as a state institution has the backing and the authority of constitutional law.

For analytical purposes, the significance of the legal foundation of armed services is that it enables us to differentiate them from all other organizations that are specialists to one degree or other in organized violence. Armed services can, thus, immediately be seen in sharp contrast with illegal violent organizations, such as criminal gangs, guerrilla movements, terrorist groups and mobs. They are also differentiated as a result from organizations whose possession of the means of violence, including firearms, explosives and other specialized equipment, is also legal, but whose existence is not laid down and provided for in constitutional or statutory provisions. In this sense, armed services cannot be confused with such organizations as private security firms which, in many states, have a legal right to operate and bear certain categories of weapons, yet which are not covered by any constitutional provision.

The constitutional basis for the existence of armed services within a state presupposes, first, that there is a higher political authority that can confer legality on them; second, that they have an established existence which thus ensures continuity; and third, that they are entitled to assume a high degree of exclusivity. Armed services are indeed exclusive inasmuch as they are alone in performing in the name of the state particular functions which involve the constrained application of violence; they also manifest that exclusivity by enjoying, in law, an absolute monopoly of particular types of highly complex, very destructive, and wholly dangerous weapons and equipment. Even in states such as the USA where there is the right for the public to bear arms and for civil organizations to provide weapons to members for security purposes, the types of arms and equipment permissible are carefully and narrowly defined in law and rigorously enforced. The underlying juridical basis of the constitution, whether it be *de jure* or *de facto*, is only of secondary importance, and is, therefore, only a contingent consideration.

Given that armed services necessarily must be legal, and their prime function the management of the organized use of violence, two further considerations follow automatically: first, armed services are a social phenomenon in that they are human organizations which have, second, a legal, institutional status. As organizations they manifest many of the more common characteristics of most social groups, but what is particularly special about them in this respect is a consequence of the purposes they customarily serve, and the roles they normally perform. These are invariably, but not necessarily always, written into the constitutional provisions that provide for the existence of armed services and used as terms of reference. Where this is not the case, their purposes tend to be more customary and traditional. Generally, armed services are paid from the public purse to defend the nation-state, that is to say the citizens, territory and institutions, from external attack, or to deter aggression that threatens perceived vital interests. In recent years, however, the purposes of armed services have expanded, and it is now not unusual to find that even in wealthier and maturer states, the protection of citizens and their core values against all threats, external and internal, are included. In other words, purpose is only a contingent condition to our stipulative definition of armed services, and is not a necessary one.

With internal roles added to their more normal external ones, the usual distinction between armed services and such state organizations as the Police and internal security agencies is no longer as clear-cut and well defined as before. Ironically, as armed services are employed more frequently to cope with internal threats, so police forces and security agencies have themselves apparently taken on more external functions. It would be too arbitrary here to separate totally armed services from these other organizations for purposes of analysis; nonetheless, the differences between them should be noted and constantly borne in mind. In respect of the study of the relationship of armed services and society, it is the involvement of organizations that have legal backing and which are specialist in the managed application of violence internally which matters. The issue is really one of emphasis, in which the armed services tend to be more externally oriented, and police forces and others, such as secret intelligence services, more concerned with internal matters.

From the above discussion, a working, stipulative definition of armed services has slowly emerged. The term 'armed services' clearly refers to that state organization, or group of organizations, which is permanently established by constitutional law, enjoys a monopoly of certain categories of weapons and equipment, and is responsible for the constrained application of violence or coercive force to eliminate or deter any thing or body that is considered to threaten the existence of the nation-state (that is to say the area within recognized territorial boundaries) and the interests, singly and collectively, of its citizens. With this definition, which is considerably narrower and more precise than the more general and looser terms, 'military', or 'armed forces', a taxonomy of a particular category of state institution is provided, on the strength of which, a number of sub-categories of types of armed services can be identified.

First, armed services have been typed according to the environment within which they predominantly operate – land, sea, air or space. The customary distinction in most states is between the branches of the armed services, delineated according to the environment within which they normally operate; hence, we find armies, navies and air forces. Such, however, is the technological development in the artefacts of modern warfare, and the range of uses to which they can be put, that these traditional distinctions no longer apply in all states. In some instances, more branches of the armed services have been added, such as those that take account of the existence of weapons of mass destruction as in the Soviet Strategic Rocket Forces; that accommodate the need to defend the state from within as well as beyond boundaries, as in France's Gendarmerie Nationale; and that operate in more than one environment, as in the US Marine Corps. Because of the changed nature of war, some states have even seen fit to break down the traditional institutional boundaries between the separate branches of the armed services, both for planning and operational purposes, and have introduced a single defence service instead. Canada was one such state; the experience was found to be less than satisfactory however, and currently Canada is in the process of reintroducing service distinctions and the armed services' institutional separateness.

As well as distinctions between armed services according to the environment within which they normally operate, they also exist according to functions. In days past, armed services were invariably equipped and even paid by their commanders or political leaders; alternatively, they were recompensed for their service from looting and the spoils of war. Today, the cost of permanent standing armed services is borne by the state, largely from taxation; the cost can also be offset from the sale of modern weapons abroad. Since armed services in virtually every state, rich or poor, are standing, permanent institutions, they cannot rely, certainly in peacetime, upon the spoils of war for their pay, equipment and logistic support.

With the sophistication, complexity, cost, exclusivity and destructiveness of modern weapons, coupled with the integrated and complex nature of modern warfare, today's armed services have also had to provide their own logistic support in battle. This is a provision that they have no longer been able to leave to civilians, either in time of peace or war. For this reason, a further distinction within the branches of the armed services can be made, between those branches of armed services and the units within them, that actually are trained and organized to engage the enemies of the state in combat – sometimes referred to as the 'teeth' arms – and those (the 'tail') that provide essential logistic and administrative support.

The distinction between the fighting side of armed services and logistic support is one that has altered significantly the nature of today's armed services compared with those of the past. It has also altered extensively their relationship with society. In particular, the armed services' recruitment priorities for men and women are different and the qualifications that are required have changed. Even the career patterns and, indeed, the cohesion of the armed services themselves have taken on a new significance. Equally important is the number of civilians who today fulfil essential roles on behalf of, and for, the armed services, though they themselves are neither subject to the legally defined conditions of service that apply to those who serve, nor are ever likely to be involved operationally in managing the application of violence or find themselves directly in a combat situation. Most of these people are engaged in weapons research and production, or in manning and running the large organizations that give the service branches and operational command headquarters administrative and bureaucratic support.

Another distinction worthy of mention is the terms of service of those who are in the armed services of a state. It is the exception rather than the rule to find in any branch of the armed services today only people who are exclusively 'military', in the sense of their being totally 'non-civilian'. It is also the exception to find all those who serve having either the same conditions of employment, or a relationship with their service branch in common with those in other branches. There are many people, for example, who are part-time, conscript, and even paramilitary who are attached to, and serve with, the armed services in one capacity or other. In addition to these personnel are the numerous reservists who, on leaving the armed services, nonetheless have a legal obligation to continue to train for a minimum period each year, or who have binding legal commitment to be available at relatively short notice to serve up to a certain age, but who are not required to train on an extensive or regular basis. Today's armed services comprise a mixture of men and women whose terms of engagement are very varied indeed; only a few states, however, have services made up predominantly of volunteer, full-time professionals. Most maintain a nucleus of full-time professional military staff and augment them with conscripts, part-time reserves and numerous categories of reservists. As the terms of engagement differ, and as the requirements of each branch of the armed services differ, so also does the degree and extent of training and terms of engagement that each armed serviceman or woman receives.

It is important to recognize the differences between each of the branches of the armed services, and their numerous categories of personnel and varying of terms of engagement. Service experience and training has an immediate bearing on how those who serve view the world, perceive defence priorities, and relate to society. Care, therefore, has to be exercised especially when referring to the 'perceptions' of the service men and women, or making statements about their 'attitudes'. In society at large there is a broad spectrum of opinion on most issues; within the armed services that spectrum is not necessarily any less wide, despite the stress that is customarily placed on personal discipline, uniformity and conformity. Evidence would confirm that most armed services throughout the world are not the monoliths that popular opinion would suggest; were these perceptions correct, inter-service rivalry and conflict, for example, would not be as prevalent as it is almost everywhere.

However comprehensive a taxonomy may be, complete success is invariably elusive. Consider, for example, in the light of the above discussion, how such institutions as the French Gendarmerie Nationale, the United States National Guard, Britain's Police Special Task Forces, the Spanish Guardia Civil, the Italian Bassiglieri or the Russian KGB might be categorized; each more or less fits the above definition of an armed service, but no one is like another or conforms to the popular conception of what an armed service should be like. Within the definition there is also a place for state intelligence agencies, legally armed private contract security companies, and national units serving with international peace-keeping forces. At the margin, consideration might be given to national liberation armies such as the Palestine Liberation Organization (PLO), which enjoys international recognition and some degree of diplomatic status, even though it has neither territory nor constitutional status.

Despite these numerous definitional complications, the important, and necessary, condition is the legal basis of armed services as the principal, and frequently the sole, state agency responsible for the security of all citizens and national territory against external physical threats; other responsibilities, either external or internal, are purely contingent with one possible exception. This is the implicit responsibility of the armed services, in the event that the structure of the nation-state is faced with disintegration, to intervene and assume overall authority. With this basic definition, it becomes possible to address the next question, whether or not there are characteristics of armed services, as organizations, which would enable general statements to be made about them and, as a corollary, whether or not comparisons with other state institutions might meaningfully be made.

The problem that is immediately raised when armed services are compared with other state organizations is the former's terms of reference. Armed services are formed, equipped and trained either to deter conflict, or to do battle against an adversary. Their preparation is not so much to compete (in the sense that there is a marketplace in which one side attempts to gain direct advantage over another) but to make it clear that in the event of a head-on clash of armed might, the outcome would be victory. 'Winning' in this context means the defeat of the adversary – to force capitulation, withdrawal, or surrender. 'Losing' means the probable imposition of conditions by the victor that are inimical to the interests of the state, or its citizens, or, at an extreme, the demise of the state itself and the dismantling of its major institutions. This would, of course, inevitably include the armed services, that very institution which normally is also perceived to be a symbol of independence, national sovereignty and territorial integrity. Armed services are thus uniquely engaged in a sphere of state activity where the stakes are not just high; they are often total. This characteristic of armed services should be neither dismissed nor belittled; it is at the core of what differentiates them from all other institutions, whether public or private.

The ideal military strategy for any state is to have armed services whose combined capability is sufficient to dissuade or deter any likely adversary from adventurism, or from taking the risk of using physical or coercive force to achieve its political objectives. The challenge is, however, to balance that combined military might with the resources available, so that the state is not bankrupting itself in the process of acquiring and maintaining a credible capability. A further consideration, however, arises in the event that an adversary were to take such a risk and threaten to attack; under these circumstances, the armed services have a duty, and, therefore, are expected to respond to the utmost of their ability. This is an assumption that is made about all armed services and of the men and women, each and every one, who serve in them. This is frequently referred to as the serviceman's 'unlimited liability', inasmuch as the armed services' institutional obligation to the parent society is always to respond to outside aggression and one which carries with it the real possibility of their members being killed in the course of carrying out their duty.

This 'unlimited liability' condition of service is accepted by those who serve as an occupational hazard. Whilst there are invariably compensations it is nonetheless one of armed services' several institutionally constraining characteristics. Equally significant is the effect of the combat environment in which armed services must expect to operate in time of war. Studies of battles, campaigns and wars have provided graphic illustration of what might most accurately be referred to as the 'ecology' of war. The battlefield, whether in the air, on the ground or at sea, is one of short and intense periods that are thoroughly dangerous, extremely frightening and wholly disorientating, interspersed between long periods of boredom and inactivity. For armed service units to be able to function effectively in such a noisy, dangerous, unpleasant and hostile three-dimensional environment with any expectation of success, and for the individual serviceman or woman to stand any reasonable chance of surviving the ordeal, great emphasis has come to be placed on personal and organizational discipline. Without the self-discipline of the individual or the cohesion of the various sections that make up the whole fighting unit, no operational commander could expect to be able to lead or direct those men and units under him. How that discipline is generated and acquired, and then maintained, in a changing military environment with limited resources is a continuing matter of analysis and debate. One difficulty is to avoid making preparations for a war like the last one, and to adjust constantly to meet the contingencies of the future.

As organizations, however, armed services do not differ in their basic characteristics from other, even civilian, organizations. Where they are distinctly different is in their emphasis, and perhaps in the detailed terms of engagement for serving personnel generally incorporated in legally binding service regulations. Above all, the dominant consideration affecting armed services as organizations is the prospect of their members being killed in the course of fulfilling their duty; it is this that dominates their organizational practices. Central to this notion is the transfer of individual values to those of the group, since it is accepted from experience that individual survival in combat is ultimately dependent on the cohesion, morale, discipline and preparation of the fighting group of which each person is a part. It has been said that the interrelationship of organization and destructive potential is the distinguishing characteristic of military practices. The objective of defending society by physical means is the dynamic force behind service organizations, and it is this, more than the details of strategies, tactics and military objectives, that determines their essential characteristics.

The organizational structures of armed services provide the framework that interrelates and integrates functions, ascribes authority and defines office. Service units accomplish their objectives through their organizational structure. Over time, however, military objectives change, sometimes quite radically, as a consequence of technological developments both at home, and with regard to the potential enemy. A requirement of service organizations has to be the ability to adapt to these changing circumstances, while at the same time maintaining their own organizational cohesion, identity and unity. As change has accelerated in the past 30 years, this has proved sometimes to be difficult.

Organizational structures are designed to achieve two objectives: the maintenance of a high level of discipline and morale among personnel, and the achievement of maximum combat effectiveness and operational efficiency. They therefore provide a framework of responsibilities and authority that links functional groups together. As a general rule, this framework in armed services follows the 'line and staff' concept, since this has been found to be best suited to meet the requirement of combat unit morale on the one hand, and operational flexibility under the stress of battle on the other. The line, or scalar, type of organization fixes authority and responsibility along a direct chain of command. It is with this chain of command, and the clear identification of levels of authority and responsibility that the armed services' distinctive rank structure is associated; and it is with these clear rank differences and the hierarchical distinctions between officers and other ranks that the general public is most familiar.

The strength of the line system and rank structure lies in its clear definition of responsibility of each level in the chain of command. As a

31

consequence, group discipline, and therefore operational effectiveness, is easier to maintain. The weakness of the system is in the complexity of modern warfare, where those at the top levels of the chain command are expected to understand and master the plethora of detailed information that is generated from below by those in the field, and to exericse effective control. The complexity and speed of modern battle makes this virtually impossible, despite recent developments in information technology, modern communications systems and data handling. In response to this difficulty, a 'staff' system, first introduced in the nineteenth century, has been maintained and developed and has been integrated into the chain of command system. Essentially the staff concept is a functional development from the line system, whereby those appointed are responsible immediately to those in overall command for specialist advice and to assist operational commanders in the field acquire a more comprehensive picture of the overall situation facing them. The introduction of the staff system encouraged a high degree of sub-specialization in armed services, yet also helped give greater organizational flexibility without adversely affecting the essential chain of authority and command.

Of all modern complex organizations, armed services attach the greatest importance to the maintenance of high morale – not that civilian organizations are indifferent to, or undervalue, its importance. Morale is that indefinable attribute which inspires individuals and groups to exceed organizational expectations, and holds men and units together under extreme stress. It is essential to all military organizations, given the acute stress they are likely to experience in war. How morale is generated and nurtured within service units is still an indefinite and imprecise problem, especially in time of peace; nevertheless, factors such as the quality of training; a normative commitment to the task to be fulfilled; a strong sense of identity with the unit to which the individual is attached; a pride in the specific job that he or she has to do; and a certain degree of patriotism and love of one's country must be included. One particular factor, however, has been demonstrated to have had both an adverse and positive effect on organizational morale, namely, the quality of leadership. Armed services have always recognized its importance, and it is the search for this highly subjective quality that is given high priority in the recruitment and preparation of future officers, and taken into account in their promotion to senior rank.

Leadership is the art of influencing the behaviour of others so as to accomplish a mission in the manner desired by those in command. Leadership can be a matter of appointment to rank, either by acclaim or as a consequence of circumstances. In armed services, leadership is conferred by appointment to rank, since it is only with rank that organizational responsibility and authority is conferred. The immediate distinction that this introduces within armed services is between the officer corps, being those who lead; the non-commissioned officers, being those who organize and manage according to given directions; and other ranks, who are, in essence, the operatives, as those who are led.

Since the organizational structure and chain of command of armed services emphasizes leadership and these in turn directly affect morale, operational effectiveness and organizational efficiency, it is important to identify what personal qualities are considered necessary or desirable in the officers of today's armed services. Leadership is a product of individual personality traits. These are highly subjective, but relate to the psychological make-up of the officer, and to his or her capacity to command the attention and respect of others. Whilst the 'trait' theory of leadership has been seriously questioned, leadership qualities are generally accepted to encompass two elements: first, there is the officer's social and moral orientation, including such qualities as integrity and maturity, the ability to tackle complex problems with intelligence, judgment, and practical common sense; second, is the ability to operate within a service organizational and group context, which, by definition, must include the responsibility for both the operational effectiveness of the unit under his or her command, and the lives of the people in it, in difficult and dangerous situations. The expectations placed on officers who serve in today's armed services are considerable, and far removed from the popular, but anachronistic, stereotype of the patriotic, but rather unimaginative and courageous, 'heroic' type so frequently depicted in books and films.

Leadership, however, is not precisely the same as command, though is closely related to it. Officers who rely on their position of authority as a foundation for leadership do so at their cost. Command has little to do with the personal qualities of serving officers; it is, in formal terms, the authority that an officer in the armed services lawfully exercises over his subordinates by virtue of rank or assignment. Leadership does not depend on organizational or legal rules to be effective, though the ideal is to have those in command also with the desired qualities of leadership.

In earlier centuries the structures of military organizations were markedly more simple, and leadership qualities and command could be related more directly and closely to the requirements of combat. Indeed, military commanders would head their forces into combat, leading and commanding frequently by example. Today the battlefield is more extensive and movement more fluid, the action faster, and the equipment more varied, complicated and destructive. The effect has been to put a premium more on the officer's managerial qualities than on leadership and charisma. Furthermore, the distinction between combat and logistic units – the 'teeth' and 'tail' of today's services – has had the effect of introducing new and different officer attributes. These have been simply differentiated between 'executive leadership', which stresses managerial, 'staff' qualities; and 'operative' leadership, which emphasizes personal qualities that bring out the best in small organizational units confronted with the physical stress of battle. In today's armed services, especially those of the modern advanced industrial societies, the problems that these two requirements generate for the recruitment, retention, promotion and training of officers are numerous. But above all, they belie the single stereotype of the 'typical' service officer.

All organizations stress leadership qualities, management skills and authority; service organizations not only put different and, invariably, more, emphasis on leadership and command than most, but also have to relate these with the changing, and increasingly bureaucratic, nature of their affairs. Although the character of leadership and command has radically altered with the introduction of modern weapons technology, the structure of service organizations and the armed services' well-defined command chain still serves to set them apart from most other organizations.

The question that immediately arises from this is the extent to which armed services are different. To a degree, the answer has been provided by Erving Goffman, who noted that armed services fell clearly, along with prisons, lunatic asylums and monasteries, within the category that he labelled the 'total institution'. Total institutions are those whose essential characteristic is the barrier that they build between themselves and the outside world. The purpose of such a barrier is to restrict the interaction between the institution and the outside world so that the purposes for which the institution exists can be most effectively pursued without external interference. In the case of the armed services, the dictates of secrecy and the requirements of national security effectively determine that such a barrier, both physical and procedural, is considered an essential requirement. The potentially dangerous activities with which the armed services are normally engaged are another good reason for secure barriers, not merely to allow the services themselves to train without impediment, but more especially to protect civilians, ignorant of safety procedures, from getting injured.

The purpose behind erecting barriers is to achieve the institution's objectives. In the case of the armed services, this is national security. The features of total institutions, according to Erving Goffman, are that: all aspects of life are encompassed within the institution; all activities are carried out collectively; all 'inmates' are treated alike; the day-to-day activities of the institutions are tightly scheduled; and all activities are directly related to the official aims of the institution. Where the armed services are concerned, and the multifarious units and commands of which they are comprised, these characteristics are more evident in time of war and where there is conscription than among peacetime volunteer professional establishments.

In the light of these characteristics, Goffman noted that there was likely to be a division between those with only restricted access to the outside world – the inmates – and the staff, who supervise, control and manage the institutions. The obvious suggestion here in respect of armed services is the distinction between officers and other ranks, but there is little evidence, at least in advanced industrial states, that outside access is limited to either group. In less developed states this tends not to be the case. The important consideration that this phenomenon raises is the degree to which military facilities and installations – the metaphorical 'barracks' – are divorced from civil society on purely functional and practical grounds, thereby creating the impression that they are separate and 'totalistic'. In most cases this separation is geographical, in that the physical training requirements of armed services dictate that they are located far from populated areas.

Armed services nonetheless have much in common with other totalistic institutions, though again it is a matter of degree. One common characteristic is the process of induction to which all new recruits, whether officers or not, are subjected. This process is designed by means of an intensive and disorientating experience, to break down the system of supports and values that the recruit had before entry, and to replace them with those of the institution. The more totalistic the institution, the more intense and rigorous the process. For this reason, Goffman prefers to refer to it as a 'mortification', rather than a 'socialization' process. In the case of armed services, there is no question not only that all new recruits are put through a comprehensive process of this kind, but also that it is variable according to which of the armed services they join and the particular branch within them. It is this feature of armed service life which puts it in sharpest contrast with civilian.

Another feature of total institutions with which armed services have much in common is the right that staff, that is to say the officers, have to discipline and punish. Generally this is a legal right where armed services are concerned. No armed serviceman or woman is above the law and all are subject to the law of the land. Additionally, servicemen in most states come under martial law for acts of negligence, incompetence or disobedience. In time of war, and especially when in action, armed services also have a residual authority to conduct hearings and pass judgment on their members as a matter of expedience. Without these extra powers, the armed services are not in a position to enforce the compliance of their members in times of stress.

A third feature concerns the use and allocation of privileges. Not only are such rewards given in return for compliant behaviour – good conduct, long service and so on – but they can also be withdrawn as a form of punishment. Armed services use these normative rewards and withdrawals to an extensive degree, something that is only possible while they are predominantly separate from civilian life. Some states do this more than others: the American armed services, for example, extensively issue ribbons and medals for achievements and reliable service; the British services prefer to use other privileges and rewards.

Had not armed services manifest to an extensive degree the dominant features of a total institution, the problems facing armed servicemen and women on retirement and rehabilitation into the civil community would not be as difficult as they frequently are. The armed services of the advanced states go to considerable lengths to make this transition as smooth as possible through special courses and careful preparation before retirement. Even then, ex-servicemen find greater security among veterans associations and regimental clubs than among civilian groups.

A second insight into how different military organizations are from civilian was offered by Amitai Etzioni in his *Comparative Analysis of Complex Organizations*. Etzioni was interested in the question why individuals accepted the position they held within an organization, and the duties and responsibilities that were incumbent upon them. His conclusion, in essence, was that they did so as a consequence of 'compliance', that interrelationship between the power that the organization could exercise over the individual and the interests of the individual in remaining in the organization. Taking these two dimensions, Etzioni suggested broadly that the power of the organization fell into three broad categories: coercive, remunerative and normative, and the involvement of the individual into: alienative, calculative and committed. The precise definitions of these six categories are not important here, except in so much as they create a matrix of nine possible interrelationships (alienative–coercive, remunerative–

calculative, and so on). His conclusion was that compliance, the interaction of personal involvement and organizational power, concentrated in most organizations into one of three out of the nine possibilities on his matrix.

From the armed services' perspective, his suggestion was that the alienative–coercive basis of compliance was dominant. This conclusion is based on the assumption that armed servicemen and women are forced to serve and that they are kept there through the application of coercive organizational power. Such a conclusion is grossly misrepresentative, despite the legal powers that armed services have to discipline and punish their members. It is misleading in that it applies predominantly to conscripts who are required to do a period of service, often against their preferences. Most states operate a system of national military service, and the number of all-volunteer armed services is very small. But at least this point highlights one very important difference between the armed services and all civilian organizations, namely they are the only ones where people, mostly young men, are required by law to join and serve for a period of time.

The suggestion that the dominant compliance relationship in armed services is alienative–coercive is misrepresentative also because it ignores the vast number of career servicemen and women who are volunteers and highly professional. Their involvement is not one that requires organizational enforcement; they serve because they have calculated that it is in their interests to do so. The power of the organization is to direct the particular functions they perform, and their commitment is retained through the level of pay and meeting 'job satisfaction' expectations like variety, travel, excitement, and so on. As armed services have become more diverse in their functions and as more specialist tasks have to be done, so the variety of jobs and opportunities within the armed services has increased; the net effect has been to widen the calculative element in individuals' involvement, to the extent that it is not unknown for them to use a period of service in the armed service as a means to acquire specialist training and qualifications for subsequent use in civilian life. Diversity also raises another problem, which is that many military tasks have civilian counterparts, making comparisons of pay and conditions of work easier. One of the major tasks facing thëarmed services in advanced industrial societies is to retain skilled servicemen in the face of civilian competition which offers, invariably, much higher remuneration and less anti-social conditions of work.

Yet there is undoubtedly an element in the armed services that serve because they see it as a vocation and a national duty. The armed services induction process places great emphasis both on nationalism and patriotism, and the symbols of the nation-state (the monarchy, flag, anthem, tradition) are predominantly displayed. In peacetime they are themselves symbols of national sovereignty, and in wartime or domestic crisis they are also the manifestation of national independence and integrity. In a crisis or emergency, armed services are constitutionally recognized as the institution of national last resort. Many servicemen and women are involved out of a sense of service, and for them purely financial considerations are of secondary importance. This point, however, highlights another fundamental consideration concerning armed services and society – whether or not the state is at war. The relationship between the two and the involvement of people in and attitudes to the armed services, changes fundamentally in war.

Etzioni's concept of compliance does not immediately identify why armed services, as organizations, are distinctively different from civilian organizations; but what it does do is to highlight a number of important variables that have to be borne in mind when analysing the relationship between armed services and society. These include whether the context is one of peace or war; advanced or less developed states; volunteer or conscript systems; 'teeth' or 'tail' military units; advanced or simple weapons technologies; and officer or other ranks. To talk about armed services in generalities without first considering some or all of these context questions could lead to very misleading conclusions about their relationship with society.

In the advanced industrial states, where armed services are permanent, and there is a nucleus, at least, of full-time, volunteer servicemen and women, it is reasonable to expect that there is a high degree of professionalism. The concept of professionalism is valuable in that it provides another insight into what is different and distinctive about the armed services compared with civilian organizations. Much has been written on professionalism, but substantially less on military professionalism, despite the armed services not only perceiving themselves to be 'professional' but one of the oldest professions of all. There are some who would contest that the armed services of the state are properly professional on the grounds that their purpose is never to be used, or that military values are the antithesis of liberalism, the political philosophy upon which Western concepts of professionalism are based. Neither of these opinions, however, should prevent exploration of the concept and its applicability to the analysis of armed services as organizations.

Of the many studies of professionalism, that of Greenwood is perhaps the most comprehensive. He asserts that there are five attributes to a profession, and all must be in evidence at the same time. First, a profession must be related to, and founded upon, a body of systematic theory. This incorporates the notion that the performance of a professional service involves a series of unusually complicated and difficult operations, the mastery of which requires a lengthy training. The resultant skills must be supported by a fund of knowledge that has been organized into a systematic body of theory, the understanding of which is essential. It is not sufficient to have a practical professional skill, there must also be an intellectual ability. In the case of armed services, the theory and practice of the managed application of violence would constitute the required body of systematic theory, independent of all the technical, managerial, financial, and logistic skills that are also required.

Second, there should be an authority based upon a specialist expertise which differentiates the professional from the layman. Normally this can be seen in the distinction between a customer and a client. Customers have the freedom to appraise their own needs and judge how best they can be satisfied; a client has to accede to the professional judgment of experts since he lacks the requisite theoretical or practical skills or knowledge to diagnose his needs or to discriminate among the possibilities to meet them. A client's subordination to professional authority invests in the professional a monopoly of judgment. Different professions, generally supported by legislation, enjoy a monopoly within specific spheres of competence. In the case of the armed services such a monopoly does exist; however, as modern strategies shift the focus of attention from winning wars to deterring future ones, and strategic debates move towards the hypothetical and the abstract, there has been a civilian intellectual challenge to certain areas of expertise of the professional armed services. Futhermore, there is serious debate where armed services are concerned as to who is the client. Society (or the government) looks to the armed services for professional judgment about defence and security and in that sense, it is the client. Conversely, most states subscribe to the principle that armed services are a state institution and, as such, are subservient to society and the government. In this case, rather than being client, the government is master. This raises a complication in the relationship between armed services and society, especially in liberal democratic states, and is often at the root of many of their problems.

The third attribute is that of community sanction. Each profession enjoys a number of powers and privileges granted to them by society. For example, professions enjoy autonomous control over admission, training, standards and examinations, whilst having the community accept those who are qualified to be allowed to practise. One particular privilege is that of confidentiality; this is considered a prerequisite for the professional to exercise his skill, since it means that clients can freely divulge information which they would not do otherwise. Another privilege is that the profession itself is the determinant of competence, it being judged that professionals can only be assessed by their peers. Finally, professions are accorded a monopoly by society; they alone are legally entitled to practise their skills. Most of these particular features of a profession apply to armed services: they are the sole determinants of admission, minimum standards of competence, and the content of training, and they enjoy in law a monopoly of particular skills, particularly in respect of the application of certain types of coercive force.

The fourth attribute of a profession is the most critical for all professions, but particularly for armed services: this is a regulatory code of ethics. It is through the profession's ethical code that its total, unconditional commitment to society becomes a matter of public record. The code governs the professional's relationship with his or her client and also the relationship between one member of the profession and another. In respect of the former, it is expressed in terms of emotional neutrality, universalism and disinterestedness, and is manifest in the professional rendering his or her services when and wherever required, even at personal cost or inconvenience. It also implies that the professional or the profession would never capitalize on a monopoly position for personal or collective gain. In the case of the armed services, this code of ethics is encapsulated in the concept of the serviceman's 'unlimited ability' to defend society even at the risk of his or her own life, and to obey without question orders of a higher political authority. The latter aspect of professional ethics, that which governs intra-profession relations, refers to such attributes as cooperation, supportiveness and openness. Professionals are assumed to be of assistance to one another not only in the interests of clients, but also to further their professional knowledge and service to the community. Professional journals and conferences are designed to assist this objective, and competition within the profession by withholding information and knowledge is discouraged. This raises some problems for each of the branches of the armed services, inasmuch as they are collectively responsible for the overall defence of society but individually have a number of exclusive skills; it is this variation that is behind inter-service rivalry, a phenomenon that is often considered detrimental to the interests of defence, yet is not inimical to the pursuit of high professional standards.

The fifth attribute is that of professional culture. Professions operate through a network of formal and informal groups, institutions, organizations and associations. Because of the special relationship between armed services and the nation-state, it is unusual to find a professional association representing the interests of the armed services in the sense of forming a union acting or as a lobby group. Behind this omission lies one of the distinctive characteristics of armed services as a profession, and which gives a subtle insight into the nature of the relationship between them and society. They are not seen in the political arena, normally, and distance themselves from open, public debate. This does not mean, however, that there are not numerous informal associations of retired armed servicemen and women, or service-oriented civilians, who articulate views and demands which support, as they see them, the armed services' interests and views.

Another aspect of a professional culture is that of values, norms and symbols. These are the characteristics that give the profession both its mystique and its distinction. The values of the profession lie in its unshakeable belief in the essential worth of the service it extends to the community; its norms provide a guide to the behaviour of members, particularly in respect of clients; and its symbols refer specifically to the distinctiveness of the professional group, covering such things as formal qualifications, insignia, dress, and so on. One further cultural distinction is the language of the profession, which is often exclusive and little understood by the layman. In today's armed services, the use of professional jargon and acronyms is so extensive that whole lexicons have been compiled to give concerned laymen a translation into simple language of what is being talked about in the world of strategy, defence and weapons.

Armed services fulfil to a significant degree all the usual attributes of a profession. There are some doubts in respect of the professional–client relationship and the code of ethics, where intra-professional cooperation conflicts with the problem of whether or not the branches of the armed services should be seen as separate from, or as part of, a single defence profession. Both these caveats should be borne in mind when discussing the wider relationship between armed services and society.

There was no doubt in Samuel Huntington's mind that the armed services in the United States were professional, nor in the opinion of Morris Janowitz. Although their focus of concern was on the United States and their attention was directed at the involvement of American armed services in politics, they were the first to conceptualize the attributes of the military *qua* profession. Huntington, in his pioneering work *The Soldier and the State*, identified three characteristics that armed services displayed which, he said, gave them the right to be called professional: expertise, the direction, organization and control of an organization whose primary function is the application of violence; corporateness, the legal right to practise a skill limited to a carefully defined body or organization with its own culture, training, discipline, traditions and sense of distinctiveness (*esprit de corps*); and responsibility, the acceptance of the principle that the application of particular skills should be used only for socially approved purposes. Janowitz, in *The Professional Soldier*, added a number of further considerations which were that: only the officer corps could reasonably be considered the professionals since they alone, as the elite, exercised the greatest and most relevant amount of actual or potential power; professional responsibility really only operated during the conduct of war; modern armed services were highly specialized as a consequence of new technologies and this had introduced for the officer corps new career patterns, ideologies, skills, and value systems; and finally, in the United States at least, an objective had been defined which was that the armed services would never have to perform the function for which they were constantly preparing – a notion he termed the 'constabulary concept'.

Both Huntington and Janowitz helped to highlight the distinctive professionalism of the American armed services, but opened the way for analysis of all armed services as professional bodies. In doing so, they identified the differences between the armed services and society, suggesting that professionalism lay at the heart of the relationship between the two. Bengt Abrahamsson, in his study *Military Professionalization and Political Power* was less persuaded: he did not suggest that the armed services were not professional, but challenged the assumption that armed services would not be politically involved because they were professional. Indeed, he raised the point that it was precisely because they were professional that armed service chiefs had a responsibility to press home their professional judgment to their clients, the government, and not as servants of the state merely awaiting orders. In this he highlighted again the anomalous professional–client relationship between armed services and society, and added his support to Samuel Finer's point, in *The Man on Horseback*, that there are certain circumstances when, as a matter of professional responsibility, armed services should act independently for their client (the society they serve) and not stand by and await instruction.

This chapter has been constructed to argue the point that it is through the armed services of a state, a more precise concept, that a better approach to the study of civil–military relations is to be found.

The suggestion is also made that armed services fulfil a highly specialized function, the effect of which is to separate them entirely, and geographically to a great extent, from civil society. In organizational terms they are distinctively different, and although they conform to accepted definitions of a profession, practising their craft is done on behalf of society as a whole and not for the individual. Furthermore, the objective of the craft of the professional armed services is that ideally it should not be used. The picture, then, is of a highly specialized corporate set of institutions which have little in common with civil society – frequently referred by armed servicemen as being 'outside' – with their own set of values and ways of doing things. They almost form the 'state within a state' which is a phrase that has been used to describe the Prussian Army within Germany in the late nineteenth century. If this were indeed an accurate picture of armed services, then the notion of a functional imperative would be accurate; and if the functional imperative does apply, relations between armed services and society would be based on an interaction between two, distinctively separate, bodies which have clearly defined boundaries. To judge whether or not this picture is accurate, attention must now be turned to the other side of the coin: the question whether or not armed services are essentially a product of the societies that created them.

3

The Societal
Dimension

If the armed services of nation-states were distinctively different from their parent societies, because of the function they perform, they would have, each of them, much in common. Indeed, there would be sufficient commonality that comparisons would be relatively easy to draw. However, it takes only momentary reflection to conclude that this is far from the case. Leaving aside obvious differences, such as uniforms, traditions, ceremonials and so on, there are clearly significant and marked areas where the armed services of one state are very different from those of another. In other words, whilst the functional imperative has a major influence on the structure, procedures, composition and attitudes of all armed services throughout the world, each is, nonetheless, a product of the society that brought it forth. For all their evident similarities with others, the French armed services are clearly French and their like could not be found in Britain, the United States, Japan or elsewhere.

This was very much the approach adopted by General Hackett in his study, *The Profession of Arms*. He did not take issue with sociological interpretations of professionalism and was largely in agreement with Huntington's categories; what concerned him, as a historian, was the need to see the armed services 'with a distinct place in the society that brought [them] forth'. For this reason he sought to examine the place that they occupied within society and not view them as specialized, professional groups outside and distanced from it. His approach is compatible with other historians who have sought to analyse and explain the changing role of armed services, or individual branches, over time, such as, in the case of J. M. Brereton's social history of the British soldier from 1661 to the present day, *The British Soldier*; or Corelli Barnett's *Britain and Her Army*. Many other examples can be found for armies, navies and air forces throughout the world. The important point to recognize is that the armed services of nation-states are shaped, the policies they pursue and the roles they assume, by social, political, economic, technological and historical forces as much as by the functional imperatives of the constrained management of violence in war. These forces are ever-changing, and must be judged how, when, and in what direction.

These social, political, economic, technological and historical forces, however, have first to be identified before the discussion can move towards an examination of which influences, functional or societal, and which variables are most likely to shape the pattern of relationships between armed services and society. As a point of departure, and principally because it is most closely related to the professional expertise of the armed services themselves, the impact of technology will be explored.

Of one thing there is no doubt: the technology of war has changed radically over time. Not only is it weapons and equipment that have changed, but also strategies and tactics, as well as the structure, composition and organization of those institutions responsible for waging war. The simple wooden club of primitive man has been replaced by the multiple independently targeted re-entry vehicle, with a thermo-nuclear warhead launched from a nuclear powered submarine operating beneath the surface in the middle of the ocean, and conveyed to its target up to 5,000 miles away by an intercontinental ballistic missile with a target accuracy of less than one-quarter of a mile. This is one of today's weapons; the prospects for the future, if the American Strategic Defense Initiative (SDI) and the Soviet Union's space defence research are anything to go by, bring the technologies of war-waging, if not war-deterrence, into the realities of what not so long ago was confined to the imaginations of science fiction writers and strip cartoonists.

All significant technological developments in weaponry have also had a substantial impact on the armed services of nation-states. Sometimes the new technologies emerge in advance of change in the structure of armed services; at other times, the armed services themselves change and, in so doing, create the opportunity for new technologies to be introduced, or adopted for use in war. However, the overall change in military technology over time has been so profound that it is helpful first to clarify how this has happened and what appears to be the driving force behind it.

Perhaps the most radical effect of military technology has been the geometric (or, more accurately, the logarithmic) increase in capacity for destruction. Weapons that were once restricted to individual combat have today been made more diverse with varing degrees of impact.

Modern thermo-nuclear weapons are those of mass genocide and ecological disaster. But their destructiveness, even with a thermo-nuclear warhead, is relative to the target at which they are aimed, assuming that operational performance is as designed and intended. Furthermore, over time, there have been advances in the capabilities of weapons both of attack and defence. Within the spectrum of conventional war, the relative balance between the two has remained in equilibrium over time. But whilst the balance may have been constant, the effect of the weapons available to states on what they can do in war, and the potential destruction of the environment they can cause have increased enormously. Compare, for example, the aftermath of the Battles of Blenheim, Agincourt or Sadowa with that of Verdun, Casino or the Tet Offensive; and, now, compare them with the estimated destruction of one tactical nuclear weapon. The cumulative effects of entire wars or campaigns tell the same story: with the quantum jump in destructiveness opened up by thermo-nuclear weapons and modern missilery, the issues of who is to exercise control over their use, and who is to be responsible for their maintenance, state of readiness and security become a major concern both to the single nation and the international community. If anything should provide the *raison d'être* for the study of armed services and society, it is surely this.

But then, modern weapons have become increasingly capital-intensive, complex and expensive. As weapons technologies have changed, so too has the need for skilled service manpower. Fewer soldiers, sailors and airmen today are required than in the past for the same amount of destruction; yet the intellectual quality and educational standards of that manpower have risen substantially. No longer are armed services drawn from the lowest stratum of society (where they were traditionally recruited and where suitably qualified civilian recruits are not available); the armed services have to take on the task of training and educating their manpower to meet the necessary requirements. The need for a certain minimum standard in professional manpower has placed the armed services in direct competition with civilian organizations, and the two sides confront one another in the labour market. Only with conscription is this not a problem, but this alternative brings with it other difficulties. Moreover, their demands are sufficiently similar to the civilian sector that the distinction between certain categories of civilian and armed servicemen has become comparatively small, giving rise to what Janowitz observed in the introduction to his edited volume, *The New Military*, as a narrowing differential, particularly in management skills.

Concomitant with the increased destructiveness and greater technological content of modern weapons, has been a change in military and national strategies and operational defence planning. Weapons are generally conceived and designed in the light of existing scientific knowledge, either to meet new problems arising out of experience in the conduct of war, or as a consequence of a continuing process of scientific and technological research and experimentation that is perceived by the military, or offered by industry *inter alia* for commercial reasons to open opportunities for future application in the conduct of war. In the latter case, the harnessing of the potential offered by particle physics, and its application to the development of the fission (atomic) nuclear bomb, is one example; in the former, the development of the tank to overcome the stalemate of trench warfare during the First World War, or of radar in the Second World War, might be cited. But targets are only important in relation to the political objectives for which armed services are maintained; weapons are a means to an end, not an end in themselves. It is the question of who defines these objectives that lies at the heart of any civil–military relationship: should the armed services' perceived need for new weaponry take precedence over the political purposes for which it is needed.

There are, broadly speaking, two schools of thought over the stimulus behind scientific and technological developments which have direct application to war. J. F. C. Fuller, on the one side, noted the rate of scientific discovery during the late nineteenth and twentieth centuries and its impact on the conduct and outcome of war; he concluded, in his *Armaments and History*, that superior weaponry was the critical factor that determined victory. The implication behind his observation was that war, and preparation for war, was a major stimulus to scientific discovery and technological inventiveness. Whilst few could agree with Fuller's somewhat extravagant claim, none would deny that the exigencies of war have had an effect on the rate at which scientific knowledge has been applied to weaponry, or that new weapons and new technologies introduced during the First and Second World Wars had a significant influence on their outcomes. Whilst the post-1945 Cold War between East and West does not qualify as strictly as a war, the relationship between both sides has been sufficiently distrustful and hostile as to stimulate what has the outward appearance of a qualitative arms race, most evident in scientific research and its application to military technology and weapons systems.

Fuller represents an extreme point of view, though there are many who have followed his line of argument, suggesting that war has also had a significant effect on shaping society and its values. Lewis

Mumford in *Technics and Civilization*, and Ralph Nisbet, in *The Social Philosophers*, are two among many who have argued that security considerations were principally behind the formation of the nation-state, and, furthermore, have had a dominant influence on the structure of political and social relationships. Though adopting a different view of civilization, Arnold Toynbee, in his *War and Civilization*, nonetheless acknowledged the powerful influences that war and the profession of arms have had on shaping the values of society. In his opinion, Christianity was once the world's great civilizing force; it was largely responsible for the creation of Western civilization and inspired the human spirit that made it possible. He profoundly regretted today's preoccupation with warfare and the lack of charity and understanding this had generated; these he considered in turn to be the cause of the breakdown of civilization both in material and spiritual terms. These modern societal values he labelled as those of Valhalla.

Maurice Pearton, in his *The Knowledgable State*, analysed the relationship of weaponry and diplomacy, and in so doing pointed again to the importance of domestic arms technology as a significant influence on the conduct of states in international relations. However, a more direct focus of this line of argument is provided by the social historian, John Nef. In his book, *War and Human Progress*, he postulates the opposite argument to that of Fuller. Nef does not reject the contention that war has an impact on scientific and technological development and therefore on society, but asserts that it is attempts during time of peace to limit war, rather than in time of war to win, that has had the greatest impact. Of course, science and technology are not the only forces that shape society and its attitudes, even though they are becoming increasingly significant. Arthur Marwick's study, entitled *The Deluge*, in which he examines Britain's experiences of total war between 1914 and 1918, has also demonstrated that during the abnormal circumstances of war the structure of society, male and female working patterns and the procedures of employers, not to mention the social basis of human relations, change, sometimes permanently.

There is no overarching theory which explains the effect of scientific and technological development on the relationship between armed services and society. It is certainly not, as Fuller implies, the armed services' drive for new weaponry that is the dynamic force behind scientific endeavour, with society benefiting from whatever can be turned to civil use once the needs of the armed services are satisfied; nor is it only the societal drive to limit war, as Nef suggests. It is an interactive process whereby weapons technology sometimes has civilian application, and sometimes civil developments can be adapted to meet

48

the requirements of the armed services. Other considerations, such as whether society is at peace or war, the health, size and level of development of the national economy, the level of education, and prevailing public attitudes have also to be taken into account. Nevertheless, on occasions, there have been many technological developments where clearly neither societal nor service considerations have had most influence: for example, in his *The Social History of the Machine Gun*, John Ellis contends that the machine gun is a by-product of the revolution in industrial production, and its appearance on the battlefield would not have been possible otherwise. On a somewhat grander scale, Fred Cooke's *The Warfare State* takes the line that the demands for national security in the USA has created, since 1945, an armaments industry of immense size, one that was not only a new experience in American history, but also one that posed a threat to its system of democracy. That permanent armaments industry, and those like it in other advanced industrial states, have for some time commanded a major share of national resources, both human and material, and used for scientific research and development into new weapons technologies. These are, of course, resources which might have otherwise have been used to meet civil needs and often expressed as the opportunity cost of guns or butter.

Although this issue is more one of degree than of kind, armed services do not exist in a vacuum, inasmuch as they largely reflect the level of technological and economic development in the parent society. The exception, to a degree, is those states that have the capacity to purchase advanced military equipment from abroad. Since 1945, however, the technological dimension to the relationship between the two would appear to be moving towards one of armed service dominance as the demands of national security appear increasingly to take priority. This does not only apply to the advanced industrial states, either; the less developed and emergent states of the Third World have also invariably looked to acquire advanced technology and modern weapons as a high priority, over and above, in many instances, considerations of their own economic and social development, the construction of a sound infrastructure, and a basis of political stability. Lacking an industrial base, technological know-how and necessary resources, these less developed states have looked to, and depended on, the advanced industrial states to provide the desired arms and technologies. Most of these states, as a glance at the *Military Balance* shows, possess armed services equipped with modern sophisticated weaponry that is often far and away more advanced and complex than their levels either of economic strength or industrial and technological development could justify.

Armed services are not independent primarily because they must rely upon society to provide the necessary resources. Technology is one such resource, and has had a major influence on the shape, structure, size and composition of armed services, and has provided stimulus for their demands for new weapons. Since 1945 these demands have increased and have also become more exotic and extravagant. They have had three broad implications for society: first, they have been responsible for the establishment of permanent, professional standing armed services to maintain, at a constant state of readiness, the weaponry that modern technology has made possible. Second, they have been responsible for the creation in the advanced industrial states of a permanent arms industry which is not only concerned with sophisticated, state-of-the-art technology, but also dependent on the services' requirements for new weapons continuing virtually unabated. And third, they have diverted a large proportion of national scientific research and development resources exclusively for the armed services' purposes. In sum, taking the advanced industrial societies as a whole, armed services have expanded their influence well beyond the immediate executive responsibility of war fighting almost to one of determining the content and direction of national scientific research and future industrial activity.

This situation is not new; the difference, again, is more in degree than in kind. The 'advanced' states of sixteenth- and seventeenth-century Europe were ruled by either an absolute or a constitutional monarch; each clearly understood the relationship of military technology to the exercise of political power. Aside from the critical consideration of cost, for military technology has never been cheap, the crowned heads of Europe during this period made sure that they, or the state in their name, exercised an absolute monopoly over arms production and weapons technology. This they achieved either by making the possession of certain weapons illegal, or by controlling, through a legal or *de facto* monopoly, the production of certain categories of weapons and munitions. The same arrangement, but in a more sophisticated form, exists today; although the state arsenals have been replaced by nationalized, or privately owned arms manufacturers, their activities are closely monitored and in most cases defined and controlled by law.

In today's advanced industrial states there is a symbiotic relationship between armed services and industry, and it has to be recognized that this is a relatively new phenomenon. Whilst a relationship has always existed between the two, as for example, the knight and his armourer, the colonel of the regiment and his gun maker, the navy and its shipbuilders, what differentiates today's world from the past is the scale of arms production, its high cost, and the constant effort that is put into the advanced preparation for, or the deterrence of, possible future wars. The services–industry relationship can be conceptualized as having passed through three stages: the craft age, where weapons were hand produced for personal use; the industrial age, where they were mass produced to equip a mobilized population; and, last, the technological age, where permanent armed services are maintained at a high level of instant readiness armed with the latest weapons, to defend the state with forces-in-being. Armed services thus tend to reflect the state's level of technological advance, not merely because services' requirements are technologically the most advanced, but also because most research and development funding to industry is devoted to them.

A further influence of technology on shaping the composition and equipment of armed services and the activities of industry is its high cost. Modern weapons are extremely expensive. For armed services to acquire what they consider necessary to meet their commitments and responsibilities to society, they have to compete for scarce resources with other societal needs. How this is done varies between states. The general argument is that without modern weaponry the state would be left vulnerable. A more frequent assertion, as history has demonstrated, is that weakness is an invitation to the adventurism of others and that therefore constant vigilance is the most prudent course to follow for the maintenance of peace. It is for this reason that armed services claim that without adequate defence all other societal values and interests are precarious and that the cost, albeit high, of armed services and modern weaponry should best be seen as a form of insurance premium. This line of argument also explains why armed services' weapons requirements are 'threat driven', in the sense that their specifications are based on perceived future enemy capabilities. The consequence of this perpetual drive for modern weapons is that representatives of the armed services have to lobby for funds within government, put across their message to the politicians and the general public, and work in close liaison with the industries that develop and produce the weapons they require. In other words, technology has a prime responsibility for a blurring between the military and the civilian worlds.

The relevance of technology immediately raises the question of culture. Much has been written about 'culture' and there have been many gross misunderstandings as to its meaning. Culture is taken here to be 'a set of shared symbols and their definitions'. What distinguishes one culture from another is the way people perceive situations and respond to them. The very process by which people think and communicate is through the use of symbols, for people use linguistic symbols (for the most part words) to define situations, objects and ideas. People respond to definitions or understanding of their meaning rather than the things being defined themselves; what distinguishes one culture, or one society, from another is the extent to which its members share definitions and symbols. According to their choice of symbols or words, individuals can either communicate factual information, or seek to evoke a particular response. Propaganda involves the highly skilful use of cultural symbols to evoke particular responses and reactions on the part of the target subject. Culture influences the way people define reality; that is to say, the way they see the world, or their *Weltanschauung*. How particular societies come to view the world in a particular way depends on a whole host of factors, from geographical location to historical experience.

This brief digression on language is by way of background to the proposition that the culture of a society has a major influence on the characteristics and, moreover, attributes of its armed services. No matter how assiduously new recruits are put through a rigorous induction process on entering the armed services, in order to alter their attitudes and substitute what might be called a military ethic or culture, there would, nonetheless, be much by way of residual civilian attitudes and belief systems that would be irrevocably ingrained. This should be expected, for armed services are more than functional automata; they are often seen as, and project themselves as, the epitome of what society stands for, particularly in the sense of its traditional values. Indeed, armed services often emphasize and reinforce what they perceive to be the dominant values of the parent society in their training.

With regard to the relations between armed services and society, much will, therefore, depend upon society's view of the world, compared with that of the armed services. Not only is it a matter of how the world is perceived, but also of what is considered the appropriate means of defence of that society against what are believed to be alien pressures and threats. Many factors influence these perceptions and opinions, such as its level of education, degree of literacy, type of religion, demographic composition, geographical location, political ideology and historical experience; not least among these influences is that of the armed services themselves, and whether or not there is, for example, universal conscription and a common military experience.

A society in which there is strong armed services' influence, both on government policy and on the formation of public attitudes, is generally considered to be 'militaristic'. That is to say, the culture of that society is one in which the civilian population's view of the world and the criteria they generally feel should guide government policy towards other states is similar to, or compatible with, that of the armed services. Perhaps the most comprehensive study of militarism yet produced is Alfred Vagts's *A History of Militarism*. In it, Vagts distinguishes between what he calls the 'military way' and 'militarism'. The former he sees as the objective course of action by society to improve the efficiency and effectiveness of its armed services relative to (it has to be assumed) an informed and balanced appreciation of enemy threats to the state. Militarism, conversely, he views as the opposite of civilianism, and implies 'a certain orientation in foreign policy, a certain balance of power in society, the predominance of certain values, an elevated status of certain groups, and a certain widespread distribution of a certain style of life'. It has been defined elsewhere as the compound of military values, preponderance of the armed services in the state, adulation of military virtues and militarization.

Various indices of militarism have been identified by scholars who have attempted to categorize and label particular states, and who have sought to explain why those states have pursued certain aggressive foreign policies. The more common indicators of a militaristic nation-state include a high percentage of annual GDP devoted to defence, a frequent incidence of service intervention or interference in politics, the participation of service personnel in decision making bodies, a high content of military subjects in the artistic, literary, and recreational life of the people, a coincidence of military values and priorities in the everyday life of the nation and, perhaps the most relevant of all, the extent of aggressive, service-backed, foreign policies. In other words, the concerns of the armed services are largely synonymous with, or parallel to, the general concerns of society at large. In fascist and totalitarian states, these indicators are more manifest than are likely to be found in the liberal democracies.

Abrahamsson in his book *Military Professionalization and Political Power* argued that it is the armed services' professional duty to persuade society of their interpretation of world affairs, and noted that it is in their interests to do so. The expansion of defence-related, high technology industries has also served to expand military influence considerably. However, it should not always be assumed that influence only flows in one direction. It has also to be borne in mind that no matter how the armed services may view the world, when something goes wrong and society faces a crisis, either domestic or international, it is they who have the responsibility of doing something about it. This is the basis of the serviceman's unlimited liability, a legal, as well as professional, condition of employment that does not apply to a civilian.

Moreover, there have been many instances in history when civil society has displayed greater militaristic tendencies than the armed services as, for example, in Britain during the period of the Falklands War in 1982, and the 1956 invasion of Suez, or in the United States, during the earlier years of that country's involvement in Indo-China.

Whilst it is relatively easy to identify and list indicators of militarism, they either need quantifying or a qualitative judgment made of their significance. One indicator alone does not mean *ipso facto* that a nation-state is militaristic, nor, necessarily, does a combination of indicators. Use of the concept 'militarism' to classify any nation-state must be made with extreme caution. For example, the United States, with a record of high defence spending, interventionist foreign policies, a conservative *realpolitik* outlook on the world, an arms bearing population, a high incidence of military influence in decision making, and a large defence industrial base, nonetheless has a long and strongly held and popularly supported tradition of anti-militarism. Were this not the case, President Eisenhower, once a service commander himself, would not have warned the American people in his farewell address to the American nation in 1960 against the trend towards undue influence being exercised by the military and defence corporations in their domestic affairs.

The concept of militarism has a number of disadvantages, the most serious of which is that it is invariably used pejoratively. As with the cultural use of symbols, it is invariably invoked to suggest disapprobation of the policies, style of government, or domestic climate of other states. When used in this way, it lacks analytical precision, and has come to be little more than an insult. Another disadvantage is that it tends to be interpreted in absolute terms: a society is either militaristic or it is not. It would seem that there is no room either for degrees of militarism, or for the manifestation of militarism under one set of circumstances, but not under others.

To meet this problem, Stanislav Andreski in his *Military Organisation and Society* preferred to break the concept down, reserving the quality of militarism for a situation where four attributes are present together at the same time. These four necessary attributes were as follows: first, where there was undue military influence, for which he used the concept 'militocracy' and by which he specifically meant the preponderance of the military over civilian personnel in spheres of authority; second, he used the term 'militancy', by which he meant an aggressive foreign policy; third, the term 'militolatry', which he defined as a situation where there existed an ideology that propagated military ideals; and, finally, 'militarization', which he saw as having connotations with the extensive control by the military over social life, coupled with the subservience of the whole society to the needs and demands of the armed services. Although somewhat more cumbersome, this use of four different attributes of a society where there was evidence of extensive influence on the part of the armed services has distinct advantages, one of which is to demonstrate how imprecise the use of the single term 'militarism' has become! But it should be remembered, if his terminology were to be used, that societies can display any one or a number of these attributes without their necessarily being militaristic.

From a socialist ideological standpoint, all capitalist states, by definition, are militaristic. The basis of this claim rests on the assertion that capitalism is by definition competitive and exploitative. Capitalism is a system which, it has been argued, serves the interests of a ruling class at the expense of the proletariat, or working class. The system, and the relationship it sustains between rulers and ruled, is supported and maintained by coercion. This is seen as a major function of capitalist armed services. Another aspect of capitalism, imperialism, was the acquisition of overseas territories and the protected access to raw materials and markets; this was also seen as a function of armed services. Trade was seen to follow the flag. It is no coincidence, therefore, that Engels had a close interest in the armed services, and made the observation that if anyone wanted to discover where in society power lay, the armed services should be examined first. There have been many who have argued the militaristic side of capitalism as a system, among whom Karl Leibknecht figures prominently with his *Militarismus, Anti-Militarismus*.

Vagts's distinction between militarism and the military way raised another important consideration; how is society to know, or ever be able to judge, whether or not the resources allocated to the armed services are only appropriate to enable them to fulfil their ascribed functions efficiently and effectively? Possibly it could simply be a matter of trust on the part of society in the integrity of the armed services; but even if that trust were well founded, the secrecy around which the policies and activities of armed services are generally cloaked, and the enlightened self-interest of the services in acquiring as much of the nation's available resources as they can, makes such a position difficult to sustain. Indeed, the nature of service culture itself would be such as to suggest that the armed services' perceptions of the external threat and of their own needs to meet it would be, respectively, more pessimistic and demanding than those of civilian society.

The question of militarism arises mainly as a direct consequence of the place of the armed services in post-Second World War society. Never before have nation-states throughout the world maintained such large standing armies in time of peace, or invested so much in terms of scarce human, material and financial resources to sustain them. Security and defence issues, which had hitherto been subsumed under broader issues of foreign policy, have become increasingly associated with domestic and civilian concerns, involving such major considerations as the state of the economy, scientific and technological research and development, employment and, even, education. In the Soviet Union for example, the service chiefs demanded to be represented on Gosplan, the central economic planning body, because economic policies, they argued, could not be separated from security and defence issues. The impact of having large, expensive and permanent armed services in peacetime, however, goes beyond policy making. The nature of modern warfare and the permanent threat posed by new weaponry to all societies has meant that the frontline in war has effectively been brought to everyone's doorstep. Warfare is not the exclusive concern of armed services and governments, as the number of nuclear free zones in cities and towns around Europe and the United States reflects.

In the past, it was simply assumed that the armed services would engage the enemy in battle, at a location which would be distanced from cities, towns and centres of population. The First World War, though still largely fought in the countryside, gave the first indication of what the future had in store when German Zeppelin airships bombed English towns in East Anglia, and when whole villages in France and Belgium were destroyed by artillery and aerial bombardment designed not necessarily to defeat the enemy in battle, but to devastate his homeland and thereby diminish his will to continue the war. The Second World War witnessed what could be done in this respect with new technologies. Many great cities were devastated by strategic air and missile bombard-ment – London, Coventry, Hamburg, Dresden and so on – though the expected effect on popular morale and the will to continue the war did not materialize. The strategy, however, reached its apogee with the nuclear atomic bomb attacks on Hiroshima and Nagasaki in 1945. Whilst it is still open to debate whether or not the strategy in any of these, and other conventional, cases worked, the experience over Japan pointed to the inability of states to prevent every strategic bomber or future intercontinental ballistic missile from reaching its target, and that the nuclear fission bomb would always promise devastation on an unprecedented and unacceptable scale.

Three consequences followed from this Second World War ex-perience: first, it opened up a new field of strategic theory, based not so much upon the lessons of the past, but upon projections of future wars and the appropriate strategies with which to prepare for and face them. Second, it shifted the emphasis from a strategy of defence and war winning to one of war avoidance through deterrence, either by policies of denial or the threat of punishment, because the effects of nuclear weapons were, rightly, considered unacceptable. Although deterrence was not a new concept, it assumed after 1945 a totally new significance, and not merely for the nuclear powers. Third, it focused attention on the desirability of making some provision for home defence, particularly in respect of damage limitation and the provision for the maintenance of government and effective administration after a nuclear attack, should the strategy of deterrence and war avoidance fail.

Each of these three considerations has meant that the clear distinction between armed services and society in the advanced states has been further blurred, and to a considerable degree. Whilst there remains a likelihood of armed conflict limited to non-nuclear, conventional weapons, fought away from large conurbations and exclusively between opposing armed services, the possibility of such wars being brought to civilians is not remote. To a greater extent than is often realized, the armed services of states threatened by strategic bombardment of any sort, nuclear or conventional, have worked for many years in close liaison with civilian authorities and other non-military security organizations.

Some concern has been expressed that armed services have had to assume this internal, home defence role. The belief is that it could have an undesirable influence on people's attitudes. Alternatively, it is felt that because the armed services are an agency of the state, their involvement in internal matters could turn them into a potential political force acting on behalf of the government and for which no adequate legal or practical safeguards exist. The internal role of armed services in advanced industrial societies has expanded steadily over the past 20 years, less for reasons of civil nuclear defence and more for reasons of the emergence of new techniques of war, particularly those associated with terrorism and guerrilla movements.

Open, democratic societies are especially vulnerable to terrorist acts perpetrated by those who either have no interest in, or are impatient with, established liberal democratic procedures. Few advanced industrial states in recent years have not had to deal with both indigenous and internationally supported groups of terrorists. Most have delegated the responsibility for combating these violent groups to the armed services. A once rare occurrence, such as armed servicemen on patrol around civil airports, has today become almost commonplace; the sight of troops patrolling the streets in pursuit of terrorists is not unusual. An added dimension to this problem is the expectation that any Soviet intention to attack Western Europe would be accompanied by civilian disturbances orchestrated by sympathizers in the West, and the arrival by parachute of Soviet special forces, *Spetznaz*, skilled in sabotage techniques.

If these spectres of 'low intensity warfare' on the home front were not enough, armed services have been seen by their governments, when faced with industrial action and a breakdown of basic domestic services (electricity and water supply, communications, refuse collection, and so on) as a fallback line of 'defence'. Increasingly armed services have been used to support government policy and provide essential services during industrial disputes. Aside from the question whether this is a prudent course of action, or even legal, it has meant that the armed services, rather than being remote and distanced from civil life, have had to become aware of domestic political and economic affairs and to acquire the necessary political and diplomatic skills when required to intervene, in order not to polarize the dispute further or heighten tension. On top of all this, armed services are invariably on first call during times of national emergency and to help rescue civilians in difficulty.

The picture that emerges is one of modern armed services becoming inextricably ever more involved in the civil affairs of the state. This is in stark contrast with the earlier image portrayed in Chapter 2, of armed services as an institution geographically separate, organizationally distinctive, administratively autonomous and functionally specialist to such a degree that they are for all intents and purposes a state within a state. There is some ambivalence in liberal states as to which of these two images is preferable. The former ensures that armed services and society are less likely to be alienated from one another, but carries the disadvantage that the armed services can become excessively politicized in the process. The latter has the advantage that the armed services are more easily monitored and their terms of reference clearly delineated; the disadvantage is that a gap between them and society in attitudes and behaviour could more easily develop, leading to the alienation of one from the other, conflict, and even direct physical intervention and military government.

The suggestion of armed services being either wholly separate from society or being absorbed into it is, of course, misleading; it is neither one nor the other. The Manichaean device of suggesting two extremes is merely to help isolate those variables within the armed services themselves, and within society, which are most likely to affect the relationship between them. There is one area, however, where there is clear overlap between the two, and which demonstrates that the reality of armed services' relationship with society is organic and never constant, yet never fluctuates to extremes: this is the area of recruitment. There are today very few examples of the past practice of engaging outsiders – mercenaries – to defend the state. Those instances of this practice have been to augment national armed services, as in the engagement of the Ghurkas in the British Army; to carry out extra demanding and difficult tasks in addition to those already being performed, as in the case of the French Foreign Legion; to fulfil roles that the indigenous armed services cannot themselves accomplish, as in the case of Pakistani, South African and Israeli jet pilots serving in the air forces of some African states; to serve in foreign armed services under the terms of an arms sales contract to provide new weapons systems plus the necessary support; and as a consequence of some international treaty or commitment to provide a defence capability, as in the case of British forces in Belize or Oman. Armed services operating within international alliances do not count as mercenaries, even though they may well be contributing to the defence of other states. The critical question is, essentially, one of who pays.

Mercenaries and *condottieri* are virtually a thing of the past, except in small terrorist wars, wars of secession, or national liberation struggles. As Machiavelli pointed out from his experiences of mercenaries hired to defend the Italian city states, they are fickle, expensive, unreliable and, often, unprofessional in the proper sense of the word. Invariably, their efforts were directed at internal politics and personal advantage rather than external defence, adopting in the process a praetorian attitude to those they ostensibly served. It is far better for armed services to be recruited from within their own society, since there is a reasonable assumption that their patriotism, at least, would not be in question.

Recruitment is the point at which the civilian world initially meets that of the military, especially in states where national service is a compulsory requirement. When an individual leaves the former for the latter, he or she enters, metaphorically, a new world; but this does not mean, necessarily, that all connections with the parent society are severed. Certainly new recruits will experience an intensive induction process which is designed to mould them into people from whom the service will derive most benefit; but this is not done at the expense of their commitment to the society they will serve. Different states approach this problem in different ways, and these also have changed over time. In the seventeenth century Oliver Cromwell, for example, needed officers to lead his New Model Army and looked for men who, he said, 'made conscience of what they did'; in India only those from the warrior caste would be recruited to fight and defend society; in some Arab states, leaders would only recruit from particular tribes who, for traditional reasons, were trusted, known to be loyal and particularly skilled; and, today, in West Germany, concern that the reputation of the past should not arouse suspicions either among allies or enemies alike, has determined that recruitment is taken very seriously, and those who do join, either as full-time servicemen and women, or as conscripts, are constantly reminded that they are first and foremost civilians in uniform. This is interpreted under the concept of *innere Führung* as a requirement that they must, as a matter of duty, always maintain an awareness of their duty and obligation to society.

Officer recruitment has often been a contentious issue because many have felt that the criteria for choice of officers have more to do with class interests than with the strict requirements of the armed services. Recruitment figures for the advanced industrial states demonstrate that a disproportionately high number of officer recruits come from upper middle-class backgrounds, have a particular sort of educational background, are restricted largely to one racial grouping, come predominantly from one geographical region, and/or invariably have armed service family connections. Surprisingly, these sorts of figures do not vary greatly even in totalitarian, one-party states, except that party political connections are there more immediately significant than income or schooling.

This tendency continues throughout their service careers, with men and women who attain highest rank being those who come from particular regiments or branches of their service, a particular service academy, have service family connections, or have had 'advantageous' command postings. If this were not sufficient, the future of senior officers after retirement in industry, commerce or administration suggests that military service is a common and important experience in the lives of a fairly close-knit and highly influential group in society, and possibly more so than any other experience. These phenomena are more widespread than is commonly assumed, and although there are differences in degree, rather than in kind, they are also to be found in both the less developed and totalitarian states.

This sort of evidence suggests that there are elites from which, invariably, the officer corps of the armed services is drawn. This is arguably what Engels had in mind when he said that if the concern were to find out where power in society lay, then the armed forces should be examined first. In a way this should not be surprising, since the armed services potentially present the most powerful physical challenge to any civilian political authority. From a somewhat different perspective, this was what Oliver Cromwell wanted in his officer corps: those 'gentlemen' who could be relied upon to be loyal to their political and military leaders. He wanted to be able to trust them unquestioningly. From his standpoint, who better than those who both shared his political commitment to the Commonwealth, and who had a personal financial, political and social status stake in its survival?

This attitude carried over in Great Britain for the next 250 years, and indeed in other countries, where the recruitment of the officer corps in the armed services was almost exclusively drawn from that stratum of society which had, and could be seen to have, a political, economic and social stake in the *status quo*. Social change, the effects of industrialization, the failure of the political and social elites to provide enough adequately educated, or disposed, young men to meet the needs of modern war, the ambition of the middle classes to penetrate and gain access to the officer corps and the experience and disillusionment of total war, combined in the first quarter of the twentieth century to see the recruitment of officers drawn from a wider social net.

Elites have been defined in many ways, but, essentially, the term refers to the influential, or, more directly, those with power. Power and influence is derived from many sources – authority, wealth, birthright, intellect, for example – but the most obvious and direct basis of power is physical coercion. Whoever has access to, and control over, naked physical force has to be in a position to exercise influence. Mao Tse-tung recognized this when he made the simple, but obvious, observation that political power came from the barrel of a gun, a fact that ordinary people have recognized and experienced throughout recorded history.

The study of elites can reveal much about the relationship between armed services and society, sometimes with unexpected dividends. In his extremely imaginative, eclectic, yet challenging study, *Military Organisation and Society*, Andreski observed that the one constant theme running through the history of human society was an 'omnipresence of struggle'. Since struggle and conflict is an essential ingredient of politics, he was saying no more than man is, and has always been, a political animal. And politics is, ultimately, about the exercise of power. He was particularly revealing in the conclusion he drew from this observation; namely, that considerations of force (that is to say military considerations) have not only been the central medium of this omnipresence of struggle, but have also influenced the structure of society and the behaviour of its members, more than anything else. According to this thesis, the armed services have not only been a constant feature of society but have also played important roles within it.

These roles have often proved to be dominant. The crucial question, however, is whether or not the armed services have performed them as an independent actor within society, or as a dependent element in some larger, more complex grouping. It is generally assumed that recourse to violence and coercion is the final resort when individuals, and indeed whole societies, seek a solution to dispute and conflict. The more civilized a society, the lower the propensity to use force in order to arrive at some consensus, and the greater the likelihood of appealing to accepted rules, laws and procedures. Armed services enjoy a monopoly of a certain level of physical violence in society, either because of their legally sanctioned function and position, or because of their access to superior coercive power, with the consequence that they are always in a position to intervene as final arbiters in any dispute, or to resolve the conflict in favour of one or other party.

Given this assumption, it can be claimed that, by definition, armed services are not merely powerful, but have to be considered an elite. Those with access to armed services, or the armed services themselves, also have the potential to use that power and influence to further their own ends, rather than those in the interests of society as a whole. To Andreski, armed services and military organizations have not just determined who in society enjoyed access to power, wealth and status, but also (on the assumption that these were the ends and ambitions that man was forever seeking to acquire and satisfy) have influenced the nature and structure of society itself. Whether or not he was correct in his analysis, one inescapable result emerges from it; namely, that armed services are influential, and can be used within society for purposes of good and ill, in society's interests as a whole, or for purely selfish or sectional reasons.

In the study of armed services and society, the important consideration is not just that armed services are influential and powerful, but the degree of influence they exercise over the direction in which society is developing, especially in respect of such considerations as the sharing of decision making power, choices about society's priorities, and above all, the nature of society and its political system. A corollary of this is the question of who controls the armed services and how it is done. The fundamental issue, in the words of the much quoted aphorism from the first century Latin satirical poet Juvenal is, *Quis custodiet ipsos custodies?* – who shall guard the guardians themselves?

There have been many theories which have addressed these problems, each adopting a different approach to the role of elites in society. These are well worth considering briefly, not as comparative elite theory, but for the different insights they give regarding the relationship between armed services and society. In the light of the discussion above regarding the recruitment of those into the officer corps who had a stake in society and the *status quo*, it might be helpful to begin with the Marxist interpretation. Here, the elite is synonymous with a ruling class, and is a self-perpetuating phenomenon. Although the power of a ruling class is considered to be derived from its ownership and control over the means of production, and is therefore essentially materialist and economic, the agent of control over those who venture to challenge its position of power is the armed services. Either the loyalty of the armed services has to be bought, or their officers have to be drawn from the same, that is to say, ruling class.

It is no coincidence that the socialist revolutions that have succeeded have always been accompanied by a revolt among the ranks of the armed services; those that have failed, such as the Spanish Civil War, did so because the armed services ultimately united and held fast. The 1917 Bolshevik Revolution was accompanied by just such a revolt within certain sections of the armed services. In the ensuing civil war between forces loyal to the old Tsarist regime and those supporting the Revolution the final outcome was by no means a foregone conclusion. Had the Red Army not defeated the White in the winter of 1921–2, it is doubtful that the communist revolution would have been able to succeed.

Gaetano Mosca wrote in repudiation of the Marxist thesis, arguing that elites were a necessary and inevitable phenomenon; they had nothing to do with a conspiracy to maintain ruling class dominance. Just as organizations could not manage their affairs from day to day without some sort of leadership or direction, so society, he argued, would not survive without people with the ability and talent to organize, and others to protect and defend it physically against coercion from outside, thereby guaranteeing its continued existence. To Mosca, the armed services therefore constituted an inevitable elite in society, for they were to be found at the point of contact where two necessary societal attributes, organization and military prowess, conjoined. This stress on organizational skills and the relevance of the armed services was also a feature of Robert Michels's analysis of elites.

Vilfredo Pareto thought along similar lines, except that he placed greater emphasis on particular human attributes. He developed the argument that individuals rise to positions of power and authority on account of character and personal talents. He did not restrict these attributes to the more customary puritanical traits of hard work, dedication, commitment, integrity and skill, but recognized other, equally likely traits for success, including wit, deviousness, acumen and ambition. Many of these attributes are valued differently from one society to another, and what would be admissible in one culture as a means of rising to positions of authority would be considered amoral, corrupt, even illegal, in another. Whilst armed services in most states place high value on professional integrity and patriotism, there is ample evidence to show that many high-ranking officers have not been reticent in using their senior positions to blackmail, threaten, or by-pass normal political or social procedures. Machiavelli recognized this trait from firsthand experience among those who commanded armed forces and was under no illusion as to how these individuals could gain positions of immense influence and power. It has to be recognized that the temptation and opportunity to exploit a position of access to, or control over, coercive force for personal political advancement is ever present, requiring constant vigilance on the part of the political leadership.

Modern society is complex and its structure changes rapidly. There are those, like Burnham in his *The Managerial Revolution* and Milovan Djilas in *The New Class*, who feel that a new elite has emerged in the advanced industrial societies of the world as an immediate consequence of these fundamental changes. Their argument is an extension of those of Mosca and Michels, in that the mounting complexity of society, with its multiplicity of social, political, economic and cultural activities going on simultaneously, stimulates an even greater demand for organizational leadership and direction. These attributes, and those of the new elite, were to be found, they argued, among those who were the managers of the new large industrial corporations and conglomerates. These people were not, strictly, the owners of these corporations, but the top executives who understood how they worked and how they could, in a pluralist society, survive in an open, aggressive and competitive world. In the case of a totalitarian, one party state, as Djilas demonstrated, the new elite was drawn from those who had the skills to manage a centrally run politico-economic system and the massive nationalized industries within it.

Neither devoted any close attention to the armed services in their analysis, but a hint of what was likely to develop from their approach can be found in J. K. Galbraith's *The New Industrial State*, in which he noted that 'there has been a steady accumulation of evidence on the shift of power from owners to managers within the modern large corporation'. Ownership had become diffused and had moved away from personal control to institutional bodies representing a wide spectrum of financial institutions. These institutions, in turn, were increasingly dependent on managers' advice and direction over the operations of their industry. This new group of senior managers who formed the decision making elite in modern corporations he labelled the 'technostructure'. One characteristic of this group, he argued, was its close identification with the achievement of goals, not merely the goals of individual corporations and whole industries, but with national and state goals, such as economic growth, stability, technical and scientific advance and, 'most notable, national defence'. Although Galbraith's emphasis was on the ideological and cultural compatability of the priorities of the technostructure with national and state goals, and the common requirement for planning and estimates of performance, he did not develop his argument further, except to point out the readiness of the technostructure to 'identify itself closely with the goals of the armed services and, not infrequently, with the specific goals of a particular service'. The effect he said, was that the technostructure acquired immense influence over the definition of defence policy and security, and the weapons requirements of the armed services.

From a different perspective, the coalescence of interest of the armed services and the large defence–oriented industrial corporations was the focus of C. Wright Mills's argument in his study of power in the United States, entitled *The Power Elite*. Mills's study was, to some extent, a synthesis of Marx, Mosca, Burnham and Pareto, arguing from the premise that elites are closely associated with the roles they perform. By extending his analysis of these roles to incorporate the roles of the central bureaucracy, the armed services, as well as the big industrial corporations, he was able to point out that, together, these three sources in a pluralist society constituted in reality a single power elite. As such, this elite was not necessarily self-perpetuating, or based on birthright, merit, or any other attribute; if anything, it was on a national scale, and was closely related to, and dependent upon, the largest national institutions which had the greatest amount of capital and the widest spheres of interest. In his opinion the three institutions in the United States that most nearly met these criteria were the armed services, the central bureaucracy and the big industrial corporations. Together, these formed what was later referred to as the military–industrial complex, a grouping of immense influence and power.

During the United States' involvement in Indo-China, the power of the military–industrial complex became a focus of criticism by those who opposed the war. They felt that the continuation of the war, despite its unpopularity, was a consequence of the military–industrial complex using the conflict to further their own economic and political interests. Such was the power of the complex that it was able, so the critics claimed, to ignore democratic processes, control information, bypass legislation, and ride rough-shod over the economic principles upon which the American political and economic system was based. Illustrative of this line of argument are Victor Perlo's *Militarism and Industry*, Richard Kaufman's *War Profiteers* and Seymour Melman's *Pentagon Capitalism*.

A by-product of this clear statement of a powerful, central elite, by many analysts of the American political scene during the 1960s, was a revival of a Marxist interpretation of how American and, moreover, Western, society had developed. Baran and Sweezey's study of *Monopoly Capitalism* argued that the American confrontation with the socialist world and the subsequent Cold War was necessary to the growth and stability of capitalism in that it stimulated growth and prosperity, to a point that the economics of the West had become artificially dependent upon a continuing high level of defence expenditure. The same point was put by Michael Kidron in his *Western Capitalism since the War*, basing his argument on the multiplier and accelerator effects of spending on armed services and the annual service budget as important regulatory and control mechanisms in capitalist economies. Both studies were concerned with political capitalism, namely the use of public funds by those in power to maintain both the political system and a class structure. The notion of class as a concomitant of the military–industrial complex, which was central to C. Wright Mills, is also to be found in William Domhoff's *Who Rules America?* and Ferdinand Lundberg's *Rich and Super Rich*.

There is a wide variety of interpretations of what constitutes an elite, from where its members emanate, and how it is formed. All recognize that the armed services figure somewhere, for functional, institutional, ideological or imperative reasons. It is, therefore, necessary to establish whether it is more accurate to view the armed services as part of a single, ruling elite, like the power elite of C. Wright Mills or the ruling class of Marx, or more accurate to adopt a pluralist approach, which sees the armed services competing with other groups and organizations for influence over political decisions or future policies which affect society. The professionalism of the armed services and emphasis on the functional imperative would favour the latter; a more holistic view of modern society, and stress on the societal imperative, would emphasize the former. Liberal democracy, with which the West broadly identifies, would have to recognize the latter, since the separation of civil from military and the accountability of the one to the other is central to its ideology; but such an imperative should not prejudice the outcome of any analysis of armed services and elites in society.

In reality, neither approach is wholly sufficient; in most, if not all, instances, armed services behave as a pressure group in competition for influence over policies and decisions with other groups in society whilst, at the same time, through its membership and composition, having close identity with a single socio-political-economic elite whose influence transcends overt, legally established decision making procedures and notions of legitimacy. Where the emphasis is to lie in this synthesis of the two approaches to armed services and elites depends largely on the nature of the society that is being examined, and the problem that is being addressed. Compare, for example, the influence of the armed services in societies where there are traditional or political oligarchies, such as the Arab sheikdoms or Latin America, with the liberal constitutional democracies of Europe, North America and Australia. Neither of these two categories, however, is mutually exclusive, and decision making authority can only be explained in terms of probabilities.

If elites are characterized by the influence they exercise, the earlier question can be repeated: should armed services be considered as part of, or as, an Elite? In which context should armed services be seen, that of the formal processes of decision making, or the informal exercise of discussion and manoeuvre, characterized by such notions as that of the 'inner circle', the 'old boy network', and the 'establishment'? The answer can only be given in the most tentative terms and as a recommendation: the most fruitful insight into the influence of armed services is to look at recruitment into armed services, and to compare it with the social, class, educational, ethnic and national origins of those who enter other professions and organizations in society. In this way, the interests, loyalties and attitudes of service officers can be weighed against civilian leaders. In Britain, where these comparisons have been made, the results tend to confirm that 'the military's political loyalties have never been seriously put to the test'. Cromwell's dictum would seem to live on, not least because there exists an identical community 'held together by many formal and informal contacts and shared experiences and enjoying influence, through the position and association of many of its members, over important areas of British social and economic life ... The military career is not the least important of the common factors of this community.' The same would hold true in most other states, irrespective of the nature of their political systems.

The acid test, of course, comes when the armed services are in conflict with either the government, or other powerful groups in society, over problems in which they have mutual, but possibly exclusive, interest. In other words, the issue, which by definition must be one in which the stakes are high, transcends social, class or political loyalties; the armed services have therefore to compete for influence or remain quiescent in accordance with their professional ethic. Such a predicament could be, and often is, resolved only after resort to power politics, involving the use, or threatened use, of physical force. Under these circumstances the armed services can be, and have often proved to be, the decisive factor. Lenin recognized this when he noted that 'no revolution ... can triumph without the help of a portion of the armed forces that sustained the old regime'.

There is no doubt that the armed services, by nature of their function, and their potential political significance, form part either of a single elite or can exercise considerable influence within a pluralist society. In more complex societies, features of both elitism and pluralism can usually be seen simultaneously. Only when society faces radical change is overt, independent action of the armed services likely. For the most part, they have proved adept at ensuring their institutional interests are well satisfied without necessarily compromising officers' individual values and loyalties.

Armed services do not exist independently of the nation-state; they are, by definition, an integral part of the society that falls within national territorial–state–boundaries. Whilst ethnic and cultural groups may transcend national and state boundaries, armed services do not, since they are by definition, a state institution. There are no 'international' armed services; at best there are alliances of national armed forces that serve together in pursuit of a common goal, as in the cases of United Nations, NATO or Warsaw Pact forces. But the proposition here is that armed services of states also reflect the society of which that state is largely comprised; in them can be found the predominant cultural characteristics of that society. Similarities between the armed services of different states are primarily functional, organizational and procedural.

On the assumption that these similarities are not sufficient to understand the essential relationship between armed services and society, it is necessary to isolate those societal characteristics that are most evident in the features of the armed services and which affect their relationship and interaction with society. In this chapter, three of the most dominant characteristics of society have been discussed: first, the level of technology in society and its associated prerequisites, the standard of education, industrialization and the strength of the economy; second, the particular culture of society and the associated connotations of history, tradition, political ideology and system, and *Weltanschauung*; and, third, the social and economic structure of society and, in particular, the existence of elites. All three have a strong bearing on the sort of armed services a state has and govern to a large degree the dynamic relationship that exists between them and the rest of society.

The overall picture is highly complex: on the one hand there are forces separating armed services from civilians, making them functionally distinctive, professional, and structurally subservient to a political authority: on the other there are equally strong forces drawing armed services closer to the parent society which strengthen common values, overlapping functions and shared interests. The challenge for the student of armed services and society is to find or construct some overarching theory that can offer some explanation why the relationship between the two is different between states and societies. Chapters 4, 5 and 6 consider this challenge.

4

Approaches to the Study of Armed Services and Society

Between nation-states, the relationship between society and the armed services will be different, although they will share many common features. Because each society has, almost by definition, a different culture and faces different problems in the international arena, there is a strong case for avoiding any attempt to formulate a partial or an overarching theory about armed services–society relations, and to treat each case as being exceptional or unique. Were this to be the preferred approach – and there are sound intellectual grounds why this should be so – the particular factors and variables to be taken into account would, in all probability, be the same in almost all cases; in which event, the grounds exist, at best, for the formulation of a general theory, or at least, for partial theories that have wide application.

Many scholars have formulated theoretical propositions which attempt to explain, or provide an explanatory method to find the answers to particular problems that have interested them concerning the relationship of armed services to their parent society. This chapter examines some of the better known scholarly contributions and offers some suggestions why they should be given serious attention. But before looking at specific examples, one important caveat has to be borne in mind: each theorist was essentially addressing a different problem, or posing a different question, regarding the relationship between armed services and society, for which reason conclusions have varied, different emphases have been placed on relevant factors, and the hypotheses offered have not always appeared to have much in common.

This, however, should not present a problem since our interest is to learn about armed services and society relationships in all their manifestations; in many instances a partial theory, or one that specifically addresses one type of society or one sort of problem, is often preferable to one that is overarching or universal, and which misses specific details. No one problem is like another where armed services and society relationships are concerned; most of the theoretical approaches that are selected here have the capacity to provide a way of tackling the more likely problems facing most societies' relations with their armed services with an acceptable degree of thoroughness and depth.

The first post-Second World War scholar of any significance in the field to whom attention should be given is the sociologist, Stanislav Andrzejewski (now, Andreski). This is not simply because he was the first to publish a major contribution to the study of armed services and society (in 1952), but more especially because his study has had enduring relevance, having been revised in a later edition in 1967. This continued relevance stems from his looking at the armed services and society relationship from a general perspective, and the range of hypotheses he formulated in the process. The overall problem he addressed was that of the influence of military organizations (the armed services) on the structure and development of society, an area which he felt had not been given adequate attention because of the 'insidious utopianism that pervades sociological thinking'.

His book, *Military Organisation and Society*, which he described as 'a reconnaissance flight which only succeeded in locating the most important issues', was a bold attempt to remedy the situation and fill the gap. Its major contribution, aside from mapping a way forward in a heuristic and engaging way, was to give proper emphasis to the self-evident fact (better appreciated perhaps outside the advanced industrial world than within it) that 'military organisation influences social structure mainly by determining the distribution of naked power or, to use another word, the ability to use violence'.

On the premise that there has been throughout recorded history an omnipresence of struggle, that man is in other words basically self-seeking, desiring power, wealth and status (glory) – ends which he encapsulates in one of his many neologisms, 'ophelimities' and later redefined as 'invidious values' – and that he is more than ready and prepared to use naked force and coercion to acquire and retain them, Andreski procedes to construct a complex model of the many variables that affect one way or another the influence of military force on social structures. Among the more salient of these variables he identifies the size of the political unit, the effects of war, technology, the extent of government authority and regulation, the degree of militarism within society, and the level of economic development.

The resulting model of military influence on social structure is too complex to be summarized here, though his central thesis is both

71

enlightening and straightforward. The important point to remember is that he is centrally concerned with social structures; everything else is secondary. On the premise already outlined, he asserted that society is pyramidical in shape, with a few forming the elite at the top, enjoying power, wealth and status, with the rest below increasing geometrically in number as they go down the social scale. The critical question he then posed was how those at the top, with so much privilege, gain and retain their positions. His conclusion, quite simply, was that they had access to, and control over, coercive power.

Andreski did not insist, however, that this control over naked physical power was the only element; it was merely the most important one, omnipresent, and the arbiter of 'last resort'. When faced with a challenge to their position of power and wealth, either from outside the state or within, the elite is confronted with a dilemma: to meet the challenge from their own resources, by themselves, or to use their resources by 'buying' support, or promising privileges and other normative rewards, in return for assistance from lower strata in society. In the past, this meant engaging foreign mercenaries (though this often proved unreliable), or making concessions to indigenous groups, such as the granting of freedoms or land ownership, to those who would come to the elite's defence.

It is this dependence by elites on armed support to counter challenges to their authority and position of advantage that lies at the heart of Andreski's model. The indicator he uses to gauge the extent of this dependence is the military participation ratio, defined as the ratio of military utilized individuals to the total population. In war, the ratio automatically goes up, and it is in war that concessions are invariably made to those who are prepared to rally to the flag; it is no coincidence, as Arthur Marwick has demonstrated in his study, *Women in War*, that the cause of women's rights and emancipation was greatly helped during both the First and Second World Wars; the same phenomenon, as far as black rights in the USA is concerned, happened during the period of the Vietnam war.

As a general proposition, Andreski argued that the higher the ratio, the lower the height of social stratification. This is the same as saying that the disparity in wealth, status and power between the elite and the masses diminishes the more the latter become involved in defending the state, and the political leadership, against attack. The optimum ratio is that which pertains when the state and its leadership is able to protect itself effectively without wasting resources, given existing levels of military technology and so on; the actual military ratio is the one which prevails at any one time due to the interplay of many factors, not least of which is the quality of the leadership itself, the legitimacy of the regime, and the prevailing political culture.

Despite his heuristic initiative, Andreski's book did not stimulate either the range or sorts of studies that might have been expected. Nor did the book attract the attention it deserved, irrespective of whether his basic premises about man's motivations in life were acceptable. It is more probable that his observations about the sensitivities of sociologists were the correct explanation, especially at a time when the world was still trying to recover from six years of total war, and was coming to terms with a period of undisguised and overt conflict between two powerfully armed and antagonistic ideological blocs. Instead, the problem most analysts of armed services and society preferred to address was that concerning the intervention of the armed services in civil affairs, and, in particular, in government.

Under the circumstances, this was hardly surprising. The intervention of the armed services in the conduct of government had become a relatively regular occurrence throughout the world, ranging from overt interference in governmental and political processes, to intervention and the supplanting or replacement of governments by means of a *coup d'état*. Intervention is the stuff of high drama and is always newsworthy. The number of films featuring steely-eyed, hard faced generals taking over the high office of state by force is legion, and a whole lexicon of terms has been created, covering the wide array of means, techniques and styles of armed services' intervention in the political affairs of states. But perhaps the most immediate reasons for scholarly concern to find explanations for armed services' intervention in politics are not only that it happens so frequently, but also that there are so many states in the world (about 60 per cent of the total in 1958) that are governed directly or indirectly by members of armed services. The military regime is still the most common form of political system today.

In the late 1950s, the incidence of coups instigated by members of armed services became so frequent that, quite properly, sound explanations were sought. Most of these coups took place in the newly independent states of Africa and South-East Asia, though for almost a half century a succession of coups, military regimes, and military counter coups had already occurred in Central and Latin America. The particular concern for an explanation in the late 1950s, however, was prompted by an unease among the ex-imperial powers, and especially in Britain, that the political systems that had been established in their ex-colonies after independence were neither robust enough to withstand internal threats, nor to exercise proper authority, nor to guarantee democracy. Since most of these political systems had been modelled on those of their colonial masters, such a frequent breakdown in democracy and in the capacity of civil government to cope raised serious questions about their appropriateness and efficacy. The coups of the 1950s and 1960s in the newly independent, but nonetheless less developed, countries of the world raised ripples of doubt and, to a degree, undermined the confidence of the advanced states themselves, in their own political systems.

The first person who addressed this general problem in any great depth was Samuel E. Finer, and the results of his analysis appeared in his book *The Man on Horseback*. The initial question he addressed was why armed services intervened in politics; it was not long, however, before he came to the conclusion that this was not the most relevant way of approaching the problem. With immense insight and imagination, he simply reversed the question, asking why it was that armed services did *not* intervene in politics, thereby recognizing, along with Andreski, what has been the case throughout history, that individuals with access to, and control over, physical force have influence and immense potential political power. The critical question for him was clearly why those who are in such a position choose not to use it.

Finer was not alone in expressing concern that the incidence of military inspired coups constituted a threat to Western democracy and liberal systems of government; like the others, he worked from the assumption that armed services should not meddle in areas that were properly none of their business. Specifically these were civilian matters, and there was a consensus that there was a clear distinction between what was the armed services' sphere of responsibility and action, and what was not. The one should not usurp the other, except that, as in any liberal democratic political system, the armed services should be subordinate and accountable to the civil government. From Finer's perspective, this distinction between civil and military, or more accurately between armed services and the rest of society, was a structural one. The all important dividing line was drawn between the armed services as a state institution, with clearly defined institutional boundaries, and all other civil institutions. For this reason, the intervention of armed services in politics or in government was the assumption of the duties and responsibilities, normally ascribed in law to civil institutions, by representatives and personnel from the armed services.

The attractiveness of Finer's approach is that it is premised on a clear, unequivocal structural distinction between what is proper for the armed services to do, and what is the power and authority of

74

government. The relationship between armed services and society is clearly prescribed by a legal definition of the powers and spheres of responsibility of the armed services; and if the political system is to be maintained, and if democracy is to be assured, the armed services should not venture beyond, or penetrate, these boundaries. For this reason, Finer's focus of interest is the institutionalization of the military on the one hand, and the degree to which different societies attach importance to state institutions and to the formal and legal processes of government and decision making, on the other. The thesis he develops is that different societies attach varying degrees of importance to state institutions and legal processes; the lower this importance becomes, the lower is the restraint on the armed services not to intervene in public affairs.

The significance that Finer attached to the structure of government and public respect for the rule of law enabled him to categorize societies according to their political culture. Political culture he saw reflected in the level of respect, support and importance accorded by a population to the institutions and processes of government. In societies where this respect was low or minimal, he found that there was a greater likelihood for armed services' interference and intervention in politics and government, and concluded that this was because they would not be restrained by prevailing customs, traditions, ideology or political ethics. Military intervention he defined as the 'armed forces constrained substitution of their own policies and/or their persons for those of the recognised civil authorities'. Finer's hypothesis, therefore, is that armed services intervention is less likely the more mature the political culture of a society. The coups of the 1950s he reasoned were a reflection of countries with a low, or minimal, political culture, where respect for the democratic institutions and processes of government had not had time to develop or become established.

Finer's explanation for the reasons why armed services are more likely to intervene in politics and government, based on notions of levels of political culture, opened up further discussion of the methods and opportunities of which armed services could take advantage; in this respect, his contribution is enlightening. But as a general explanation why armed services intervene, his thesis is limited for two reasons. First, having based his analysis on structures and institutions of government, whole areas of armed services' involvement in the affairs of the state and of society are excluded, such as in cultural, social and economic affairs. Second, the thesis is not an explanatory one and certainly has no potential for prediction. The difficulty is that his argument is axiomatic, in that armed services' intervention is most likely in societies of minimal or low political culture, and societies of a low or minimal political culture are those where armed services intervention is most likely.

At best, *The Man on Horseback* provides the student of armed services and society a comprehensive *tabula rasa* of factors that should be taken into consideration when analysing military intervention in politics. This is a most valuable contribution and should not be overlooked; but the task of working out which admixture of variables together help explain why, when, and how the armed services act the way they do, remains the responsibility of the analyst. Regrettably, Finer offers no predictive or explanatory theory. This is illustrated by the book's being unable to provide any explanation why states with a mature political culture are either confronted by, or experience, armed services intervention – as in the case of France in 1961 or, moreover, rumours to the same effect in Britain during the early 1970s.

Arguing along similar lines, and from a similar premise, as Finer, Wilson MacWilliams in his volume, *Garrisons and Governments*, places great emphasis on the respect with which different populations hold their institutions of government. In a manner of speaking, however, MacWilliams reverses Finer's ideas by emphasizing the importance that the armed services, rather than the population as a whole, attach to institutions of government. He notes that one fundamental duty of armed services is to defend government institutions; in the absence of their having any respect for these institutions, armed services are not only unlikely to perform this duty, but are also more likely to be responsible for their removal, no matter what popular opinion may be. The trouble is, however, that the armed services, as an institution of government, are closely identified with the rules of the system, that is to say they are encompassed within constitutional law and convention. Frequently these rules require the armed services to be involved, without the public at large realizing it, in a wide sphere of activities that often go well beyond their immediate, formal, legal duties. The extent of these 'hidden' rules differs between one society and another, but it would not be unreasonable to assume that the more advanced and complex the society, the greater this is likely to be the case.

Complexity is a factor that has to be taken into consideration when addressing the problems associated with armed services intervention. This is implicit in Finer's thesis, since societies of mature political culture are not only older, with well-established political traditions, but are also more complex, economically advanced and socially integrated. The opposite is the case with states of low or minimal political culture, which tend to be younger, poorer and smaller. This line of argument was also suggested by Gino Germani and Kalman Silvert, in the conclusion to their study of military intervention in Latin America in the 1950s. They found that the majority of military dictatorships were to be found among those societies that had a simple social structure, and where the requirements – and public expectations – of government were relatively modest. In contrast, the explanation why the idea of an armed services coup in Britain in the 1970s was scarcely worth entertaining, even if some service personnel might have welcomed the prospect, was that the task was too complex and too burdensome for them to begin to undertake, even with the active assistance of the central bureaucracy, if that were forthcoming.

The prospect of armed services meddling in government and exercising undue influence in the political affairs of the nation has haunted American analysts and scholars right from the days of the Founding Fathers. Indeed, the experience of colonial rule enforced by the British army and navy persuaded the framers of the American Constitution that the very existence of armed services within society was more than a potential, but a very real threat to democracy. As they made provision to ensure that there were effective checks and balances against the accretion of too much power within the three branches of American government, so they also incorporated special provisions to prevent the armed services exercising undue power and influence.

One such provision was to make the President of the United States of America, an elected office, Commander-in-Chief of the armed services. Another was that only the Congress was empowered to declare war. The object was to reduce American armed services to the barest minimum, sufficient only to meet the strategic situation the country confronted. 'Standing Armies', Congress declared in 1784, 'in time of peace are inconsistent with the principles of republican governments'. As if to place a constraint on even the few servicemen remaining, the Constitution initially limited the life of the Army to two years before further appropriations were permissible, though no such provision was made to cover the navy. In the event of war, or a real and present threat to the Union, the necessary forces were to be raised from a national militia system in which all males were obliged to serve.

These general principles have been maintained in the United States, and a public wariness of large peacetime standing armies and undue military influence has been evident since the Revolution. Nowhere has this been better traced than in Walter Millis's *Arms and Men*; in his book he demonstrated that the experience of the Second World War and the advent of nuclear arsenals and confrontation with the communist states in the East introduced a change in traditional American attitudes towards armed services and their relationship with society. The theme was taken up by C. Wright Mills in his book, *The Power Elite*, a study of power in the United States during the 1950s, but the concern received its biggest boost when President Eisenhower, in his farewell address in 1961, warned the American people of the increase in the influence of armed services and the emergence of a new phenomenon in American experience, the so-called military–industrial complex.

After the nation had been at war, it was customary for the United States to demobilize; conscripted servicemen would return to civilian life, the professionals would return to barracks, and surplus equipment would be melted down, metaphorically, to produce ploughshares. The international circumstances prevailing at the end of the Second World War which led to the polarization of world society, the responsibilities that devolved upon the United States as the only state with the economic and military power to police the world and deter further armed conflict, and the impact of new weapons systems and nuclear arsenals, determined that full demobilization was not politically expedient at the end of hostilities. The era of large American peacetime professional standing armed services involved in an Alliance, in a state of permanent hostility with another militarily powerful adversary, and engaged in a qualitative and sometimes quantitative arms race was born. With these new circumstances came the attendant dilemma of the maintenance of a permanent nuclear capability which was designed not to be used, and which, if used, could not, as Mills concluded, 'be brought rationally to bear upon the decision of any of the political, economic, emotional or philosophical issues by which men still remain divided'.

Concerned at what this development meant for the United States but in particular for American democratic principles, Samuel Huntington in his book, *The Soldier and the State*, attempted to find answers. In so doing, he not only gave recognition to the importance of the relationship between armed services and society, but also provided a theory of that relationship. In the first instance, the theory was directed at an explanation for the prevailing relationship within the United States and, in the second, at providing a guideline for other states that were also concerned about the growth of the influence of their armed services.

His particular theoretical contribution was to demonstrate that a distinction had to be made between the operational side of national security policy, concerned with external and internal defence, and the institutional. The latter dealt with 'the manner in which operational policy was formulated and executed'. National security decision making encompassed the institutions of government, the armed services themselves, and the political processes by which the public at large was involved in questions governing its protection. The objective was to ensure adequate security without sacrificing other societal values, much along the lines of the aim of the Founding Fathers to have armed services of only sufficient size to meet existing strategic conditions. In more practical terms, as implied in Huntington's distinction between functional and societal imperatives, the objective was to achieve the right balance between the functional requirements of the armed services on the one hand, and the societal values of the public at large, on the other.

Central to Huntington's search for an answer to his question whether or not American liberal ideals of democracy had been compromised by increases in the size, budget and scope of the armed services, was the concept of professionalism. Characterized as being a special type of vocation involving expertise, responsibility and corporateness, professionalism held, according to Huntington, the key to civilian control over the armed services. It was far preferable, he argued, to stress the professionalism of the armed services as an objective method of control rather than by the subjective means of maximizing civilian authority over them. Better that the armed services themselves were prompted to promote military efficiency whilst recognizing their subservience to the state, than impose civilian values and directives to the probable detriment of military efficiency and, ultimately, national security.

The attraction of Huntington's theory at the time was its compatibility with a distinct change in American ideology, from nineteenth century liberalism to a 'realist', new conservatism – a shift in attitude that bore on the relations between armed services and society, and was born out of the post-Second World War experience. Whilst the liberal philosophy had been hostile to armed services and generally looked to subjective means of control and the civilianization of servicemen, the 'new conservatism' of American society recognized the need for standing armies with a high degree of skill if national security were to be guaranteed. Professionalism, as a service ethic, gave some assurance of a balance between the operational needs of security and adequate civil control, since encompassed within that ethic, by definition, was the ideal of responsibility. What responsibility meant in this context was the commitment of the armed services to the highest standards of defence and readiness and, more importantly, their obligation not to pursue policies or to take action which were inimical to the values and preferences of the society they served.

Huntington's argument, like Finer's, was axiomatic inasmuch as civil control over the armed services was best served by maximizing professionalism, and professionalism was the best solution because it recognized and encompassed, *a priori*, civilian control. Whilst his theory might be challenged on these grounds, and, as at the time it first appeared criticized for his dependence upon the American armed services' own definition of professionalism as their assurance to him of disinterest in the civil affairs of government, his study did point to some important considerations for the student of civil–military relations. Foremost among these is the awareness that no matter how much the armed services stress pure professionalism in the sense of their exclusive expertise and corporateness, they are not independent of society, and emphasis of this fact during their training and education is not incompatible with the objective of maximizing efficiency and national security. Indeed, the Federal Republic of Germany has, under the watchful eye of allies and adversaries alike, made careful provision to ensure against a repetition of German or Prussian militarism by indoctrinating all its servicemen, professionals and conscripts alike, with the ideal of *innere Führung*, that is to say, the social responsibility of the serviceman to the society he or she serves.

To some extent Huntington recognized the limitations of his theory when he extended his interest beyond his immediate concern with the United States. Recognizing that the relations between armed services and society operate on two levels, the power of the officer corps relative to civilian groups and the compatibility of the professional service ethic with the prevailing political ideology in society, he had to concede that there were states in the world where the prevailing ideology was wholly incompatible with Western concepts of professionalization, except in terms of armed services being paid experts. The ideal ideology for his prescription would be conservatism; less suitable would be Marxist, socialist and early liberal ideologies. For Huntington's theory to be relevant, and for there to be a balance between the requirements of the armed services and the values of society in respect of national security policy, not only would ideal circumstances have to prevail, but there would also have to be a clear, and universally understood appreciation of the security threat that faced society. Such ideal conditions obviously do not exist; for this reason his suggestion that more objective military professionalism should be encouraged as a means of promoting adequate civil control over the armed services should be treated with great caution.

Not only are the preconditions for Huntington's theory unrealistic; his assumptions about professionalism have also been challenged. Finer, in *The Man on Horseback*, noted that in certain circumstances the armed services of a state may be required either as a matter of legal, constitutional requirement, or as a matter of being the nation-state's institution of last resort, to intervene in government and assume the responsibility for ruling society. To respond under these conditions would be a matter of professional duty, thus demonstrating that professionalism alone is not a guarantee of non-involvement in politics. Furthermore, it should also be pointed out that in many states it would be an exaggeration to refer to armed services as 'professional', except in the loosest sense of the term.

It would not be appropriate to end this discussion of theories of professionalism without reference to Morris Janowitz's study of the American *Professional Soldier*, since he also addressed the questions whether or not the post-Second World War expansion of the armed services in the USA had resulted in their greater domestic political involvement, their social and intellectual distancing from the rest of society, and their lack of appreciation of the proper purpose of military power. He addressed these problems by looking at the American professional officer corps, noting that, whilst there had been changes in the armed services' organizational style, skill differential with civilian groups, recruitment patterns, and degree of political awareness, the American armed services had indeed retained their professional distinctiveness and integrity. This professional ethic, he concluded, was adequate to maintain 'civilian political supremacy without destroying required professional autonomy'. Moreover, Janowitz proceeded to note that the surest guarantee against excessive armed services involvement in domestic politics was their own disagreements over security policy and defence budget resource allocation, and inter- and intra-organizational rivalries and ambitions. In varying degrees, these observations also apply to other states, especially where there are standing armed services, a high level of defence spending, and the use of advanced equipment.

The most detailed criticisms of professionalism as a basis of contemporary civil–military relationships is Bengt Abrahamsson's *Military Professionalization and Political Power*. He did not so much offer a theory of civil–military relations as point out that military professionalism alone did not provide an answer, either to the relationship, or to what underlay it. His argument was that armed services are like all other organizations, in that they are goal-seeking and concerned primarily with growth, improvement, and, ultimately, their own survival. The image of subservient, armed services submissive to governmental or civilian dictates based on purely professional grounds, he concluded, was incorrect. Armed services by nature were, he suggested, conservative in approach and attitude to most social and political issues, sometimes extremely so; their training focused directly on the organization's goals, and these they were expected to prosecute not only in combat against an enemy, but also within the political arena, and in competition with civilian groups. Far from being distanced from society, armed services, Abrahamsson contended, should be seen for what they were in reality: a politicized, highly active and motivated interest group, one that not infrequently also had strong political views.

Those who have asked why armed services intervene in politics, or how they might be prevented from so doing, have sought to underpin their answers with reference to a body of theory. None has succeeded completely, though each recognizes a number of factors that have to be taken into consideration. These factors broadly fall into one of two groups: the functional imperative of the armed services, such as professionalism; or the societal imperative, such as ideology. The admixture of these two groups of variables, that is to say the relationship between the two, is taken to determine the degree of likelihood of armed services intervention.

Not all scholars, however, have limited their inquiry merely to the question of intervention of the armed services. Some, like David Rappaport, have seen the relationship between the armed services and society as being a determining influence on the type of society that emerges. His argument was premised on two factors: first, the power that armed services have at their disposal; and, second, the function that they are called upon, or are expected, to perform. The theory is that only particular types of society would have armed services fulfilling particular functions. On the strength of this premise, Rappaport is able to categorize three broad types of society. The first, and most prevalent, is the society whose armed services are engaged by the government, or the political leadership, primarily in internal security and policing duties. In reality, these services exist more often than not to defend the person, or persons, of those in power and authority, than to maintain internal law and order. He labels such states as 'praetorian', after the personal guard that was created to protect the person of the Roman Emperor. The potential for the services in such a society to abuse their power and exceed their prime function is, of course, considerable. Evidence from such states, where the armed services functions are primarily internal, points to their being relatively poor economically, with a small, wealthy oligarchy and a large, mostly rural, poor and scattered population. The structure of these societies is fairly simple and they are likely to have an inept or undisciplined administration. Invariably in such societies the armed services emerge as the only institution with any degree of discipline, training and cohesion; for this reason, they are a focal point of political intrigue among those in power or those who aspire to it, including the service leaders themselves. Military regimes, by definition, are a form of praetorian state.

The second broad category Rappaport identifies encompasses those states whose armed services essentially exist to defend society against external attack and to act in support of its foreign policies. As external defence is the armed services' principal function, internal political stability is assumed; indeed the use of armed services internally would constitute 'the threat system of the state turned in on itself', and destroy the political equilibrium that is one of the hallmarks of such a system. He refers to this category as the civil and military polity to differentiate both the separation of the armed services function from society as a whole and the subservience of the one to the other. One feature of this arrangement is the professionalism of the armed services and the constrained military obligations required of its citizens. The 'mature' states of Western Europe, North America, Scandinavia and other Western-style nations fall easily into this category.

The third category based on armed services' functions is the nation-in-arms. Here the dominant function of the armed services and of each citizen is public duty. Military service is a direct personal obligation that befalls all citizens, irrespective of status, wealth, ethnic origin or, sometimes, gender. The 'nation-in-arms' category encompasses those states that either have adopted a political system which does not differentiate between civil and military, with everyone subject to a common political ideology and a single party authority, as in communist states, or face a threat which is total, in the sense that the very existence of the state and its entire population is constantly at stake. Israel would be the clearest example, for it is the declared objective of some of its Arab neighbours to see the country's extinction; consequently it becomes the commitment of every Israeli citizen to contribute, as a matter of patriotic and national duty, to the continued existence of the state. Such an arrangement blurs the distinction between what is strictly an armed services matter and what is purely civilian.

To base such a general theory of the relationship between armed services and society only on the function that the armed services are called upon to fulfil is far too ambitious. It cannot provide answers to questions why the functions were what they were, or explain change, either to the armed services or to society. However, Rappaport provides a simple taxonomy upon which to base a typology of civil–military relations and, by extension, categories of state. Although very general and not amenable to detailed scrutiny, the typology is nonetheless a valuable point of departure for further study of armed services.

The work of Amos Perlmutter, and in particular his *Military and Politics in Modern Times* follows naturally from the contribution of Huntington, Rappaport and Abrahamsson, since he is concerned particularly with professionalism on the one hand, and praetorianism, on the other. Rejecting idealistic 'deterministic' distinctions between military and civil functions of state that were characteristic of past views of armed service and society relationships, Perlmutter emphasized that in the modern state there was a wide area of overlap between the two. The degree of overlap, based on a symbiotic relationship between armed services and other state institutions in the determination of national security policy, would, however, vary according to prevailing ideologies, orientations and organizational structures. In seeking an explanation why these relationships should vary, he appeals to the 'fusionist' theory, which recognizes that 'bureaucracy and politics as well as government and administration, are all symbiotically connected'. From the point of view of the armed services, he is stipulating that their military professionalism, the development of exclusive expertise and corporateness, becomes linked with their bureaucratic function as participant in overall defence and security management.

In other words, he considers that professionalism alone is not sufficient to explain civil–military relationships. In the modern state, where power in society is diffuse and essential functions are performed by complex, differentiated and interdependent organizations and institutions, the armed services are inextricably involved in policy making processes. As a consequence, in some states, especially the more complex and advanced ones, the armed services, as professionals, are drawn into national policy making; in the less advanced countries, they become involved in politics and not infrequently assume charge of both military and state bureaucratic functions.

By adopting this fusionist, or sharing of governmental responsibility, approach, Perlmutter is offering an approach to the study of armed services and society relationships which is essentially praetorian in complexion. All states are to a degree praetorian in as much as the corporate nature of government and bureaucracy draws the armed services into the affairs of state. Old vertical relationships between governments and armed services, he concludes, have been replaced by horizontal ones, and conflicts occur not between the services and civilians, but between corporate organizations in contention over the direction of national policy, resource allocation and political orientations. These are the very issues to which Abrahamsson referred when he noted that it was in the corporate interests of the services to persuade government and society that their view of 'reality' (*Weltanschauung*) was necessarily correct. Only on the strength of the armed services' professional expertise in matters of security can they expect to prevail in such debates.

A determining factor of the extent of intervention by armed services in society and its politics is the sort of organizations they are. To Perlmutter, modern armed services are characterized by their corporate professionalism. This is not only a new social type, but it also provides the premise underlying his subsequent analysis. As professional, the armed services determine the minimum standards of expertise and behaviour of their members; as corporate, they work to maintain themselves in existence and protect their exclusivity, a difficult undertaking in modern pluralist states. It is in the corporate aspect of armed services that the key to Perlmutter's thinking can be found, since the emphasis on exclusivity will influence the extent to which he expects them to be prepared to intervene in politics in the face of social, economic, political and ideological changes within the nation-state. As the institution 'most closely identified with the political regime', and 'most dependent of all the bureaucracies within the modern nation-state', the armed services are most susceptible of change. In consequence, the corporateness of the armed services is both a restraint against intervention in politics and a stimulus for it.

He concludes that armed services will only intervene, or go extensively beyond their immediate professional concerns, when their corporate or bureaucratic management roles are threatened. No matter what the prevailing political regime or ideology, armed services are involved in the political affairs of all nations. The nature of their involvement has enabled him to categorize three broad groupings of armed services in the modern nation-state: the strictly professional, the praetorian and the revolutionary. Each arises in response to the type of civilian institutional authority. The professional corporate armed services are mostly found in the Western liberal democracies; the praetorian in military dictatorships and in those states where civilian authority is weak; and the revolutionary where there is a strong ideological component which encompasses the whole of society. In the first two, the desire of the armed services to maintain their corporate exclusivity is high; their only difference is the degree to which they take independent political initiatives. The revolutionary soldier, whilst ideologically 'corporate', would be unlikely to exist; were he to be so, he would automatically fall outside the ideological conditions laid down in the provisions of the state.

Perlmutter adds to the body of theory on armed services and society by incorporating, more comprehensively than Huntington did, contemporary corporatist theories of the state. He also provided a useful synthesis of Huntington and Rappaport in that he identified three categories of state, each very similar to Rappaport's types, and related them to the modern corporate, professional armed services. The bulk of his study then explored the experience of different states that came within his three categories. Regrettably, however, his fusionist theory did not provide the explanation why particular states experienced military coups, or why particular states experienced revolutionary change; all it could do was to note that there had been change, and, as a consequence, the characteristics of the armed services and their participation in the affairs of the state also changed, prompted by their desire for corporate independence and integrity.

Theories of civil–military relations should provide explanations not only for why the relationship in any one state is what it is at any one time, but also why the relationship changes over time. As Finer could not give an explanation why mature societies could experience intervention by armed services just as much as societies with a low political culture, and Perlmutter could not explain with his corporate theory why praetorian or revolutionary armed services appeared in the first place, so the contribution of Maury Feld fell short of the requirement to explain change. Nonetheless, his study, 'A typology of military organisations', is important, for he is the only one to base his argument on the 'role and the position specific armies claim in the social structure and the form of the popular beliefs in which such claims find expression'. His hypothesis is that these claims and beliefs underlie the attitudes of armed services, which determine, in turn, their use and organization. In other words, the role that armed services is called upon to perform not only reveals something about them, but also about the society and its ideology, of which they are a part.

Building on this hypothesis, Feld proceeded to identify five types of armies – navies and other armed services did not figure in his analysis. He did this according to their structures and the political systems from which they emerged. The first was where the army leadership was an alien body ruling a conquered society in an imperial role; the second was the same leadership that had integrated itself within the indigenous community to form what was essentially a feudal society; the third was a military leadership that was part of society as members of a political elite within a nation-state under a single, absolute sovereign; the fourth was the military that had a role in a representative society as a consequence of particular (professional) skills and expertise; and the last was a military that was part and parcel of a totalitarian system, fulfilling that role prescribed by the prevailing political ideology.

According to Feld, the five categories reflect the states of mind about armed services and society open to both the serviceman and woman and the civilian. Furthermore, they each reflect social–military relationships inasmuch as the roles ascribed to the military reflect the needs defined by the parent society. The first and last represent the poles of social–military relationships with the former reflecting an absolute military dominance and the latter a totally communal one. Conflicts between the military and society occur when the roles adopted by a given military group and those assigned to it by society are at variance. The greater the consensus between military and political elites, the greater the stability of the political system. At the two extremes this can be achieved through coercion, or by ideological conformity.

The fascination of Feld's typology and the theory embedded in it, lies in his apparent chronology. Taking the Roman Empire as the starting point, Europe has witnessed the expansion and control of the armies of Imperial Rome as the instance of external military dominance over society; after its decline and fall, there was the emergence of the feudal system. Next came the establishment of the nation-state under an absolute sovereign, to be followed by the nation-state under a consti-tutional monarch or republic. Finally, we witness in the East the creation of a single party communist system. Regrettably, he made no attempt to explain why societies should change from one type into another, or indicate clearly what was the role of armed services as instruments of change. Nevertheless, Feld's typology and the emphasis he gave to the roles that armed services have adopted, or have been given, are significant contributions to the understanding of the relation-ship of armed services with society over time, and help to explain why conflicts between the two break out, and why sometimes they coexist reasonably harmoniously.

None of the theorists discussed so far offers any theory about armed services and society relationships that has any predictive capability. This could not be said of Harold Lasswell, whose best-known contri-bution in the field of political studies is, arguably, his analysis of civil–military relations, which he formulated under his garrison state hypo-thesis. Lasswell was concerned to understand and explain the direction of events during the late 1930s, and in particular the inexorable trend within Europe towards war. Finally published as an article in the *American Journal of Sociology* in 1941, the garrison state hypothesis represented an extension of Lasswell's concern with the role of specialists in society, not unlike Perlmutter's later interest in corporate professional bodies. He argued that these specialist groups represented powerful interests and exercised immense influence within society. He concluded, therefore, that the intensity of security crises and the threat of war would affect the interests of these specialist elites and prompt them, and in particular those with security interests, to become more and more involved in policy making and government. The greater the threat to the state, and the greater the insecurity perceived, the more that the intervention of particular elites (those that Lasswell categorized as the 'specialists in violence') would be received favourably. Ultimately, Lasswell concluded, external and domestic politics would come to be dominated by specialists in violence; that is to say, the armed services, police and intelligence agencies would expand their influence, and the world would become dominated by garrison states.

Lasswell's hypothesis is important because he not only pointed to the direction the world was going at the time, but also noted that the conditions of modern warfare encouraged permanent military influence; but most especially he is significant because he introduced the important link between domestic politics and changes in the international environment. The two are interdependent, and the more there is instability in the one, the more it affects the other. The article then looked at the domestic and external conditions that cause the emergence of garrison states, and described their essential characteristics. These were that the professional armed services had, in the interest of maximum fighting effectiveness, assumed the role of 'manager and promoter of civilian (arms production) enterprise', and taken over the control of the handling of information and propaganda in order to maintain morale. Given that the final objective was the survival of the state in a hostile and technologically changing world, the armed services were becoming the paramount consideration of government. Projecting these requirements forward in time, Lasswell reasoned that, ultimately, the armed services would be in a position to justify centralized control over most aspects of civil life, including patterns of work, scientific investment, education, and even social welfare. Soon after he had formulated his hypothesis, the Second World War broke out, and because the requirements of security and the needs of the armed services to prosecute the war to a successful conclusion were paramount, Lasswell's prediction could be said, in very general terms, to have been correct.

Lasswell deplored the world he predicted, and encouraged everyone to do what they could to prevent it. The garrison state was fundamentally undemocratic; it was a society ruled by specialists in violence who would be prepared to use violence to maintain themselves in authority, albeit on the premise that this was necessary for security. The dilemma for Lasswell was that if the hypothesis were correct, and there were an inexorable movement towards the establishment of garrison states, then there would be nothing he or anyone could do about it. In a later book, *National Security and Individual Freedom*, written after the Second World War, he appears almost resigned to the garrison state being inevitable, and appealed that some elements of democracy and liberal values should be retained.

In a manner of speaking, Lasswell envisaged in 1940 a world of states ruled by armed services, a world of military regimes. In 1960, he had the opportunity to review his hypothesis in the light of subsequent international events. Whilst he could not see any less likelihood of garrison states becoming the dominant political form in the future, their characteristics would not be as total. The only ground for optimism he could isolate was a reduction in world tension, even though the United Nations had failed to live up to expectations; the Cold War had not entirely disappeared, the technological arms race between the major powers had accelerated, and arms transfers had become a feature of international commerce. However, nuclear deterrence, states' interdependence, and forms of communications had, he reasoned, helped to ameliorate differences and raise the threshold of conflict. Nevertheless, Lasswell already recognized the emergence of subversion and international terrorism as a problem leading to the expansion of domestic control and further restrictions on civil liberty.

Superficially, Lasswell's hypothesis has proved to be correct, but more in kind than degree. The post-1945 world has seen greater armed services and police involvement in the internal affairs of states, particularly in decisions affecting the content and direction of new weapons technologies. Security considerations have become paramount in modern states and standing peacetime service establishments are now the norm, not the exception. The percentage of the world's resources devoted to armed services in peacetime, both in absolute and relative terms, has indeed steadily increased. But his ultimate prediction has not finally emerged; armed services, whilst influential by dint of their being a specialist corporate body, do not either dominate or control society in the manner envisaged in his garrison state construct; and when they do, as in the cases of the military regimes of the developing states, it has not been for the reasons he put forward. The explanation, as Lasswell to his credit started to recognize in the early 1960s, was quite simply that modern states are governed in a corporate manner, in which highly specialized, technical groups share involvement in decision making, rather than one dominating the rest. In this respect, at least, Lasswell and Perlmutter complement each other in giving a comprehensive view of contemporary relations between armed services and society.

This chapter ends with one of the lesser known studies of the relations between armed services and society, but one that comes closest to a general theory. This is Claude Welch's and Arthur Smith's study, *Military Role and Rule*. Their approach is to draw back the veil of prejudice and myth about armed services and get back to basic principles. First, they assert, no armed services are apart from a nation's politics; second, every state has armed services and police forces; third, the needs of armed services for resources to fulfil their tasks are extensive, which makes them powerful political actors; fourth, armed services, in order to fulfil their customary tasks, are organized, cohesive and disciplined; and fifth, the political influence of armed services differs between states, but in each the critical question is not whether there is influence, but how much, or what kind, and when it is exercised.

In a systematic way, they proceed to identify those factors that bear on these three questions, differentiating those that are of an internal sort – that is to say, come from within the armed services – and those that are environmental, pertaining to the social, economic and political conditions prevailing in society. With this background, they combine the 20 factors they had identified which bore on the question of armed services and society relationships, and ordered them into four major variables. These four, together, formed the basis for both categorizing and explaining the relations between armed services and society in different states. The four variables were: the extent of popular participation in decision making; the strength of civil institutions; the political strength of the armed services; and, finally, the relationship between military and civil institutions, expressed in terms of the degree to which they are separate, with 'integral' boundaries, or overlap, with fragmented boundaries. The former would reflect the 'ideal' of Huntington's objective control of the military or of Rappaport's civil and military polity type of state; whilst the latter would have more in common with the fusionist theory of modern corporate government, and the nation-in-arms category of state. To a considerable degree, their resultant matrix has much in common with that of Robin Luckham, in a study of military intervention published in *Government and Opposition* under the title, 'A comparative typology of civil–military relations'.

Armed, so to speak, with these variables, Welch and Smith were then able to construct a matrix by cross-referencing levels of political participation and the political strengths of the military against the relationship of civil–military institutions in both praetorian states, with weak civilian institutions, and civil politics, where civilian institutions were strong. The result was that they were able to place most states in the world within the matrix, and on the strength of the factors that they had earlier incorporated into the matrix's variable groupings, to give not only explanations of where states were located, but also some indication of how they might alter their position. They were able to do this because their theory was based on the assumption that their four summary variables interacted in such a way as to define the involvement of armed services in politics. The strength of their theory lay in their ability to provide explanation for the whole spectrum of armed services' role in politics, from the exercise of influence along recognized channels to the overt, direct and total replacement of government by military violence.

Welch and Smith achieved a general, comprehensive theory of armed services and society except for the little attention they gave to international considerations, and they did not consider adequately the corporatist view of modern government. One explanation for this apparent oversight is their principal preoccupation with praetorian type military regimes, and less with advanced industrial states, or with communist political systems. Even so, their contribution is significant, and if any general theory is to be developed, there is a good case that their work should be taken as a point of departure.

One of the reasons why an overarching theory of the relations between armed services and society has taken so long to emerge is the preoccupation of scholars with more narrow problems. Either they have a particular interest in particular states, or categories of state, or are only concerned with one aspect of the armed services–society relationship. Concern with less developed and developing states and the incidence of military intervention has dominated the literature, to the detriment of general theory. Invariably these studies have been directed more at questions of political development and modernization than at the more fundamental issue of the place and role of armed services in society. Less dominant, but nonetheless a continuing concern, has been the pattern of civil–military relations in the United States, prompted in part by anxiety over the changes in the relationship between the United States and its armed services and how these have threatened the country's belief in its own ideology and democratic institutions. In both areas of preoccupation, it also has to be remembered that the vast majority of scholars in the field come from the United States, and through financial support for their endeavours, their work tends to reflect the prevailing concern of the American administration and establishment.

This narrow and fragmentary approach was noted by Roman Kolkowicz and Andrzej Korbousky in their volume devoted to civil–military relations in communist and modernizing societies, *Soldiers, Peasants and Bureaucrats*. They observed that civil–military relations studies tended to fall into one of three categories: the developed, the underdeveloped and socialist states. They also found that the scholars concerned in each category tended to come from different disciplines, thereby making the field appear more fragmented than ever. Not only was their approach different, so also were their perceptions about the countries and economic change. The only way to overcome these criticisms, therefore, is to embark, at the outset, on constructing an overarching theory of the relationship between armed services and society which not only takes into account all relevant factors, and details the linkages between them, but also provides a means to explain change.

5

Military
Involvement
in
Politics

Each of the eminent scholars who has sought an explanation of the relationships between armed services and society has advanced an understanding of the problem significantly, and in the Hegelian tradition further refined what is salient to the question. But no final and satisfactory solution has been found and the challenge remains to extract from what has been earlier postulated the important factors relevant to the relationships of armed services and society, in order to arrive at a more satisfactory synthesis.

The problem being addressed must first be clarified; this is a lesson that was pointed out by Finer and should not be ignored. It was noted earlier that the terms of reference of past theorists have not all been the same and, as a consequence, their theoretical contributions have varied. Most have been concerned with the physical intervention of armed services in government, focusing on the *coup d'état*; as a consequence their theories have been partial, inasmuch as they deliberately do not address the wider scope of relationships between armed services and society. Where the terms of reference have been widened to include the involvement of armed services in a corporate, bureaucratic scene, in the affairs of government and national security policy making, only one aspect of the armed services and society relationship is addressed. What has not been attempted (only Lasswell really began to give it any attention) is an overarching theory of the relationship which encompasses more than the purely political dimension.

The next two chapters will, therefore, attempt two separate objectives. The first is to address the problem that has exercised most civil–military relations scholars in the past, that of armed services' political involvement in the affairs of the state. The objective is to formulate a model of armed services' intervention in politics. The second is more ambitious and is concerned with constructing an overarching theory which identifies and establishes the whole spectrum of variables that affect in one way or another the relationship between armed services and society.

One of the problems upon which studies of military intervention in politics have focused has been the concept of intervention itself. Coming from Western societies with liberal presuppositions about the apolitical nature of armed services and the proper relationship between military and political institutions, most scholars viewed any political activity undertaken by armed services as illegitimate and undemocratic. This view has taken a long time to be dispelled, but even the corporatist view of Perlmutter and the 'back to basics', realist approach of Smith and Welch, do not wholly dismiss it: they implicitly feel that there are, and should be, institutional boundaries to the legitimate concerns of the armed services, and that these boundaries should never be crossed. But the issue, really, is not whether these boundaries should or should not exist; it is a matter simply of the power and influence of armed services within society. It matters not one iota whether or not the armed services *should* exert influence in a wide area of the affairs of the state if, in fact, they do – and do so with public knowledge and support. Further, power and influence may have nothing to do with the armed services themselves, but may be merely a consequence of what others in society choose to accord them. This is obviously likely to be greater on matters of national security than elsewhere, but even here it does not necessarily follow that such influence is bad, illegitimate, or undemocratic.

The first step in constructing a model of armed services' 'intervention' in politics, therefore, is to get rid of the concept of intervention. Taking Smith and Welch's straightforward observation that armed services are found in all states, and that their immediate function is fundamental to the existence of the state, it is not unreasonable to start from the premise that armed services are involved *ab initio* in politics and public affairs because it is their constitutional responsibility to be so. This involvement can be in the name of the armed services as institutions, or of serving officers acting as office holders or, simply, as individuals with some recognized authority. Frequently, the distinction between the man and the institution is hard to make, despite the disclaimers that frequently accompany statements from servicemen that they are speaking either in a personal capacity, 'unofficially', or off-the-record.

Armed services' involvement in the affairs of states should not, in the first instance, carry with it any sense of moral disapprobation. The statement that armed services are involved in policy is not, *a priori*, a value judgment but, *a posteriori*, a statement of fact. Any act, argument, opinion, or judgment made by representatives of the armed services, even in a sphere of competence for which they are alone responsible, is, in the strict sense political in that it is directed at changing the status quo, presumably in a manner advantageous to their own interests or their perceived interest of the state. As a state institution, itself a political construct, the armed services have a permanent political label and are symbolic of, and stand for, the political ideology upon which the political and juridical principles of the constitution and the political regime, or system, is based.

Arguing from the premise, therefore, that armed services are permanently involved in the affairs of the state, it is of no value to ask the question whether or not they should be, except from a totally pacifist perspective. Instead, the most pertinent questions to ask are, first, what good grounds can be put forward why they should be involved; and, second, given that they are anyway, how they might properly be so in a way that is compatible with accepted principles of democracy, civil government and the rule of law? Any theory of civil–military relations that might be induced from the model should then be able to establish whether there is any causal connection between the reasons for involvement and its manner.

The operative word here is 'properly'. How is it possible to talk in terms of the proper involvement of armed services in the affairs of state when normative principles that have dominated Western thinking have already determined, *a priori*, that they have no legitimate role at all beyond their own immediate functional concerns? 'Proper' in this context clearly refers to the notion of legitimacy, a concept that is central to an understanding of the relations between armed services and society in all states at all times. Before addressing the issue of whether there is any causal connection between the reasons for armed services' involvement in public affairs generally, and the manner of that involvement, some attention should first be given to this core concept.

There is a tendency to view the concept of legitimacy in absolute terms – either something is legitimate, or it is not, there is no compromise position. At any one time this may indeed be the case, but as social, political and economic conditions are constantly changing, what might be perceived to be legitimate at one point in time would be considered illegitimate at another. Likewise, what is thought to be acceptable in one society would be dismissed as inadmissible in another. Prevailing circumstances have much to do with perceptual shifts, but culture and the political expectations of societies as a whole play a significant role.

'Legitimacy' is derived from the Latin *legitimus*, meaning, strictly, 'according to law'. It is a concept that was expanded during medieval times to mean 'customary', but only in the sense that it was thought to encompass something that generally received public approbation. This strand of thinking, at least in Western countries with their Judeo-Christian traditions, has continued to the present day; something is considered to be 'legitimate', subjectively, if it generally enjoys the support and trust of the population as a whole, and is believed to be appropriate to their needs and circumstances. The problem with this approach is that the concept depends, *a priori*, on the vagaries of public attitudes and fashion. A more objective approach would be to identify criteria by which to judge the legitimacy, not merely of those in authority and the policies they pursue, but more specifically the role and performance of armed services in the affairs of states.

The concept of legitimacy is most frequently linked with the name of Weber, who identified three fundamental conditions by which rulers and those claiming authority could claim a legitimate right to govern: the rational–legal, the traditional, and the charismatic. Though abstract in form, Weber's distinctions, based on the notion of what prompted individuals to take action, are valuable since they demonstrated that there was no single objective basis for legitimacy. He did not, however, address the problem of what were the norms of legitimacy, an omission that was later remedied by H. Eckstein and T. Gurr in their studies of *Patterns of Authority*. In contrast, they identified norms and values that were critical to people's acceptance of authority as being legitimate. Among these were such considerations as the openness, effectiveness, impact, and consistency of authority in respect of the everyday life of the community. Only when these norms were satisfied, they argued, could the population be sufficiently aware to exercise any meaningful judgment about the legitimacy of the authority over them.

The legitimacy of armed services is founded on their being first and foremost an institution of the state. Their existence in other words is laid down in constitutional law, which normally details their powers and responsibilities and their relationships with and to other legally established state institutions. But purely *legal* prescriptions do not in themselves confer legitimacy; it is equally possible that the constitution itself might not enjoy popular support, or fulfil the salient norms identified above. Constitutional provisions governing armed services, if they are to work successfully, must assume a public acceptance of what powers the armed services may exercise, and under what situations and conditions. In liberal democracies, these powers are popularly assumed to be minimal, which partly explains why there is so much public disquiet when armed service leaders apparently exercise greater influence in state affairs than would seem to be permitted under the terms of the constitution.

The basis of legitimacy for the armed services rests in part upon their constitutional position (for they need to be seen to have legal authority) and in part upon the public's acceptance first, of the essential function they are supposed to perform on behalf of society to defend and protect it, and, second, their manifest competence at fulfilling that function together with their professionalism. But this only applies for as long as the armed services restrict their responsibilities overtly to their immediate function. It is when they widen their scope of interest and become involved in the affairs of state which are at best contingent to, and at worst have nothing to do with, their primary and most directly legitimate function that the problem really arises. As will be demonstrated, this is a situation which is much wider in scope and more pervasive than is generally assumed, and rather than being more prevalent in the less developed states, is, in fact, more extensive in the more advanced ones.

Jacques van Doorn in his edited volume with Gwyn Harries-Jenkins, *The Military and the Problem of Legitimacy*, offered a definition of legitimacy which goes some way to providing a solution to the problem. Legitimacy, he says, is the 'capacity of a social or political system to develop and maintain a general belief that the existing social order and its main solutions are generally appropriate'. Although loose, and somewhat imprecise, this definition indicates at least that any state authority, or political action taken by it, is to be considered legitimate only if it can carry the general support and acceptance of the population. Within this definition is encompassed the relations between armed services and society, and the respective powers that military and civil leaders exercise. When these cease to be acceptable to the public, that is to say when military power and influence become excessive, or when military values and behaviour are at variance with those of the population at large, the armed services are no longer considered legitimate, and should not be viewed as such.

Armed services are a symbol of state sovereignty and independence, and it is their 'manifest destiny' to act as saviours of their country in time of emergency. This mantle immediately confers upon the armed services a latent, but ever present, public acceptance which their political adventurism and even their alien military values do not easily erode. This status and image of the armed services gives them a residual legitimacy which they enjoy, an asset which is not accorded to other state institutions. In other words, armed services can operate in the political arena with much greater freedom than almost all others, simply because of their close, and potentially disinterested, identification with the state itself. Moreover, as a publicly perceived disinterested actor, the armed services can take up legitimate demands of the public which the purely political authorities might not choose to recognize, or act upon. The extent to which the armed services in different states actually take advantage of this latitude, albeit under the cloak of secrecy and national security, without necessarily jeopardizing their own legitimacy, is a problem that the remainder of this chapter addresses.

In his study of the grievances of military coup makers, William R. Thompson suggested that the numerous studies which have attempted to explain the occurrence of military coups might be clustered into four categories: first, there were those that emphasized the 'pull' of regime vulnerability. Here the armed services were dragged into politics and ultimately pulled into taking direct action by the weakness of the political leadership or by the underlying socio-economic underdevelopment or its actual breakdown. The second cluster recognized the capability and organization of armed services relative to the civil bureaucracy and administration, from which the studies generally concluded that many military coups occurred as a consequence of military 'push', or the feeling that they were best equipped to meet the population's expectations of efficient or honest government. The third cluster placed emphasis on the effects of the international system on the perception of the armed services of states and on their subsequent action to initiate a coup. Sometimes these international influences directly affected the decisions of the armed services, and at others created the circumstances in which intervention was deemed essential. The final cluster contained those studies that recognized that military coups were inherently dangerous and risky undertakings, especially as they would be deemed illegitimate in the eyes of the population and the international community, and that the competence of armed services in running the state bureaucracy as well as their own organization was likely to be limited. From this appreciation, the conclusion was that over and above environmental or institutional reasons for contemplating a coup, the armed services themselves must have harboured serious grievances or acquired pressing motives to persuade them to act unconstitutionally.

Thompson himself concluded that none of these clusters of theories was exclusive and that each had a contribution to make to an overall explanation. But what concerned him most was the extent to which the first three, as long-term, underlying factors, were the dominant factors in most studies, almost to the exclusion of the last. To undervalue armed servicemen's grievances and the armed service motives on the grounds that they were short term, 'trigger' factors, he felt, was 'to distort what military coups are all about'. The advantage of referring to Thompson's study here is to draw attention to the concept of motive as the central, independent variable in explaining why armed services involve themselves in the affairs of state. Coupled with the notion of involvement rather than intervention, the idea of motive provides a firm foundation upon which to build an explanatory theory. Once the motives of involvement have been established, then the methods by which the involvement of armed services in politics become manifest can be distinguished.

On the premise that the concept of intervention is more relevant to the method employed, rather than the outcome, the involvement of armed services in politics can be seen as a permanent condition; the critical consideration becomes, then, one of degree more than of kind. Just how much and by what means the armed services are involved, and what motives prompt them to increase or decrease that involvement, are consequently the important questions to answer. Fundamentally, the motives usually attributed to armed services' involvement in politics can be separated, by definition, between those of military and those of civil origin. The former are more easily identified for they are generated from within the armed services and are, in the first instance, associated with self-interest.

The motives of self-interest among the armed services cover the spectrum from individual personal ambition among senior, and sometimes not so senior, officers, to the institutional interests of the armed services as a whole. Within this range falls a number of motives, sometimes generated by individual services, particular branches of a service, or individual units. The source of the motive should also be seen as separate from the particular motive itself, which often can be shared between the services themselves and even, more widely, outside the services, within the civilian community.

One constant concern of the armed services which prompts their senior staff to be actively involved in politics stems from their professionalism; this has to do with their interpretation of the threat to the state compared with that of the government or, even, the public at large. The motive to get their interpretation of world events across must be substantial, especially when it is the armed services themselves that have to act in the last resort. More often than not these professional concerns are translated into debates about resource allocation, the size of the armed services' budget, and the distribution of resources within it. When these are not satisfied, and the perceived threat remains, their professional judgment and competence are called into question.

Armed services' motives are not always so professional or responsible. All organizations have institutional ambitions and goals; these are not always compatible with those of other organizations, or with government and public policy. Armed services, generally, throughout the world have earned themselves a reputation for their corporate loyalties and inflexibility, but, on occasion, they have been in conflict with central government policy when protecting their institutional interests. Sometimes this conflict has been manifest in inter-service rivalry; at other times it has involved head-on conflict with governments and an adamant reluctance to change according to political directive.

Personal interests may be as strong a motivating force as institutional. Traditionally the pay and conditions in armed services have not been the most generous. There have been instances when the services have stepped up the degree of their involvement in politics to seek to remedy the situation. This was the case in Britain in the late 1970s when the armed services' pay had dropped to such a level that they were forced to seek redress through political action, albeit in a legal and constitutional manner. In this instance, they used their wives to do the lobbying for them!

One of the strongest motives behind armed services intensifying their political involvement in the affairs of state comes when there is an acute awareness among them that they no longer enjoy the confidence or support of the government, or even the population at large. This feeling, or perception, is made all the more acute when the state is at war, or when the armed services are engaged in disagreeable or unpopular operations, either at home or abroad. This was the experience, for example, of the American armed services in Vietnam and the French forces in Algeria; both situations led to suggestions that senior officers should have assumed a political initiative in Washington and Paris, respectively. In the case of the French, this even went so far as an order to some of the French armed services to march, or more accurately drive their tanks, on Paris in an attempt to put pressure on, or even threaten to replace, the French President.

Motives of armed services origin should not be confused with motives that are essentially civil in origin with which armed services and servicemen and women identify or associate themselves. Armed services' motives are exclusively those which are concerned with their standing, reputation, institutional health, and professional responsibilities; to use concepts discussed earlier, these are the proper concerns of the armed services in the execution of their constitutional duty to ensure the proper protection of the state and the security of its citizens.

It is, in other words, the attempt to optimize the defence of the state in a manner compatible with the 'military way', as defined by Vagts, in the face of attempts by others to prevent, or compromise, it. All such service motives, however, are legitimate and laudable.

In those states where the armed services have disproportionate power compared with other civil institutions and organizations, the motive to involve the armed services in politics can often be attributed to the ambitions of officers seeking personal advancement or naked power. Whether such motives should be associated with those of the armed services as a whole is a moot point, but in the absence of a further category, and on the assumption that the officers concerned carry their men with them – acting under orders – in the pursuit of their personal ambitions, it is sufficient to leave them in the category of motives of armed service origin.

It would be simpler if all armed services were truly '*la grande muette*', in the way that the French armed services perceived themselves during the nineteenth century. Then they would indeed be distanced from the political affairs of state. Alas, this is not the case, and their involvement is everywhere. Indeed, as Finer correctly points out in his study, there are frequent circumstances where armed services, as a matter of constitutional requirement, have to become involved in politics and the affairs of state. Such a requirement might well be contrary to the preferences or wishes of the armed services themselves, but they are legally obliged to act. Such instances have been relatively rare, but seemingly are becoming more frequent as the incidence of terrorism, guerrilla war and internal violence steadily increases. The most common constitutional provision is that of a national emergency involving everything from the outbreak of war to a breakdown in domestic law and order. It can also include, however, incidents, such as a natural disaster or crisis, that are beyond the capabilities of civil authorities and specialist agencies to handle.

Governments can also require armed services to be drawn into public policy matters, not as a matter of constitutional or legal requirement, but as a matter either of policy or expedience. Reasons why civil governments should find this course either necessary or constructive have varied, and it is wrong to assume that it is more likely in less developed states. Indeed, the converse has proved the case, especially in advanced states with a large, complex defence industrial base that has extensive economic, technological, demographic and social policy implications. This is especially evident in the Soviet Union, where as we saw earlier representatives of the Soviet armed services have had a seat on the Central Committee of the Communist Party, sometimes with one on the ruling inner praesidium, the Politburo, and have demanded representation on the government's central economic planning agency, Gosplan.

The final sources of armed services' involvement in politics, as a consequence of motives that are civil in origin, are those that emanate from the public at large. Here the distinction between motives of constitutional and government origin is important: in the latter cases the armed services are either required or are ordered to become involved for specific reasons; in the former the decision rests largely with the armed services themselves whether or not to identify with, or take up, a 'cause'. At the most general level, the armed services can take a sense of the feeling of the nation, particularly in respect of the public's attitude towards specific issues. The cases with which the armed services can make such identification depend on their awareness of civil affairs and the range of contacts they have with the civilian community. The most regular, direct, and immediate contact armed services have is with the defence-related industries with whom they share a common interest, in equipment research and development, and weapons acquisition. Other close contacts are through veterans' associations; here the two groups tend to be mutually supportive.

Ethnicity is a factor in armed services about which people are becoming increasingly aware. The ethnic composition of armed services has proved, over the past 20 years, to be important, certainly as far as armed services' involvement in politics is concerned. In advanced industrial states this has tended to concentrate on such issues as the ethnic composition and distribution of armed services compared with the society at large, and the issue of comparative civil rights inside and outside the service community. In the less developed states where tribal interests cut across armed services interests, the problems are more acute, and frequently involve the armed services in attempting to resolve internecine disputes.

Motives for armed services involvement in politics thus centre on those of civil and military origin, and, respectively, are concerned with sectional and service institutional interests. However, there is a category of motives that is neither exclusively sectional nor of self-interest, but which concerns the nation as a whole. These are referred to in figure 1 as 'national interests' which, as with the concept itself, are ambiguous in the extreme. Essentially these are motives that can be of either civil or military origin, but invariably are an amalgam of both. They are those which are perceived to be in the interest of the nation as a whole. The most obvious one, which is of civil origin exclusively because it is written down in the constitution, is the requirement that

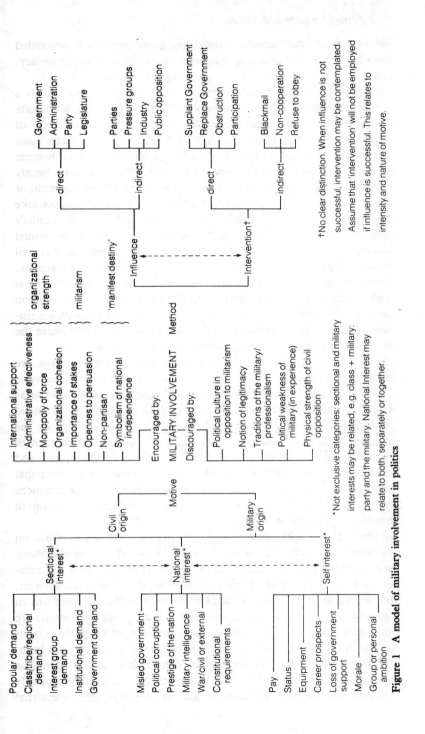

Figure 1 A model of military involvement in politics

the armed services become involved in government because certain prerequisite circumstances as defined in statutory law have been met. Here there is little room for interpretation or perception of need; the circumstances are clearly stipulated.

The remaining motives, however, are a matter of perception on the part of those concerned that it would be in the national interest of the public at large that the armed services took an active part in the political affairs of the state. It is hard to define categorically what circumstances would initiate such a requirement, or how perceptions of this order are caused; suffice to say that what might be seen as a dire situation in one country might well be considered the norm in another. Perceptions are difficult to define at the best of times, especially as they are the outcome of a long gestation period, cultural influences, personal experience and ideological beliefs. Nevertheless, there are often circumstances in any society when it is evident that things are wrong and there is a sense of urgent need for something firm, decisive or radical to be done. It is under these circumstances that the public looks to the armed services, as the most disciplined and prepared operational organization to hand, and with the least tarnished political reputation, to do something, or when the armed services themselves feel that they, as the institution of last resort, are best suited to remedy an otherwise worsening or intolerable situation.

These sorts of situation were discussed in great detail in a chapter in Harry Eckstein's book, *Internal War*, by William Kornhauser, entitled 'Rebellion and political development'. Although the concern in this study was the circumstances which might prompt a population to rise up and revolt, his argument can also apply to the armed services. The four general circumstances that Kornhauser identified which might prompt popular reaction and revolt were an inept and incompetent government; a government that was distanced and inaccessible to the population at large; a corrupt government which was essentially self-seeking; and, finally, an arbitrary government, one which was both summary and indifferent to popular expectations. Any of these circumstances might equally persuade the armed services, independently or in conjunction with civilian leaders, to increase their involvement in the affairs of the state, even to the point of supplanting the government with one more compatible with popular demand, and, therefore, more legitimate. Such increased involvement would most probably be perceived by all to be in the national interest, since it would be intended to redress shortcomings that were deemed prejudicial to the state. The critical consideration is the degree of sensitivity of the armed services to the political situation and their assessment of the performance of the government. As a state institution, the armed services not only tend to identify with the government of the day, as the established legal authority, but are also perceived in their turn to be associated with the government by the population at large.

Within the category of national interest motives for the armed services' involvement in state affairs, there is a covert element which would appear to be becoming increasingly relevant. Lasswell noted in his garrison state hypothesis, that armed services were becoming increasingly involved in domestic matters well outside their immediate professional and constitutional concern; in a covert way this trend has been increasing almost everywhere. This seemingly inexorable development stems from the concept of national security and the role that armed services have performed as both the generators and recipients of security-related intelligence. With the expansion of terrorism as a tactic employed by politically motivated groups, not infrequently with support from other states, armed services have found themselves involved more and more in internal security tasks and in that sub-national world of low-intensity operations. The precise dividing line between what is a legitimate or acceptable internal security operation against terrorists or insurgents, and what is armed services' interference in legitimate civil affairs, is blurred to say the least, and requires on the part of the armed services themselves, more than the governments they serve, a high degree of political sensitivity, public awareness and feel for popular tolerance.

Much has been made of the extent of armed services' and security agencies' penetration of personal privacy and individual liberty in the name of national security. The capacity of a relatively small group of politicially determined individuals to disrupt extensively the day-to-day running of the state and the capacity of the government to exercise its authority is considerable. Concern about this has necessitated improved intelligence, closer public surveillance and rapid, decisive action; but whilst this might be prudent preparation by armed services, police and other relevant government agencies, in the national interest, such courses of action draw the armed services into areas of political and economic life which in the past have normally been outside their terms of reference.

There is a wide spectrum of motives for armed services to want to become, or find themselves, involved in the political affairs and government of a nation, ranging from military self-interest, through civilian sectional interest, to perceived national interest; the next question is how this involvement becomes manifest. The categories of methods that are open to armed services are on the one hand to exercise influence directly on the properly constituted authorities or indirectly through third parties, or on the other to intervene by taking coercive action. The particular method of involvement that will be chosen depends on a number of dependent variables, including the nature of the motive, the intensity with which it is felt, and the degree of urgency that circumstances demand.

Each of these broad categories warrants some elaboration. Taking first the involvement of armed services in politics through the exercise of influence, this has already been noted by Perlmutter when he talked of the corporate nature of government, or by Finer when he alluded to the normal exercise of interest articulation or lobbying by armed services as a matter of professional duty and practice in more mature political cultures. Nonetheless, there is a general perception, especially in the West, that armed services, whatever their motives are to do otherwise, do not behave like outside civilian interest groups in directly lobbying governments, the administrative bureaucracy, or legislative bodies. The evidence, however, is that this is not an accurate perception, and the converse is more accurate, no matter what the political system. Indeed, studies of military–industrial complexes in many states have demonstrated that armed services are particularly effective lobbyists with the advantage that they operate for the most part with privileged access within government circles. Informal as well as formal networks of contact and access serve to enhance armed services' involvement and influence; their size, cost and scope also serve as an influence 'multiplier'.

There is substantial evidence that armed services exercise influence over a wide range of public policy issues indirectly through third parties, who are themselves active in the political arena. In the West, partly to maintain a low political profile, armed services articulate their views and position on a whole range of issues through veterans' groups and retired officers. In some states, especially those in Central and South America, the armed services are closely associated with particular political parties and there are circumstances, even, where armed services sponsor a political party, provide candidates, or, even, assume its leadership. Not least among these indirect networks of influence are the defence–industrial links that armed services establish and maintain in the course of their acquisition and development of new weapons systems.

Since the armed services are constantly involved in the affairs of state, their influence is ever present; the issue at stake is the extent of that influence and the areas in which it is most likely to be exercised. In this respect, the corporatist image of the armed services and government is probably the most accurate, but only in conceptual terms; the details would have to be added on a case-by-case basis. This imprecise nature of armed services' involvement in public affairs does not, however, apply to armed services' intervention; intervention is a positive act which, by its very nature, alters the institutional structure of government or is instrumental in replacing those who hold political office. When armed services metaphorically 'take to the streets' they are, by definition, stepping outside the legal and constitutional framework that was responsible for their existence. The act of physically intervening in the affairs of state is illegal unless there is prior constitutional provision, as in the case of a national emergency; for this reason, such action attracts attention and raises problems for other states regarding the international recognition of the resultant political authority.

Intervention can take many forms and can be employed to achieve different objectives. The tactics and methods of military intervention have given rise to numerous studies, some concerned with how military intervention might succeed and others with how it might be frustrated. Of the many books on military intervention, the best-known and most influential is Edward Luttwak's *Coup d'État*: it not only offers a guide to strategy and tactics, but has also provided the basis of films and novels amongst which may be numbered the film *Power Play*, starring Peter O'Toole and David Hemmings, and Frederick Forsyth's novel, *The Dogs of War*.

However, from an analytic standpoint, Samuel Finer's *The Man on Horseback* is probably the most helpful guide, since he points out that the motive to intervene is not sufficient alone to prompt the armed services to take action; he contends that there has also to be both the opportunity and the disposition. He also points out that the physical intervention of the armed services is not simply aimed at supplanting the government with a body of senior officers; equally likely they intervene to replace one government with another that is more sympathetic to their own interests or the interests of the population at large. He does not, however, consider a third possibility, that of military intervention on behalf of the existing government in order to restore an otherwise deteriorating internal situation, or to prevent its being replaced by an alternative party or faction whose declared policies are considered inimical to either the services or the national interest.

It has not been unknown that armed services have intervened directly to frustrate or obstruct government policy without necessarily seeking to assume office or to replace the existing government. The spectrum of obstruction can be extensive, ranging from deliberately preventing necessary information and intelligence from reaching authorized agencies, to the physical prevention of government personnel and political figures from performing their proper duties. There is a likelihood that this sort of obstructive activity would increase during times of national elections where there is scope for the armed services to frustrate the established democratic process. Nor should it be assumed that armed services necessarily intervene directly in politics alone: it is equally likely that they might participate with, and lend positive support to, other political movements.

The final method of armed services' involvement in public affairs is that of indirect intervention. This is intervention at its most subtle, since it leaves little or no trace. Here armed services can maintain their public image of professional distance from civil matters, whilst behind the scenes they exert their influence negatively. By this is meant the refusal of the armed services to obey or follow through the legitimate orders of the properly constituted authorities. There have been instances over Northern Ireland when British government policy has been circumvented by the armed services refusing to obey orders, or more subtly, threatening not to obey orders. Such indirect intervention constitutes blackmail, a course of action that can assume a positive form, namely to communicate to the government that if certain policies were to be introduced, the armed services would 'react' or 'respond' in a particular, prescribed, way.

Figure 1 details the whole range of possibilities as to motive and method of armed services' involvement in public affairs and government. To identify and detail these possibilities, however, is not sufficient, since to do so would not offer any sure indication why certain motives are more or less likely to be translated into what sort of involvement. In other words we must explain why armed services' involvement sometimes remains legitimate and professional, but at others becomes more direct, interventionary and illegitimate. Initially, however, this hypothesis might be offered; that armed services' involvement in politics is more likely to assume the mantle of intervention if the motives are of civil origin and are concerned or linked with sectional interests. Motives behind political involvement that are of armed services origin and in professional or self-interest are likely to be manifest in the exercise of direct or indirect influence on the legally constituted authorities. The hypothesis stems from Finer's persuasive argument that political culture is a dominant influence on the behaviour of the armed services and on the value placed on the institutions of government by the population at large. The more the armed services extend their interests beyond their constitutional authority, the more they devalue the importance of the structure of government, with the corollary that the likelihood of their intervention in public affairs becomes greater.

It is possible, however, to extend the model beyond merely the link between motive and method. Armed services and societies do not exist in a vacuum; consideration of time and place, the influence of history and tradition, public recognition of ideology and nationality, and the services' own perception of themselves have to be taken into account. It is when these other, dependent variables are entered into the motive–involvement–method equation that a better appreciation of why armed services extend their involvement in public affairs is acquired.

The best approach to adopt is to consider members of the armed services of a country, any country, who have sufficient seniority to influence and define service interests, organizational policies and priorities, and to recognize that at their disposal is a coercive capability which is unlikely to be matched anywhere within the state. In all states, without exception, armed services enjoy in law a monopoly of coercive force, display a high degree of relative administrative effectiveness and possess, as a function of their duties, an organizational cohesion and loyalty that no civilian organization can equal. In other words, armed services display immense organizational strengths, the more so because they have to train and operate predominantly independently of normal civilian life. All the institutional and organizational characteristics of armed services identified by Abrahamsson and others, and which were discussed in Chapter 2, give armed service leaders reasonable grounds for confidence that any assertive action on their part in the civil affairs of state, beyond purely military considerations, would be manageable and controllable. The organizational strengths of a disciplined body of armed men is a powerful consideration when it comes to the matter of senior officers contemplating the increased involvement of the armed services in the affairs of state.

The standing of armed services within the community likewise can be a source of encouragement for armed services' 'adventurism'. Societies that, for whatever reason, give high regard to military values, are persuaded that high public spending on defence and security is important – even paramount – and accord a high social status to armed servicemen, are not likely to resist or object to expanded military influence over their lives or over the policies of government. The situation here could prove to be a vicious circle, in which public attitudes and the permeation of armed services into civil affairs become mutually supporting and reinforcing. Under such circumstances, the armed services themselves often become persuaded by their own propaganda, in that they identify the preferences of the public with their own policies, become increasingly open to persuasion by partial, sectional groups, and yet persuade themselves that as the one institution symbolic of national independence, patriotism and unity, they are both impartial and the disinterested arbiter of what is the national interest. Frequently, after a coup instigated by members of armed services, their justification is couched in terms of their being the institution of last resort and of being the best judge of what had been a good or necessary course of action for the nation. At the same time, those responsible also protest that their motives were entirely pure, their action having been taken only after long deliberation, and always in the interest of higher goals that, by inference at least, accorded with their perception of the 'general will'.

There is, therefore, much to encourage armed services to involve themselves in public affairs, most of it self-generated and based on their perceptions of what is needed to be done and, all too often, on the imperceptions of outside agencies or allies. Equally influential, however, are considerations that might make armed services reflect on exercising influence beyond what is compatible with the execution of their proper duties. Perhaps the most powerful of these factors is that of political culture, in which it is generally accepted throughout the world that undue military influence in the affairs of state is both threatening and inimical to the basic principles of democracy. History has demonstrated that where armed services have exercised a wide influence, relations between states become destabilized and mutual suspicion grows; and whenever ideologies which place great emphasis on military values and give high status and influence to armed services have gained the upper hand, internal oppression and external conflict have invariably followed in their wake. Before contemplating their involvement in public affairs beyond what is either constitutional or compatible with their immediate professional concerns, armed services' leaders should be aware of the probable popular reaction, internally, and international implications, externally. It was this sort of concern that exercised observers of the expanding power and influence of the American armed services, and which prompted the plethora of critical studies of military industrial complexes, and the Pentagon's and other security agencies' abuse of their power and authority since the early 1960s, and even earlier.

As was discussed earlier, legitimacy is a central concept in the study of the relations between armed services and society; it is also a concept of which armed services generally are at least aware – though they do not always go to great lengths to understand fully. But to the extent that it is understood by them, and incorporated in the training and education of armed servicemen, it constitutes a factor which discourages armed services' excessive involvement in public affairs. Indeed, the education and training of officers and of other ranks in the armed services is of vital importance in this regard, for it provides the foundation upon which their professionalism is built. Without adequate education about the nature of the relationship between armed services and society as part of their professional preparation, an armed serviceman's or woman's perception of what is legitimate in respect of involvement in the political affairs of state is likely to be insufficient or distorted. This becomes even more critical in armies that are largely conscript. The evidence tends to point to military training and instruction taking precedence over education, and relatively few states bother to give adequate or extensive time to these more fundamental, if philosophical, considerations. In totalitarian, one party states, this is less of a problem; here political education is a necessary element in the serviceman's and woman's socialization process, and plays a major role in military training. Traditions of the armed services and their degree of professionalism may certainly act as a restraint on armed services, but to be effective they need to be constantly emphasized and refined, and made constantly relevant to prevailing circumstances.

One of the more telling constraints on armed services becoming unduly involved in politics, and certainly in restraining them from direct intervention, is the practical problem of governing and administering the country, or, even, assuming responsibility for spheres of governmental activity. For all their organizational cohesion and administrative effectiveness, there is a wide gulf between the training and preparation for war, and the daily administrative tasks in the public domain. The political weakness of the armed services, especially when there is no assurance of popular support or guarantee of administrative and bureaucratic compliance, should be sufficient to restrain armed services from taking extreme steps to intervene directly. What is not so surprising, however, is that this has not proved to be the case in all states, especially those whose economy and political structure is comparatively simple; in the 25 years between the end of the Second World War and 1970, there were approximately 274 cases of direct military intervention in 59 states. Since 1970, military intervention has continued at much the same pace, suggesting, first, that the concepts of professionalism and legitimacy have had little relevance; and, second, that the precedent of a military regime gives encouragement for a second attempt, since most of the 59 states above would appear to have experienced more than one coup.

111

In the past, military 'adventurism' in politics has generally been a phenomenon generated from within the armed services themselves, but increasingly this has become less frequent. As a matter of external policy, the major arms producing states have aggressively sought overseas markets for their equipment and weapons, for two basic reasons: the first is purely economic, since external arms sales help to defray the costs of development and the overall unit cost of the weapons themselves; the second is that arms sales provide a vehicle for the exercise of political influence. Since it is through armed services that sales are conducted, major arms producing powers have been able to exercise influence through proxies, on the policies and priorities of their customer states, even to the extent (as the Greek experience showed in 1967, or Poland in 1983) of encouraging an indigenous military takeover of power. Correspondingly, external pressure can be exerted to restrain the armed services of client states from contemplating direct intervention, or, even, persuading military regimes to restore civilian government in return for financial, military and economic assistance.

It is not possible to make any positive prediction from the above discussion as to when and how the pattern and mode of armed services' involvement in public affairs, beyond their own professional concerns, is probable. There are simply too many variables which could prove relevant for it to be feasible to isolate any particular instance which might prove critical. The model described above can do no more than identify these variables as an indicator of what to look for when analysing the political involvement of armed services in society. All the variables, however, are abstract and have to be translated into empirical evidence in each case. However, the model does provide one important service: it places greater emphasis on the armed services themselves than has customarily been the case in earlier studies, particularly in respect of their own perceptions of the implications of their contemplated course of action. And if any prescription were to be drawn from this conclusion, it is that particular importance should be attached, in the education and training of the officer corps, to the nature of the relationship between armed services and society and the legitimacy, within each society, of armed services' involvement in public affairs.

6

Towards a
Theory of
Civil-Military
Relations

In the last chapter, the concept of legitimacy was seen to be central to the problem of the involvement of armed services in government and politics. It provided a framework for addressing the questions why the involvement of armed services is more acceptable in some states than in others, and why, generally, there is general disapprobation when they usurp civilian government. Although the concept itself is open to wide interpretation, it nonetheless helped to focus attention on the salient issue of whether or not the armed services' exercise of power and influence was the exception or the rule.

In addressing the wider challenge of the construction of an overarching theory of civil–military relations, the terms of reference have to be widened beyond the specific issue of armed services' intervention and involvement in public affairs. A general theory must be found, that will encompass the many facets of the relationship of armed services and society, including the political, economic, social and cultural, both in a domestic and international context. And as if that challenge were not enough, the theory should ideally be able to account for change in the relationship over time, and offer some reasons for that change.

The one methodology that offers some promise of explaining change is that of 'systems theory'. As an abstract construct, systems theory works from a set of assumptions regarding the nature of a system, its working, and its relationship with its environment; change in a system comes about as a consequence of change in the environment since the two are interdependent and interact. Furthermore, a system is made up of component parts which also interact and are interdependent, meaning that change can also be the consequence of alterations to either the elements of the system, or to the relationships between them. One of the difficulties with the application of systems theory is that of defining the system itself, and its principal characteristics. But if a satisfactory definition can be found, then the theory built around it offers wide scope.

The relationship of the armed services and society does not, on the face of it, seem to have much in common with the concept of 'system', either in a procedural or structural sense. This is, indeed, the case, since the focus of interest is on a relationship the characteristics of which are too varied and unpredictable to make any categorical prediction. This should not, however, preclude the search for a system within which the place, role or function of the armed services can be identified, along with those of society at large. One consideration, however, should guide that search: it should be pitched at a high level of analysis in order to encompass all the variables that impinge on the relationship between the armed services and society.

The single concept that would appear to meet these requirements is that of national security; and the system to which it would relate is the national security system. Such a system both encompasses the armed services, in their many manifestations, and draws in society at large, since national security, and moreover national survival, has become a major societal preoccupation. In other words, national security is both specific, in respect of the functions and duties both of the armed services and the forces of law and order; and general, in respect of the expectations and demands of society as a whole. It is this dual connotation that gives the concept both its analytical power and its relevance to the study of the relationship between armed services and society.

First, however, some attention should be given to a definition of national security, especially as it provides the foundation upon which this theory of armed services and society is to be built. Furthermore, it serves as the independent variable that determines the boundary, or parameters, of the national security system of which the armed services are an integral part. Needless to say, the search for an adequate definition is no easy task since there is no consensus among earlier writers as to what the concept means precisely. This is no better exemplified than in Arnold Wolfers' discussion of the concept in his book *Discord and Collaboration*, where he refers to national security as 'an ambiguous symbol'. The challenge here is to remove that ambiguity and formulate a definition of national security that is both workable and that clearly delineates the framework within which armed services and society fall.

The concept of security is a perceptual one. There is no condition, *a posteriori*, which can be defined that is 'secure'. Security is a condition that individuals and groups perceive, *a priori*, to prevail; as such, the concept has more to do with psychology than with the study of armed services and society relationships. Nonetheless, a number of situations can be identified which clearly influence these perceptions, in the sense of enhancing people's consciousness of being more 'secure'. Likewise, since security is not a permanent condition, the obverse is true, that certain situations generate perceptions of insecurity. Often the same indicators apply, and feelings of security and insecurity are matters of degree rather than of kind. Take, by way of illustration, the situation of a society having numerically large armed services: to some, this would suggest enhanced security since it would constitute strength and protection against outside threats; but to others, it would represent an internal threat to personal liberties and values. As with the concept of militarism, security in this context would seem to be more one of balance and priority than one of absolutes. Another example might be the possession of nuclear weapons: it is both a source of strength and potential deterrence against attack, but also one of weakness, inasmuch as their possession invites pre-emptive attack from a suitably armed adversary.

The best clue to the concept of security may be derived from the simple question, 'When do you feel secure?' Having posed this question over many years to students of civil–military relations, the answers have been varied, and sometimes surprising; but they all share a conceptual core. Usually the answers clustered around their having adequate finances, being among trusted, reliable and close friends, enjoying robust and good health, gaining a lucrative and interesting job, or putting distance between themselves and sources of trouble and difficulty (even in one instance when they were fast asleep!). Very seldom, if at all, was any reference made to the existence of armed services, a nuclear guarantee, or the vigilance of the Police. Either these public services are taken for granted, or, security, in a defence or protection sense, is not seen as a high priority or something related to the concerns of everyday life. Furthermore, no-one ever mentioned security as being equated with political stability, thereby suggesting that in a state, such as the UK, there is a general acceptance, at least among university students, of the working of the governmental system and of a degree of fairness and social justice that acts as a cushion against violent disorder and insurrection.

These students can scarcely be taken to task for their responses since their experiences have largely been limited to a country that has enjoyed a high degree of political, economic and social stability. The answers would likely have been very different from those coming from totalitarian states, or states which have experienced armed services'

115

intervention, civil war, or the disintegration of the social and economic fabric. To a degree, the students' responses reflected one common theme which is central to the concept of security; no matter what their answer, they all were seeking a condition in life which enabled them to cope with the unexpected. Ideally, the best condition of security is one of foreknowledge, to be able to predict the future and thus enable appropriate preparations to be made. But this ideal is not possible; as history repeatedly demonstrates, crises occur for a whole host of random reasons which even the best laid plans and careful preparations have failed to anticipate. In the absence of the ideal, security has to do with the activity of forward planning and deciding on those courses of action which afford the best chance, with available resources, of being able to cope with both the anticipated and the unexpected. Armed with the firm belief that the future can be faced and all problems and threats can be coped with, the individual or society can be perceived to be 'secure'.

At the individual level, and in a domestic context, the prescriptions of Lord Beveridge, outlined in his book, *The Pillars of Security*, are worth noting. Architect of Britain's social welfare system, Beveridge was charged during the Second World War with addressing the problem of the reconstruction of British society. Working on the assumption that at the cessation of international hostilities, peace among nations would prevail, Beveridge focused his attentions on creating conditions within British society that would enable the population at large to be able to cope with the vicissitudes of modern life. Recognizing that, if left to their own resources, many would founder, he recommended that it was the responsibility of the state to provide the foundations of a civilized society that guaranteed the basic requirements of life. If these basic requirements were assured, he argued, not only would each individual be secure, but society as a whole would be free from internal conflict, be confident in itself and be healthy.

It comes as no surprise, therefore, to find that Beveridge's approach to the concept of security was based on a series of negatives. Security was a condition where there was an 'absence of want, disease, ignorance, squalor and idleness'. The state, he recommended, should assume the obligation to ensure that for all the citizens there would be adequate food, health provisions, education, housing and employment. Perceptively, he recognized that, of these five conditions, employment was the most difficult to guarantee. In somewhat utopian fashion, Beveridge felt that if these five conditions were met, society would be stronger, and that internal dissension and conflict would be diminished to the point of irrelevance. For this reason, he ignored in his definition

116

of security the absence of fear of violence, summary arrest, persecution, and invasion of privacy, either from within society or from outside. In his scheme of things, armed services, the Police, the rule of law, and impartial and disinterested justice, were given low priority. Past historical experience and subsequent post-1945 life in Britain and elsewhere have demonstrated that even with the introduction, albeit in partial and incomplete form, of Beveridge's recommendations, assumptions about the absence of external threats and internal harmony were unfounded. Indeed, anxieties about internal strife, state sponsored terrorism, and increases in domestic and trans-national crimes of violence have steadily mounted over the past 40 years, generating with them demands for security provision of a more positive and active sort.

The importance of Beveridge, however, is that he gives further emphasis to the notion that security has something to do with giving the individual, or society, the means with which to cope with the unexpected. The emphasis here is on security as a means, one which is shared with Arnold Wolfers in *Discord and Collaboration*. Despite his reference to national security being an ambiguous symbol, by which he meant that the concept was subjective and *a priori*, Wolfers finally concluded that security was best seen as the 'protection of internal values'. This approach has proved immensely valuable because it opens up two lines of reasoning. The first is that security is a means, inasmuch as it is the method of protecting the values of society, both in a material and a cultural sense. As a means, security may take one of two forms, the negative, as emphasized by Beveridge, by which the environment is altered within which individuals and society can best cope with the problems that beset them; or the positive, which is actions taken by individuals or society to prevent the environment impinging upon their lives. In the latter form, both the Police and the armed services would figure prominently.

The second line of reasoning which is promising is that, whilst national security is a means of protecting internal, that is to say national or societal, values, it is equally possible to see security as a value in itself. Security, in other words, is both a means and an end. As an end in itself, security is nothing more or less than a condition perceived by the population of a society to exist and to be of value. Put the other way round, no individual or society deliberately seeks a condition of insecurity, uncertainty or vulnerability; to do so would be flying in the face of human experience and psychology. The logic of the situation that Wolfers' definition affords is that security is both a means and an end, and raises the conundrum that one of the ends of security is to protect itself as a value. Whilst at first this statement may appear nonsensical, it does have some validity. All organizations tend to be self-sustaining, self-justifying and self-interested; those institutions and organizations which are engaged as a means of protecting internal values – principally the armed services and the Police – may also see their function as one of merely existing, since their 'being around' is a perceptive value upon which society places some priority. In being around, the armed services and the Police are symbolic of society not only being protected and secure, but of its perception of being so. The actions and performance of the armed services and their relationship with society affect this perception, sometimes quite radically.

The distinction between security as both a means and an end is fundamental, because it means that armed services really exist in two contexts, or environments. One is the world of praxis, in which they take effective steps to defend society from predators that threaten its values and interests; the other is a purely perceptual environment, one of attitudes and beliefs, in which society at large feels more or less secure as a consequence of the armed services' presence. The two worlds are not mutually exclusive. Attitudinal changes on the part of society – for example when there is a shift in beliefs about the nature of the external threat, or a different emphasis on expenditure priorities as between the armed services and social welfare provision – impinge on the performance of the armed services. Conversely, manifest improvements in the equipment, operational readiness or morale of the armed services influence public attitudes. The challenge for government is to strike a balance between the two over time, and keep them constantly in a state of equilibrium.

The picture, then, is of the armed services existing in two separate, but related, environments simultaneously. But armed services are not alone in their concern for security; nor do most states permit them in law to be so. As a general rule, armed services are prevented from taking decisions about the security of society independently. This customarily is the responsibility of government and relevant administrative departments who, in a democracy, are accountable to the people, that is to say, society at large. In other words, armed services are an executive arm of government, and, in an ideal world, at the service of society. Too often, however, they become an operational arm of government, assuming in the process the praetorian characteristics discussed earlier. Nonetheless, decision making authority on matters of security is that of the government, though the armed services, as professionals, and, in some states, with representatives serving in the administration, are the government's principal source of advice.

As advisers to government on security matters, the armed services have found their exclusivity being challenged in recent decades by civilian 'experts'. This development has been particularly prevalent in the United States, partly as a consequence of nuclear weapons and the introduction of the strategy of nuclear deterrence, and partially because the armed services have demonstrated that they are not very efficient at working out a cost-effective solution to society's security needs. In the former instance, the absence, so far, of nuclear war has bereft the armed services of any immediate claim to experiential knowledge. In other words, civilian intellectuals are no less able to think through the logic of a defence strategy based on nuclear deterrence than are armed servicemen. Over three decades the American armed services and government have spent vast sums of money engaging civilians under contract to help them think through the complexities and ramifications of national defence policy. In response, numerous civilian defence 'think tanks' have mushroomed, mostly located around Washington, though one of the oldest and most pre-eminent is the RAND Corporation in California. This phenomenon of civilian advisers has not been restricted to the United States, and can also be seen developing in many other, mostly advanced industrial, states. One important point, however, has to be recognized in this context: although civilian and independent of armed services and governments, these advisers nonetheless are drawn into the government net by their having to sign undertakings, covering official secrets and classified information, not to divulge information acquired as a consequence of their contractual agreement.

The matter of the cost-effective solution to society's security needs is more complex, since it involves the incorporation of civilians into defence and security decision making circles, from outside or within the government bureaucracy, to monitor armed services' use of public money, or to advise on how that money might be most prudently and effectively spent. This development effectively started in the early 1960s, again in the United States, as a response by the Kennedy administration to the situation whereby the armed services were spending public money to meet their separate requirements with little concern for duplication and waste. Robert McNamara, Kennedy's Secretary of Defense, was charged with remedying the situation and introduced into the Defense Department numerous civilian economists and analysts whose largely academic skills were brought to bear both on general national security problems and specific issues of weapons choice. This development has not only become institutionalized, but has also developed to the extent that their advice and input into defence policy decision making invariably outweighs that of the armed services themselves. This situation is not unique to America, but can be seen increasingly in the major states of the world.

Neither the armed services nor the government can effectively take active decisions on matters of security without substantial administrative and bureaucratic support. With the complexities of modern warfare and the flexibility of modern weapons, it has become necessary in peacetime to have huge government departments supporting and administering the requirements of the armed services. The organizational structures and procedures of the central organization of defence warrants a separate study in its own right, suffice it to say here that without massive administrative support, modern armed services would find it impossible to operate. Given the size of modern defence budgets, public expectation of efficiency and propriety, and detailed control over expenditure, it is no surprise that in some states there are as many civil servants working in defence departments as there are in the uniformed armed services themselves, or that such departments are the largest of all government departments. It should go without saying that such administrative support is not without its own influence in security matters, especially as those involved are charged with the responsibility of coordinating and facilitating the flow of information with which security and defence decisions are made, and represent a continuity which servicemen lack.

Information is central to all decision making and no more so than in the field of security. The intelligence organizations of both the government and the armed services are charged with the task of gathering and collating information on other states in order that an assessment can be made, not just of whether they are likely to constitute a threat, but more directly of the form that threat takes, or is likely to take. Security and intelligence gathering are closely interrelated to the extent that the intelligence agencies are the most secret of all, and certainly the most protected. Information gathering, however, is not the only responsibility of intelligence agencies: they are also involved in the interpretation and filtering of data, two functions that give them considerable potential influence over the content and direction of security policy and decision making.

It is evident from this that armed services are not alone when it comes to defence and security matters. Furthermore, in most states they are responsible for more than external defence, having a hand also in matters of internal security. Normally – at least traditionally – there is a division of responsibility between the armed services and the Police, the former concerned with external threats and the latter with purely domestic matters. The distinction is breaking down, however, for a number of reasons, nowhere more so than in the liberal democracies where, traditionally, the employment of armed services in internal operations has been regarded as anathema and contrary to basic principles of democracy. The change in attitude towards, and public acceptance of, the armed services assuming this expanded role has been a direct consequence of new forms of warfare in which terrorism and guerrilla tactics have played a prominent part. On frequent occasions, these new tactics have been supported both in material, financial and moral/ideological ways by foreign governments, thus exacerbating problems for the domestic security agencies.

The complexity of modern society has increased its vulnerability to sabotage and other terrorist and disruptive activity, thereby making the need for vigilance and internal surveillance more necessary. In addition, it is expected in time of crisis that potential enemies will use sympathizers to cause disruption as a tactic to hamper armed services and their reserves mounting an adequate response in time. The experience of modern states in the past 20 years has demonstrated that state-sponsored terrorism is an option that governments can use, and have used effectively. In open societies, where there is large movement of people to and from other societies, the ease with which these sympathizers, agents and operatives can be planted within the community suggests that the method presents few problems.

The doubt has been frequently expressed whether or not the police forces of states have the capacity or capability to respond to these new internal security developments; and even if they could, whether or not this is a proper function for them to perform in view of their other public duties. The assumption is that anti-terrorist and anti-guerrilla roles would constitute a radical departure from the concept of policing *per se,* and for this reason armed services have increasingly been drawn into this area of 'low intensity warfare'. It is not a role which the armed services, though increasingly expected to undertake, either like or welcome. The explanation is simple: it constitutes, in so many words, 'the threat system of the state turned in on itself'. Furthermore, it more closely identifies the armed services as agents of government than of servants of society at large. Herein lies a whole area of division of responsibility between the armed services and the Police, one which demands resolution, yet which, by definition, touches at the heart of generally accepted ideas of democracy and political legitimacy.

Without attempting to resolve which organization should be charged with internal or external security matters, and what form it should take, it is evident that both the Police and the armed services share a global security concern. Allied to them are numerous other public institutions and organizations with whom they operate, such as the fire, coast guard, border guard, customs, ambulance and other emergency services. Together, they fulfil an important function in the provision of security in any state, namely the operational function. These institutions are the executive arm, the tool of government that actually makes things happen as a consequence of policy decision. They may be conceived of as an operational system in their own right, but it makes no sense to divorce them from the intelligence, advisory, administrative and decision making functions upon which they depend. It is therefore expedient for analytical purposes to include these other functions with the operational within a single system. The result is the creation of one single state or national security system, charged with overall security of the state in the face of internal and external threats.

By conceptualizing a national security system in this way, it becomes immediately possible to place armed services in their proper context, and to trace the pattern of interconnectedness they have with government, other public institutions, and society at large. Furthermore, it enables the national security system to be put in the context, discussed above, of security both as a means, to meet and eliminate internal and external threats; and as an end, that is to say, as a value that society has in perceptual terms. In other words, the national security system of states exists in two environments, one of practice, action and experience (some might say the 'real' world); and one of attitudes, values and perceptions. To trace how these relate to the national security system itself, and the armed services within it, it is necessary to follow the accepted theoretical propositions of how systems operate.

The first requirement is to establish the boundary of the national security system in order to distinguish it from its environment. It has often been said that this is both the easiest and hardest task of all, since all too frequently institutions are both inside a system and outside it, according to circumstances. In the case of a national security system, there is the immediate problem of society as a whole: every citizen has an implied security role in the sense that there is a personal duty to report any suspicious person or happening either to the Police or someone in authority. To be required in law, or merely to be morally expected, to make such reports and to be ever-vigilant (all the more so during time of war) does not necessarily make each citizen part of the state national security system. It makes much more analytic sense to restrict the national security system to those institutions and structures that are expressly charged in law to fulfil defined security and security-related tasks. Any institution or individual that does not meet this criterion automatically forms part of the 'environment'.

If the national security system itself is defined as being composed of institutions and structures that have, in law, a responsibility for the protection and security of the state, its institutions and its citizens against all forms of physical threat, a number can be immediately identified. These are the relevant government ministries and the government itself (or delegated committees), the armed services and Police and other operational agencies, the intelligence services, and relevant advisory organizations working under contract. Each of these agencies performs a necessary function in the mounting and execution of any security or defence operation.

It is a tenet of systems theory that all systems exist 'in contra-distinction with their environment'. This somewhat imprecise way of putting it means that a system does not exist in a vacuum; more than that, a system both affects the environment in which it finds itself, and is affected by it. In the case of national security systems, there are the two environments mentioned above, both of which are interrelated. The simpler and more immediate environment is that of internal and external threats to security which the national security system was originally structured and organized to combat. National security is affected by the actions of others and responds to them by deciding on, and taking, the appropriate action. That action is invariably the responsibility of the armed services, especially in an external context. For the sake of simplicity, this environment is called the military environment, since it relates mostly to those occasions, events and crises that require the response of the armed services (see figure 2).

THE MILITARY ENVIRONMENT

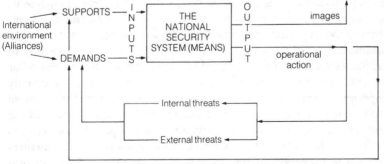

(Forward planning: military research and development)

Figure 2   Security as a means: the protection of internal values

There is another dimension to this military environment which has to be included. As a consequence of modern forms of warfare, in which deterrence and high technology have assumed a dominant influence, states have no longer been able to plan for security on the assumption that populations can be mobilized and indirectly diverted quickly to produce the necessary equipment and weapons. Highly destructive weapons incorporating the latest in high technology take decades to research, develop and produce, and at great cost. Increasingly, security has to be ensured with 'forces in being', with weapons and equipment to hand. The consequence is that one major part in the provision of security is the continuing scientific, technological and industrial research and development effort to prepare the security forces for the future. This is a formidable challenge, for wrong estimates of technology, or a failure to anticipate technological developments by a potential enemy, could leave the armed services ill-prepared and inappropriate to meet a future threat. Security, today, is indeed a matter of forward planning and 'getting it right', for which reason there is not just a strong incentive to overprovide for security and to hedge bets, but more especially to plan for security on the premise of a worst-case analysis.

Success at security planning is measured in terms either of meeting any threat and having the capacity to defeat it in a head-on confrontation, or in deterring or preventing any threat from materializing which would necessitate the use of armed force. This applies both in the domestic and the external environments. Externally, considerable emphasis is placed on the deterrence of war, a policy which places great stress on good intelligence and the acquisition of a military capability sufficient to persuade a potential adversary to think twice before taking courses of action that were clearly indicated as being unacceptable or inimical to state interests. In some instances, this has been an incentive for the acquisition of nuclear weapons; in others the maintenance of armed services permanently at a state of readiness; and in yet others, a combination of both, especially where the adversary also has access to nuclear offensive weapons. With the lengthening lead times both in the acquisition of new weapons and in building, preparing and deploying appropriate armed services structures, it is a most difficult task to judge at any one time how much expenditure and preparation in this area is enough, and on what it is most prudent to spend public money.

The maintenance of armed services and weapons in readiness to meet external threats and to deter adventurism is only one side of the coin. The other is the deployment and use of armed services to restore the *status quo* ante, as in the case of the Falklands War in 1982; to punish, by way of retaliation; to warn, as in the case of the American raid on Tripoli in 1986; or to affect a change in the international environment in order to enhance national interests or security, as in the case of the Soviet invasion of Afghanistan in 1979. This is direct operational action and, as such, is an output of the national security system. The decision about such a course is ultimately made by government in the name of the state as a whole. In the event that such action proves successful, the demands on the armed services and the national security system promptly end, effecting, in the parlance of systems theory, a negative feedback. If the response is not successful, or takes time and warrants further decisions about escalation of the engagement, the demands on the national security system are considered to be as a consequence of positive feedback. Indeed the feedback, once a course of action has been taken, remains positive until the adversary is defeated, the government decides to redefine the nature of the threat, or the adversary withdraws voluntarily.

In the domestic context, the same principles apply, except that here the adversaries are the citizens of the state. These might well include those who possibly hold greater allegiance to an outside state, those who hold ideological convictions totally at variance to the principles upon which the state was founded, or those who prosecute political objectives in a manner which is wholly illegal and, possibly, unconstitutional. The acquisition of information and intelligence on one's own citizens contradicts the very foundations of liberal democracy and individual freedom, though these political and ethical scruples do not appear to impinge on the behaviour of security organizations in totalitarian and one party states. The resolution of the problem of where to draw the line between the need for the maintenance of law and order and the protection of the citizenry from arbitrary violence and terrorism on the one hand, and respect for privacy and individual freedom on the other, is difficult, and one that would appear to be becoming more and more acute, everywhere.

Internal threats to security can occur anywhere and anytime, appear in a variety of forms and have any number of causes. For the most part they are little more than threats to law and order, involving relatively small groups engaged in rioting and demonstrations either to vent their frustrations or to promote one particular political objective or grievance. Whilst these actions might well involve violence and other illegal activities, they seldom constitute a major breakdown in law and order, or present a serious challenge to the authority of government. Indeed in most states they have come to be recognized as a legitimate form of political expression provided that they do not cross the boundary into illegal or criminal behaviour. Examples would include the anti Vietnam War demonstrations in the United States during the 1960s, the appeal by the unemployed for assistance in finding jobs in Britain during the early 1980s, the protest of the French students about their treatment when protesting the conditions in their universities in 1968, and the industrial strike action by miners and other unions in Britain and elsewhere in the 1980s.

When internal protest assumes a certain level of violence and espouses objectives that directly challenge the state constitution (such as separatist movements like the Irish Republican Army, the Basque ETA movement and the more militant wings of the Scottish and Welsh Nationalists), the question has to be raised whether or not the civil police are either the appropriate body or are adequately equipped to handle the task. In these instances, the temptation to use the armed services internally has not been one that governments have always resisted. This course of action, however, can be fraught with difficulties, not the least of which is that it might very well lose both the government and the armed services popular support.

This conveniently brings the discussion to the second environment within which the national security system has to operate: that of security as a value. This is the context in which the image and performance of the armed services in particular, but of the whole of the national security system in general, has an influence on the public's perceptions about security and its own inner confidence that each and every one of them is, quite properly, secure. Were the public to begin to feel that provisions for security seemed inadequate for any number of reasons – the armed services appearing too small, ill-equipped, of low morale, poorly led, inefficient, and so on, or the enemy too big, powerful, efficient, and armed with the latest equipment – then the national security system would lose popular confidence and expectations would rise that remedial action needed to be taken. This could be manifest either in a resolve to devote more resources to remedy any shortcoming in capability, or the converse, to redefine foreign and security policy to match the diminished capability of the armed services and reduce the resources devoted to them (see figure 3).

A more likely reason for the national security system losing support, however, is a perception that armed services are responsible for mismanagement and waste, absorb more national resources than are commensurate with their requirements to meet any potential threat, or are deliberately misrepresenting those threats in order to create a false impression of danger, in order thereby to justify more national resources for themselves. Given the relatively high proportion of public

126

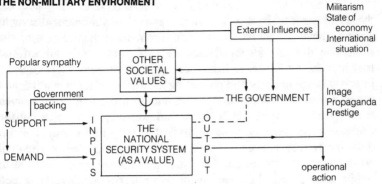

THE NON-MILITARY ENVIRONMENT

Figure 3   Security as a value

expenditure allocated to armed services today, and their being in receipt of a constant proportion of the state's GNP, this sentiment is never far from the surface, especially when seen in the context of scarce national resources and other pressing social needs such as health, education, welfare and the environment. The challenge to those responsible for national security is to gauge public attitudes so that the need to acquire the necessary resources to fulfil defence and security obligations does not itself generate internal opposition.

Armed services and governments can influence public opinion on security matters considerably, because of their almost exclusive access to defence and security intelligence and information. Again, the approach has to be extremely cautious, for to project too pessimistic and threatening an image of the threat to society could cause unnecessary alarm; conversely, to underestimate the threat deliberately could encourage overoptimism and complacency, and an eager readiness to redistribute resources from defence security to other public expenditure areas. Such attitudes prevailed for a while after both the First and Second World Wars in the UK and in much of Europe. Increasingly in the Western world, the public has become more knowledgeable about and conversant with defence and external security issues. The consequence has been to place armed services and governments on the defensive, and for them to provide the public with more detailed justification not just for total limits on defence expenditure, but more frequently on the weapons, forces, strategies and tactics that have been developed to meet the supposed threat. Moreover, the definition of the threat itself has also been challenged, since it provides the basic assumption behind all subsequent armed services' funding.

As Abrahamsson and Perlmutter have pointed out and as has been discussed earlier, the armed services, as part of the national security system, have an active interest in promoting their interests and projecting their professional assessment of world affairs, the threats they and the state face, and the most appropriate ways of securing the integrity of the country and protecting its interests. In other words, the national security system has a second output; according to our systems model it is an output which has nothing directly to do with military operations against any known physical threat, but is one that endeavours to maintain good relations with the population at large and create an acceptable image of the national security system as a set of public institutions. This endeavour to project and persuade is little more than a public relations exercise, but should not be underestimated or belittled for that. The success that it achieves not only brings the armed services dividends in terms of moral support, but also makes the resources requested by them easier to acquire.

The interface of the national security system with society at large tends to be more with the Police and armed services than with either governments, intelligence or bureaucracies. Putting the role of the Police to one side, since they are not our immediate concern, the armed services have many ways of projecting themselves in the public eye aside from their normal military duties; as public servants, they are, in a manner of speaking, accountable to society, and it is not uncommon to find their representatives going round the country providing information, giving lectures and setting up exhibitions explaining their roles and describing how each service contributes to the overall national defence. According to the society and its traditions, as far as possible, the armed services usually have to avoid making any public value judgment about security policy, since to do so would be deemed both unprofessional and a transgression of that sensitive line between political authority and military execution. For the most part, these presentations are restricted to factual, non-classified information. Not unnaturally, such performances also provide a graphic account of the enemy, his intentions and capabilities, sufficient to justify maintaining if not increasing public spending on defence, but not so pessimistic that it generates public alarm or despondency. With more knowledgeable audiences in the West and well-prepared arguments by peace movements, particularly on questions to do with control over nuclear weapons and deterrence strategies, these public occasions between armed services and the public have proved, at best, stimulating and at worst, acrimonious.

During the course of the war in South-East Asia, popular opinion in the USA and elsewhere steadily changed from outright support, through tacit acceptance to active hostility. Many factors contributed to this shift in attitude, the most significant of which was the day-to-day coverage of the war on television, giving graphic details of an ugly and extremely vicious conflict. As the war progressed and casualties mounted with little or no prospect of an outcome, favourable or otherwise, so public sympathy turned not just against the policy itself and the administration, but also against the American armed services, or more specifically, the military hierarchy and the central defence organization. To stem this tide of public sentiment, the Pentagon embarked on a massive propaganda campaign designed to play down the lack of progress in the war, to project a more optimistic view of the outcome, and to win support for the armed services. The policy proved unsuccessful, and ultimately counter productive in the face of a sceptical population that became increasingly cynical about the real beneficiaries of the war (whom many perceived to be the arms manufacturers and the central bureaucracy).

Normally in time of war, public sentiment supports the national armed services. This was nowhere more evident than during the Falklands War of 1982. Despite strong reservations among many sections of the British public about the long-term wisdom of the government's policy over the Falklands, the need to dispatch a task force to regain them after the Argentinian invasion, and the cost of the whole operation, there was open and massive support and concern for the servicemen engaged in the fighting. Indeed, the operation did not need the same public relations support that the American troops did in Vietnam, and, if anything, the relatively small and highly selective amount of information, and its tardiness in getting to the British public proved a source of frustration during, and criticism after, the war. The prevailing ideology and culture of society must be relevant here, since the important distinction between the Falklands War and Vietnam is the public's perception of the legitimacy of the operation. It is difficult to persuade any public of the justness of any recourse to war, particularly in a better educated world of rapid communications and easier access to information than ever before, and whilst such decisions are political, it is generally assumed that armed services will have had some involvement in the decision.

Times of crisis and war are exceptional; normally the pattern of public relations and image-building by armed services during times of peace is held at a low-key, but constant, level. Ceremonies, pageants, festivals, shows and tattoos nearly always feature the armed services in one way or another. Memorial services to the fallen in war have a spiritual dimension, whilst also serving a more practical purpose to keep armed services and the need for security in the public eye. Those countries that have introduced national service and conscription coupled with compulsory periods of service in reserve forces, have an instant conduit through which to exercise influence over public attitudes. Whilst national service might not always be popular, the experience at least would appear to generate an appreciation, if little else, of armed services' attitudes and way of life. Countries with all-volunteer systems compensate through extremely strong and active veterans' associations, and in Britain and the Commonwealth countries in particular, the recruitment of service units from particular geographical areas, linking them with towns and cities, major organizations, or institutions helps to build a mutually supportive relationship. In France this is taken one stage further, where armed services' ceremonials, such as the transfer of command from one officer to another, is invariably done in full view of the general public.

In sum, the pattern of public relations and 'keeping the armed services in the public eye' (a phrase used by the British Army for just that purpose) is a necessary, non-operational element in the output of the national security system. All states engage in it, more or less, and they would be less than prudent not to. It influences the environment in which the armed services exist and have to operate, and makes the government's policy on defence and security easier to put across to the general public. The effect of public relations is almost impossible to quantify, for public attitudes towards armed services are dependent on many other variables. A state with a manifestly high level of defence spending which the government only maintains at the expense of other public expenditure programmes will generate public opposition and resentment. Whilst this will be immediately directed at the government and its policy, the knock-on effect is on the armed services themselves. This happened in the United States under President Reagan, whose high defence spending increased steadily and disproportionately to domestic welfare programmes. As a counter balance the more that the armed services can be seen to be helping the public at large, by providing search and rescue services, assistance during times of natural disaster and other humanitarian tasks, the better for armed services and society relations. Nowhere is this aspect of armed services taken further than by the French Gendarmerie Nationale, a military force under the Ministry of Defence, with a clearly defined defence role, but employed primarily for domestic security, policing, search and rescue and surveillance purposes.

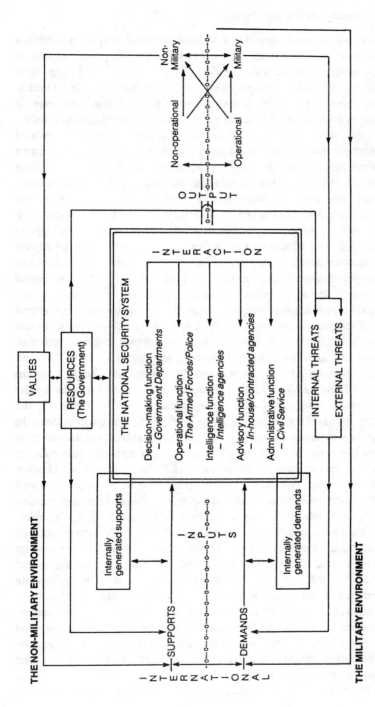

Figure 4   The national security system: means and ends

Because the presence and involvement of armed services in the affairs of the public is usually held at a low level, it tends to pass unnoticed. A close examination of most states reveals that in many and often imperceptible ways the armed services do have a presence and a part to play. This is in no way to suggest some lurking conspiracy or a potential threat to democracy. Whilst clearly they have some influence on public attitudes about security matters, this is more 'atmospheric' than of substance. It is an influence that is not likely to turn a society into a militaristic one, or encourage an idealization of the military. On the contrary, it should be welcomed and encouraged, since it keeps both parties, the armed services and society in tune with each other's attitudes, beliefs and thinking. When the two become estranged, isolated suspicions begin to develop leading to misunderstanding and alienation. The ultimate objective in all civil–military relationships is the harmonization of values and beliefs, consensus about the proper place of armed services in society and agreement on security policy and its cost to the state. Figure 4 integrates the two environments, and illustrates how a failure by government and the national security system either to prevail in the military environment, or to judge public attitudes correctly in the non-military environment, can have the effect of undermining the stability of national security.

The harmonizing of values and beliefs is, of course, an ideal objective, but one for which all elements of the national security system must strive, whatever function they perform. Fundamentally, it is a matter of trust between the public at large, the government, the security services and intelligence agencies. That trust can be bolstered when there is a high degree of openness in government and effective mechanisms for public accountability. Excessive secrecy surrounding security matters, whilst having practical value in terms of protecting vital information from potential enemies, nonetheless can generate anxiety and suspicion among the population. In the UK, the wide-ranging provisions of Section Two of the Official Secrets Act, for example, have not only brought the concept of official government secrets into disrepute, but also raised fundamental questions about democracy and the right to know. When linked to provisions for defence, and the intelligence war to combat terrorism, as was done in Ackroyd *et al.*'s study of *The Technology of Political Control*, and Duncan Campbell's book *The Secret Society*, secrecy becomes a major source of mistrust rather than of confidence at least on the part of some sections of the public. In totalitarian states, of course, secrecy and a secret police appear to be commonplace.

The responsibility for building public confidence in the provision of security is primarily that of the government. On the one hand the public must be convinced that everything is under control and that government policies regarding the allocation of national resources adequately reflect the public's priorities and reasonably fulfils minimum expectations. On the other hand, the government must ensure that the armed services and the Police have sufficient resources to meet their commitments. Leaving the Police to one side, this latter task is somewhat more difficult in the modern world, since the test of policies and planning comes only when the armed services are ordered to take action. Much has to be taken on trust that within the financial limits imposed, the armed services are at a sufficient state of readiness to meet their commitments. The state of affairs within armed services is seldom raised in the public domain, except in the most general terms of declaratory policy and their roles within it. On matters of nuclear deterrence, in those states that have the capability to adopt such a strategy, it has to be almost a token of faith on the part of the public, first that the capability is a credible one, second that it is permanently operative, and third that there is complete control over the weapons concerned to ensure against accidental use or deliberate adventurism.

Public trust is vital in the domestic arena. Where the armed services are used internally as a matter of government policy, an immediate conflict of interest arises which is absent externally. The issue is whether or not the use of the armed services is made chiefly in the interests of the government itself, either to bolster its position or to intimidate opposition, or in the wider, national, interest. The latter part of the twentieth century has seen an increase in volatile politics with whole sections of people taking to the streets in protest at government policy. Often these movements have been beyond the ability of the Police to control, necessitating the intervention of the armed services. Often, under the pretext of keeping external public services running, armed services have been used to intervene in industrial strikes and lessen their impact. Such use of armed services places them in an invidious position, knowing that they stand between disobeying legal orders on the one hand and potentially alienating large sections of the population on the other. Such considerations are less critical in totalitarian states, or those with ideologies that do not see armed services as being separate from society as a whole or make distinctions about the environment within which those services, the Police and other agencies have to operate.

The balance is a very delicate one, more delicate than is customarily supposed. The French government made a mistake in the late 1950s and faced the prospect of their armed services intervening in government; the British and American governments also made mistakes in the late 1970s when constant reductions in defence spending created a perception of weakness and vulnerability in the international arena. Insufficient attention to defence and security matters contributed substantially to the defeat of both administrations at the subsequent elections, sweeping President Reagan and Mrs Thatcher to power with a mandate to increase defence expenditure significantly. To help in arriving at the most balanced decisions, governments depend heavily on the input of information from the intelligence services, the opinion of experienced advisers, the disinterestedness of the senior bureaucracy and the professional judgment of the armed services, Police and security agencies. This suggests that there has also to be within the security system itself a high degree of integrity, a sensitive awareness of public opinion, and mutual trust.

All this activity does not happen in a vacuum. As actors on the international scene, states are affected in their security policies by foreign commitments, traditional friendship, moral scruples, and alliances with other states. Not all these international linkages carry the same obligations, the international legal principle of *rebus sic stantibus* – that no state is obliged to comply with any agreement or treaty if by so doing it would be disadvantaged – notwithstanding, but the more binding are those that tie national armed services to a regional collective security agreement involving a common military command structure. Both the North Atlantic and Warsaw Treaties come within this category; the armed services of member states are expected to mould their security policies, defence expenditures, military equipment and operational plans and doctrine to that of the alliance. To a degree, such arrangements are a limit on national sovereignty, for which the trade-off is a perceived enhancement of national security. Again, the public at large must be convinced that the benefits outweigh the costs, particularly when the alliance requires foreign forces to be stationed on home ground. Public debates in several Western European states have suggested that the benefits of a NATO dominated by one superpower equipped with independent nuclear weaponry are no longer as clearly defined as they were when the alliance was first formed.

The model of the relations between the armed services and society elaborated above has attempted to integrate the system within which armed services are located, with the dual nature of the environment in which they have to operate. The main link between the two is the role of government and its capacity to maintain a balance between the values of society, of which security is one, and the operational capability of the armed services and others to cope with internal and external threats in both the present and the future. Failure to achieve that balance runs the risk of alienating the armed services from society, or vice versa, or failing to cope with security crises when they arise. The ease and success with which this balance can be achieved varies between societies with different political systems, different cultures, and different levels of economic and technical development. But these variations are secondary to the fundamental hypothesis that the relationship between armed services and society in any state depends on the balance struck between security as a value and security as a military capability.

7

Issues
in
Civil–Military
Relations

Any theory of civil–military relations, such as that developed in Chapter 6, based on the concept of a national security system, must be capable of providing some explanation for events in the real world. The test of such a theory comes when it is set against case studies of situations where the relationship between armed services and society changes and for which some causal explanation is sought. This chapter addresses four such case studies, not in respect of any particular country, but in respect of some fundamental issues which the relationship between armed services and society has to address. Each of these issues will be discussed in the terms of the national security system model outlined above.

The four issues selected for discussion and analysis are: (in Chapter 7) national service and conscientious objection, and armed services and public accountability; and (in Chapter 8) armed services and industry, and armed services and political authority. Each issue relates to problems that the Western liberal democracies have had to confront and in some cases are still trying to come to terms with, in the past 70 years or so. They are issues that not only go to the heart of what a liberal democracy means, but also demonstrate that the essence of civil–military relationships lies in ideological perceptions of what a political system, or regime, should be. Conscientious objection raises the immediate issue of individual liberty; public accountability, that of the necessary restraint on autocracy; defence-oriented industry, the issue of the potential abuse of power and influence; and political authority, that of the sensitive balance between power and responsibility.

Conscientious objection in the simplest meaning of the term refers to a situation where an individual refuses to comply with a law, or with customary behaviour, as a matter of individual conscience. It is an assertion by the individual of an absolute right to personal freedom not to be required to do anything which is alien or contrary to his or her conscience and fundamental beliefs. Bearing in mind that all people live in one or other state (aside from the nebulous status of refugees and stateless individuals) such an assertion of residual individual liberty constitutes a potential challenge, if not a direct threat, to the society and state of which the person is a member. Rules, written and unwritten, bind people together within a society, and give that society its cohesion and its distinctiveness. Compliance with those rules, even the 'natural' or 'organic' ones promulgated by anarchists, is what gives any society or group its stability and security.

The proliferation of rules in a society does not necessarily make it more civilized or stable; it may indeed be more rigid, with less scope for individual choice and freedom. Totalitarian and dictatorial states customarily place great restrictions on individual choice and prevent dissent, albeit in the name of some ideology or common good; liberal democracies attempt the opposite, seeking to find a judicious balance between individual freedom and sound government. It is a precept of liberal democratic systems that too many rules and too much government direction over people's lives invite dissent and disobedience. The ultimate objective is to allow the maximum latitude for personal freedom and initiative compatible with the effective government of a civilized society.

With varying degrees of success, most Western societies manage in time of peace to strike a sufficient balance to avoid authoritarianism, repression and compulsion, yet permit individual scope, whilst still providing the basics of a civilized society. Cultural and ideological expectations play a major part in this, and no single model of liberal democracy would be able to operate effectively in all countries. There is one circumstance, however, when even the liberal democracies are forced to suspend their basic philosophy on individual freedom: this is when the society as a whole is faced with extinction at the hands of an alien force. The defence of society then becomes paramount, and assuming that neither neutralism nor surrender is a viable option, the whole society has to turn its hand to its survival. This means, in practical terms, diverting the nation's human, economic, industrial, technical and material resources to defence. It also means making a demand on all members of a society to restrain their right to individual liberty – that is to say, to opt out – and contribute to the common cause. Conscientious objection is the assertion of the right of the individual, on grounds of individual conscience, to refuse to comply with that demand, even in the face of a real and present danger to society as a whole, a society of which the objector is a part. It is a position unlikely to generate much sympathy from members of the armed services, even at the best of times.

Conscientious objection is arguably the most critical problem facing armed services of any state, and most especially in time of war. It is critical in the sense that it represents an immediate and direct challenge to the premise which underlies their very existence – namely the protection of the state and the guarantee of its continuation. An assertion of conscientious objection is a statement of fundamental opposition not just to war, but to the very existence of armed services and even to the state itself. Normally, conscientious objectors and armed services would not come into direct conflict, at least for as long as the armed services have no call upon an individual's time or commitment. They only meet in confrontation when legislation is passed requiring men and women to serve in the armed services as a matter of national service and when volunteers are insufficient to meet the threat. The objector rejects this legal compulsion on grounds of conscience, and in so doing presents both the government and the armed services with a dilemma.

It is appropriate at this juncture to digress for a while to point out that the notion of national service itself, whether as service in the armed services or with other public service organizations, is viewed very differently from one state to another. This has been discussed at some length in M. R. D. Foot's *Men in Uniform*, a study of military manpower in modern industrial societies. In some states, national service is accepted as the norm, in others it is seen as a clear infringement of individual liberty. These extremes in attitude stem from cultural differences, themselves derived from contrasting legal and ideological traditions. A clear contrast, for example, can be found between Great Britain and almost all its European partners: the former finally abandoned conscription in 1961 whereas the latter have retained it to the present day. British experiences of conscription were born of necessity, and brought with them considerable resentment and resistance among many of those who were 'called up'. In contrast, conscription would appear to function tolerably well on the European mainland, even in peacetime. There is some evidence of objection and resistance in Holland and West Germany, but, on balance, there is a general acquiescence to a necessary obligation.

The difference stems in part from respective histories, but more fundamentally from the philosophical and juridical foundations upon which Britain and the other European states were built. Historically, Britain, being an island nation, has been a maritime power; its defence has been effectively conducted away from its shores, either at sea or abroad, usually in Europe as Michael Howard reminds us in his *Continental Commitment*. Any land force Britain has possessed has been used predominantly to acquire and police an overseas empire, with little requirement for an army in large numbers to be stationed at home. Not even its current NATO and Western European Union commitment to station forces in Germany has required the UK to raise more forces than those it can recruit voluntarily. The European states are, however, basically continental powers, and though some have a recent history of overseas empires, their defence and security have depended upon having substantial forces stationed at home for protection against land attack. The required numbers precluded any likely possibility of raising an all volunteer force, necessitating the expedient of conscript forces to make up any shortfall.

Practical defence realities alone, however, would not vitiate individual objection or opposition to conscription; there has to be something more. It is to be found in the juridical principles underlying the Roman legal system, as established by Napoleon Bonaparte in Europe, in contrast with those of the system of common law in Britain. On a more philosophical plane, it has to do with the relationship between the individual and the state. In Europe, largely as a direct consequence of the French Revolutionary Wars and the introduction, if not imposition, of the Code Napoléon throughout most of the Continent, the prevailing principle was that man was essentially barbaric and uncivilized, and only capable of achieving any acceptable existence as a consequence of becoming part of society. In a line of argument essentially following that of Rousseau, it is society as a whole that is better placed to know what is good for the individual than the individual himself. This is clearly reflected in the procedures in the law courts of mainland Europe, where the onus of proof that the charge brought against an individual by the state is unfounded, lies with the defendant; in Britain, it lies with the plaintiff, and it is the responsibility of the state to prove, beyond any reasonable doubt, the validity of the accusation.

The relevance of this becomes clear when legislation is introduced requiring, in theory, every citizen within a state (in practice only young able bodied males of a certain age) on the continent of Europe, to come to the assistance of their society by serving in the armed services. In a manner of speaking, such legislation expresses a 'general will', which is superior to, and more enlightened than, any individual preference. In Britain, the opposite is the case. Under common law, citizenship does not impose any requirement on an individual except by common consensus and acceptable practice.

There is no single formal document which codifies the British constitution or any definitive charter conferring and guaranteeing individual liberties. Many feel that there should be. Citizens are automatically assumed to be free, and each additional piece of legislation constitutes a further infringement on that freedom. Above all, conscription into the armed services is seen as such an infringement; and for some, it is a totally unacceptable one, since it also requires that the individual should put at risk his or her own life in the interests of others. The consequence is that the conscientious objector in Britain, of whom there were a significant number in the First and Second World Wars, presented to the authorities the problem of finding suitable treatment, or punishment, for what was *prima facie* an offence against the law, or of arriving at some accommodation whereby the reasons for refusal to comply on grounds of conscience were adequately recognized. The conscientious objector on the continent, by definition, would have committed an act of treason, having set him or herself above and apart from society, and therefore having betrayed it. This explains in part why on the continent the incidence of refusal to do national service during either world war was comparatively small.

The problem of conscientious objection and the sensitive issue it raises, therefore, is largely confined to those states whose legal systems and cultural background have more in common with Britain than with the European tradition. This brings the discussion back to the earlier question, what should the authorities do with conscientious objectors? First, it has to be assumed that conscription is introduced as a consequence of an identifiable external threat to national security, for which the volunteer professional armed services are insufficient. It goes without saying that this threat places the society and its values, *pace* Wolfers – individual liberty included – in jeopardy. It is also supposed that the call to arms comes after long and careful deliberation by democratically elected representatives of the people and is made only as a final resort in the interests of the society and state as a whole. Given all this, some individuals nevertheless still prefer to defy the law and refuse to serve.

One distinction should be recognized initially, namely that between conscientious objection and pacifism; not all conscientious objectors are pacifists, and not all pacifists necessarily prove to be conscientious objectors. Conscientious objection is an extreme form of disobedience; in the words of Thoreau, it is the decision of an individual 'not to lend himself to a wrong which he condemns'. It need not necessarily be confined to matters of conscription, fighting or killing in war. Pacifism, together with the philosophy of non-violence, is a positive philosophy which contends that the resolution of conflict between individuals should never be attained through recourse to violence, coercion or war. The decisions behind this position are multifarious, taken on religious, moral, humanist, political and ideological grounds. Since conscientious objectors to conscription have tended to be pacifists of one form or another, the two are generally taken to be synonymous.

National service, and/or conscription, is the legal requirement for sections of the population, usually young men between the ages of about 18 and 40, to serve for a specified period of time with the armed services of the state, or with some approved public organization. Most states in the world operate a system of conscription, and in time of war it is rare to find a state today that does not. The rationale behind conscription varies between states, and its purpose is not always that of increasing the numerical strength of the armed services. In the less developed countries of the world, national service is an important opportunity for widening and furthering education and training beyond school age. In countries where there are ethnic diversities and regional animosities, it has been seen as a practical, effective and expedient way of generating a sense of national unity within the population, and of reducing tension. The attraction of national service is that it is a relatively cost-effective way of raising service manpower, even though there are obvious opportunity costs involved by taking young people out of the labour market (if there is one) for a period of time. As a means of mitigating the worst effects of unemployment, national service has attracted its supporters, though such a palliative, again, is not without penalties or problems.

In time of war the requirement for national service is usually self-evident: either conscription is introduced or, if it already operates, the period of service is extended. In addition, men who have done national service and who are held for periods of time in a reserve capacity, with legal obligations to train for a period of time each year to maintain their military skills, also are 'called up' to serve. Whether or not conscription is by induction, an extension of service, or a call from the reserves, the obligation is a legal one in the sense that it is a consequence of legislation. It does not necessarily carry with it any moral obligation as a matter of duty. Failure to comply with the law carries penalties, the severity of which is related to the height of public perception and anxiety regarding the extent of the danger with which the country is faced. Usually, public awareness of the threat in wartime is clear, and the reasoning behind national service legislation is patently obvious to all.

To a country ostensibly at peace, and with a defence policy based, for example, on the deterrence of war through the threat of nuclear weapons, the rationale behind national service is not so persuasive. This is a situation that many European governments are currently facing (albeit in regard to the NATO alliance nuclear guarantee) with significant numbers of young men challenging their obligation to do national service with the armed services. One compromise favoured by the West German government has been to allow protesters to serve in the community instead; another has been to reduce the period of service substantially, a course adopted by France; and a third is to limit service to non-combat roles within the armed services, and then mostly with the Army.

Superficially, conscription and national service which requires the citizen to contribute to the protection of society with little recompense, is cost-effective; but it is one fraught with difficulties. The most delicate arises when conscription does not appear to be universally applied, some individuals being exempt whilst others have to serve. Reasons given for exemption on medical, domestic, educational, or occupational grounds, are open to wide interpretation, and hence invite discrimination and injustice. This problem was exacerbated in the USA during the post-war period, and especially during the Vietnam War, when the selective draft system was in operation. Here, the number of young Americans eligible for call up at any one time exceeded the requirements of the armed services; selection was therefore left to a lottery with the less fortunate who had neither qualified for exemption nor had volunteered being selected.

With such flexibility, the system invited abuse, particularly in matters of exemption or deferment. As the experience of the Vietnam War became increasingly disagreeable and dangerous, so the loopholes in the system were more and more used and abused. The draft then operated more to the advantage of the white, middle-class sections of American society and to the disadvantage of the poorer black and Hispanic communities. This experience not only added to the increasing hostility of large sections of American society towards the war, but did much to discredit the armed services in the eyes of the community. To add insult to many injuries, many young Americans not only defied the law openly by burning their draft cards in public, but also by taking the expedient course of leaving the country by crossing the border into Canada either until an amnesty was declared, or the passage of time and the ponderous nature of the law made it safe to return.

The British experience of national service following the Second World War and then the Korean War was one which neither the armed services nor the British public strongly supported. The armed services found that the work involved in training large numbers of servicemen to a level at which they were useful or militarily effective in an operational role, was not commensurate with the return. The burden fell largely on the Army, with the Royal Air Force picking up most of the remainder on ground duties; relatively few were accepted into the Royal Navy. Many professionals were diverted from their assigned professional roles merely to deal with repeated intakes of new conscript recruits. The result was a less than satisfactory compromise of conscripts being given pointless make-work tasks which did little more than kill time; the effect was that the system lost both reason and purpose, generating at the same time a strong sense of alienation among those involved. In retrospect, this somewhat unsatisfactory episode in British military history has now become encapsulated in a rash of novels, television shows and plays brandishing such self-explanatory titles as *Virgin Soldiers*, *Chips With Everything*, and *Excused Boots*, *It Ain't Half Hot Mum*, *Privates on Parade*, and *Ginger*, *You're Barmy*. Reluctant to operate selective national service as in the United States, the British government finally abandoned conscription in 1961. The United States followed suit after the Vietnam War, moving to an all-volunteer system, reluctant to continue trying to enforce a law that had patently lost public support.

The enactment of a National Service Act, which places a legal obligation on certain citizens to serve in the armed services of the state, immediately creates a predicament as between the requirements of the state, determined by perceived military necessity, and the rights of the individual. Whilst individual rights are not independent of obligations and responsibilities to society, and are therefore not absolute, there are nonetheless some obligations which the state may not demand of people. The predicament is neither clear nor simple, as those who objected to conscription, and those who tried to enforce it, found out sometimes to their cost. It is not simply that the defence of society, the values it stands for and the institutions of the state come into conflict with an individual's refusal to comply; it is also a conflict which has to do with both the means and ends of war, on the one hand, and the conscience of the individual, on the other. Conscience here refers to the moral, political, ideological and religious determinants which dictate a person's beliefs and behaviour patterns.

J. Singer in *Democracy and Disobedience* notes two senses of the concept of 'conscience': the 'traditional' and the 'critical'. Traditional conscience refers to inner dictates, a sort of 'inner voice', which tells a person what and what not to do. It is, effectively, a 'gut' feeling which defies and does not require rational argument; above all, it does not require reason. Critical conscience emerges as a consequence of a person's seriously thought out moral convictions, taking into account any number of influences and logical positions. The person who objects to conscription as an expression of his or her objection to war is a pacifist; it is a position that, by definition, has to be total and absolute. As such, the pacifist has no alternative but to adopt the position of traditional conscience; opposition to war on grounds of critical conscience, those of reason and logic, invites argument as to the merit of the objectors' position. Experience of how states have responded to pacifists and conscientious objectors in time of war demonstrates that those of 'traditional conscience' have tended to be treated more sympathetically and favourably than those of 'critical conscience', who have argued their cases on moral, ideological or political grounds. The crucial test has tended to be the life-style and behaviour pattern of the former, which for the most part has tended to be restricted to the stricter religious sects, such as the Quakers, Mennonites, Hutterian Brethren, Mormons, and Plymouth Brethren.

Field, in his post-Second World War study, *Pacifism and Conscientious Objection,* pointed to a further important distinction, that of pacifism as policy and pacifism as individual duty. The former position is one which pacifists, and therefore by definition objectors to both war and conscription, hold with regard to resort to war by the state: quite simply, war should never be declared or fought. Their practical emphasis is on the futility of war and its inability to settle any dispute. Their general position is that alternative methods should be tried, marshalling in support the moral argument, such as that premised on the sacrosanctity of life and the immorality of killing to achieve what is at best an ephemeral, transitory material or political end. Theirs is a position which has much in common with that of non-violence, a policy advocated by Gandhi and underpinned in his philosophy of truth-force, *satyagraha*. Pacifism and non violence, Gandhi contended, elevated the human character and, as such, was a powerful moral force. He posited that means were more important than ends in any conflict, since the way in which goals were achieved had an effect on the goals themselves.

Pacifism as individual duty Field saw as being fundamentally different from pacifism as policy. Basically, the difference lay in the advocacy of non-involvement in war on the one hand, and the problem for the individual once war had broken out, or when the society was in real and present danger, on the other. 'An objection to making war at all is not the same thing as taking part in war, once it has started.' Many pacifists and conscientious objectors, he felt, often confused the distinction, and found their reasons for objection to being conscripted difficult to sustain before the tribunals on grounds of reason and logic. s Clausewitz once said, 'You may not be interested in war, but war is interested in you'; even for the pacifist, once war has broken out, no-one is left untouched.

The distinction between one who holds a pacifist position as a matter of policy, and opposes war and violence as an instrument of policy as a matter of principle and 'critical conscience', and the other who is a pacifist as a matter of 'traditional conscience,' whether war has broken out or not, can usefully be summarized in terms of the one being 'pacificist' and the other 'pacifist'. The former is pacific by dint of reason, the latter by belief.

For the armed services and the state, however, the problem is less philosophical and more practical. Once national service has been introduced, the problem is what are the authorities to do with conscientious objectors. There is need to distinguish openly between the genuine conscientious objector and the fellow-traveller, and to establish which arguments for exemption are admissible and which are not. One delicate legal point that must be established unambiguously is on whom the burden of proof should lie: the state as prosecutor, or the objector as defendant. Most countries have recognized that refusal to serve the state in war is a human right that has to be respected if the society in question has any justifiable claim to be thought civilized; but to respect a position and to admit its validity (that is to say its logical consistency) are two different things. More than that, the state authorities have to recognize the rights and feelings of all other citizens, and particularly those who do serve their country in war, thereby endangering their lives for the protection of society as a whole. The principle of equality before the law and equal treatment by the law is fundamental, especially when the existence of society itself is at stake.

Conscientious objection strikes at the very core of civil–military relations; it indicates an indifference, if not overt hostility, by individuals to the existence of armed services. When armed services, therefore, make a legal claim on the services of these individuals, the relationship is diametrically opposed. The choice of action falls between the two extremes of either accusing the objector of treason and taking the course of action prescribed in law (usually capital punishment), or acquiescing in the individual's right not to serve. Usually it falls somewhere in between, and the decision is based on the merit of the argument presented to the authorities. Significant here is the need for the authorities to set up special military tribunals for the purpose, rather than employ the normal processes of legal courts. Equally significant has been the tendency for these tribunals to be staffed in part, and even sometimes entirely, by service officers, the very group which would be least disposed to the conscientious objectors' position.

Conscientious objection is not a new phenomenon, although in the modern age of total war and the *'levée en masse'*, it has assumed a greater significance. In fact it has a long history, with records of pacifism and non-violence dating from early times, but its manifestation as a refusal to obey the law to serve in armed services in war only goes back to the First World War. Before then, pacifist thinking – *inter alia* of Erasmus, Kant, Fox, Bentham, Luther, Calvin, Confucius, Tolstoy, Lao-tzu, Isaiah – focused on how total and perpetual peace was to be attained and strove to create religious (and other) utopias on earth. It is the thinking of George Fox, however, that has most guided those religious groups of 'traditional conscience' in their opposition to violence and war, and their commitment to pacific ways.

Since these people formulated their various ideas on peace and non-violence, the conditions and nature of war have changed radically; so also have the motives and arguments behind pacifism and conscientious objection. The focus today is less on seeking to establish a utopia on earth, in which violence would be absent, and more one of trying to avoid war, now that the potential for destroying whole civilizations with modern weapons is real. Modern pacifists, such as Einstein and Philip Noel-Baker, tend to follow Bertrand Russell's line of argument that 'there never were, and are not now, absolute pacifists, but those who advocate or support peace because it is the only prudent politics in an age of potential total destruction'. Concern for the future of the world while nuclear weapons are in the hands of governments and armed servicemen has proved a powerful driving force behind such movements as the Campaign for Nuclear Disarmament (CND) which has attracted many pacifists of both 'traditional' and 'critical' persuasions.

Another reason for pacifism and conscientious objection to war is based on a revulsion against the modern weapons of war. This objection is partly on ethical and partly on moral grounds. Basically, the position is a humanist one: that human life is paramount. In past wars attempts have been made to ban certain categories of weapons (particularly biological and chemical) and to outlaw specific targets, especially those where civilians are likely to be found. For some, these bans are sufficient; for others, all forms of weapons designed to take life and cause destruction on any scale are unacceptable. As the modern inventory of weapons at the disposal of armed services widens, so opposition to their eventual use increases.

A third general reason for opposition to war and a motive for conscientious objection is political. Here the argument is that there are no ends commensurate with the cost in human life, civilization and the emotional distress of going to war. In this context, nuclear weapons represent the extreme position; as Gunther Anders observed, 'the atom bomb cannot be considered a weapon, since a weapon is a means to an end, which ought to dissolve with that end, the end then surviving the means'. A similar argument was put by Norman Angell with regard to aerial bombardment after the First World War, and by Ivan Bloch in his study, *The Future of War*, published in English in 1902, who argued that war had become economically ruinous, even to the supposed victor. These are arguments being voiced increasingly in West Germany by people who are well aware that war on the Central Front in Europe, no matter whether conventional or nuclear, would leave the whole area devastated.

Conscription causes a conflict between conscience and the law. The law requires the individual to serve in the armed services, and to lend support and commitment to combat in war. This could well require the conscript to commit acts that he considered immoral, and that were contrary to his conscience. As Einstein noted in a letter to a young conscientious objector, reproduced in his book *On Peace*, 'During the Nuremberg trials the various governments adopted the position that immoral acts cannot be excused on the plea that they were committed on government orders. What constitutes an immoral act can be determined only by one's individual judgement and conscience.' Herein lies the fundamental paradox about conscientious objection and armed services: governments expect moral behaviour on the part of its enemies in war that it does not expect of its own citizens, and furthermore it demands moral behaviour by its own armed servicemen (to exercise conscience when obeying orders), behaviour which it does not always accept among its population. For this reason, Einstein considered the conscientious objector a revolutionary, and the very antithesis of the dutiful armed serviceman.

The second central issue concerning the relationship between armed services and society is that of accountability. The problem stems from the basic supposition that armed services are potentially powerful, having access to and operational control over immense coercive physical power – what Andreski chose to refer to as 'suppression facility' – but are nonetheless servants of the state and, by association, of society at large. The public, and indeed its representatives in the legislature and those who form the government, need some tangible assurance that armed services are fulfilling their duties and responsibilities according to democratically agreed public policy decisions. It also needs assurance that they are not pursuing policies of their own which are inimical to the public interest. As the answer to the question who guards the guardians is difficult to find, so also is the answer to the question how that tangible assurance can be acquired. To complicate matters, armed services and other security agencies generally fall under national security legislation which defines most of what they do as secret, and denies public access to classified information.

It was Huntington's and Janowitz's argument, discussed earlier, that in the United States at least the public had no real need for concern that its armed services were behaving in other than a proper and responsible way because they were professional. Professionalism, they assured their readers, was the guarantee of military disinterestedness. More prudent, or at least more sceptical, people might take such professional assurances by armed servicemen with a pinch of salt, and opt for more objective evidence of their compliance with civilian authority. This requirement lies at the heart of open democratic government, and is one which holds all governments and state agencies accountable to the people for what they do and how they spend public money.

In the Western advanced industrial states, the issue of public accountability has become one of central concern as a consequence of increased government involvement in the lives of citizens, and the enormous increases in public expenditure. Concomitant with these developments there has been a radical change in the structures of government and the pattern of public administration. In all this, the armed services and government departments responsible for defence and security have not only been affected, but have led the way. Arguably, however, the most far-reaching development in public administration in the advanced industrial states is that of the massive expansion of government contracting for public goods and services. With the trend during the 1980s in both Europe and North America for the central administration to take on less responsibility for the provision of goods and services and to 'divest' itself of its assets and 'privatize', this pattern has tended to increase. It is also a policy with which even the Soviet Union has currently been flirting under Mr Gorbachev's leadership. The largest area of government contracting with the private sector is in defence procurement in terms both of value and of employment; that is to say, the purchasing of research, development and production of advanced equipment for the use of armed services.

A situation has, therefore, emerged in these countries where there are many private organizations and corporations engaged on production and the provision of services under contract to the government, and paid from the public purse – that is to say with taxpayer's money. According to standard liberal democratic theory, governments are answerable to the people not merely for policy choice, but for the execution of those policies and for the proper, authorized, disbursement of public money raised by taxation. By association, public money spent on purchasing equipment from private industry, particularly when it also involves research and development, should be accounted for; but this immediately presents the dilemma whether the government and the public at large have the right to inquire into the commercial affairs of private industry. In practice, access to such information has proved extremely difficult to obtain, and legislatures, those bodies that appropriate public money in the first place, have found that in the defence contracting field the combined barriers of official secrets and commercial confidentiality have generally frustrated their legitimate attempts. As Ed Kolodjiez has demonstrated in his monumental study of the manufacture and marketing of arms, nowhere is this more a closed world than in France. The issue presents nonetheless a challenge to the student of civil–military relations in all advanced industrial states.

Bruce Smith noted in his introduction to the pioneering volume on public accountability, edited with Douglas Hague, *Dilemmas of Accountability in Modern Government*, 'there are many devices by which a democratic government is held to account for its actions. External and internal audit, scrutiny by mass media, legislative oversight, party responsibility, the electoral process are a few of the common elements of a system of public accountability ... How can control be exercised over those to whom power is delegated?' To this central question a supplementary may be added, whether or not governments today, with their massive annual budget and wide scope in provision of public services, are simply too big, complex, distanced, amorphous, bureaucratic and diffused for any reasonable system of public accountability to operate.

Paradoxically, the public's only real chance of finding out what has been done in its name stems from some major mismanagement of a government programme which could no longer be kept hidden, such as a huge cost over-run on a weapons project. This happened, for example, with the American B-1 bomber and the British Stingray torpedo, to name but two among many hundreds of examples worldwide. Alternatively, when a public employee can no longer as a matter of conscience continue to keep silent over clear government deception of the public, and 'whistle-blows', to use the American expression, or 'leaks' the matter to the press, the public eventually finds out. By then, of course, the damage will already have been done. The cases of Ernest Fitzgerald and Clive Ponting over the C5A scandal and the *Belgrano* 'crown jewels' affair, respectively, are two examples that brought the government machine, for a while, abruptly to a halt, inflicted some political embarrassment, and obliged it to account for its action. A concomitant reaction has always been to seek some retribution on the 'whistle-blowers': Fitzgerald, Ponting, and others in a similar situation felt the full force of the administration's disapprobation in the form of legal charges, loss of job, and the discrediting of their character.

The problem of public accountability is central to democracy, and the problem is nowhere more acute than in defence. Given the problem, the challenge is to find a mechanism whereby the democratic requirement of the public's 'right to know' is satisfied, whilst at the same time the government can still retain sufficient authority to conduct its business and contract for goods and services with outside private bodies, without having constant interference from the public and their representatives. The problem is further exacerbated by the length of time that many complex weapons development projects take to come to completion, and by the inevitable requirement for military secrecy, a major consideration when new capabilities for the armed services are at stake.

So complex and sensitive is the accountability problem, from both a political and a national security standpoint, that when outsiders, such as investigative journalists like Duncan Campbell discover major secret government programmes costing vast sums of public money, there follows a massive security clamp down. As a consequence of diligent research and personal expertise in defence matters, Campbell found out that the British government had spent up to £500 million on a military signals intelligence (SIGINT) satellite codenamed Zircon, and revealed the fact in the *New Statesman*. There is nothing intrinsically wrong in such a policy, *per se*, except in this case Westminster was totally unaware, as were many members of the government and Cabinet, that the programme even existed. Public money in huge amounts had been 'laundered' under the noses of Parliament in numerous ways within the government's overall accounts, with the result that neither Members of Parliament, nor the public at large, were aware of what was afoot. In fact, and not for the first time, they were kept totally in the dark. This discovery happened in the wake of an earlier 'scandal' concerning the £1 billion British Chevaline nuclear warhead project about which the public had been kept unaware for nearly ten years through the use of similar 'laundering' techniques. After this experience, both the Labour and Conservative Parties jointly undertook in public statements not to allow such behaviour to happen a second time, whichever party gained power. Over the Zircon disclosure, the Conservative government again invoked the Official Secrets Act to prevent publication, but by the time they had acted, the article in question had already appeared, and had attracted media coverage.

The crucial consideration, however, is not the problem of implementing public accountability generally, and in defence and armed service matters specifically, but what is meant and understood by the concept in the first place. David Robinson, in the Smith and Hague volume, helped the discussion by suggesting that, in reality, public accountability was a balance of three kinds of accountability which applied with varying degrees of intensity to governments, the administrative bureaucracy and outside, generally private, agencies. These three areas were fiscal, process and programme accountability. To this three, a fourth should be added, that of policy accountability, one that has particular relevance in the context of defence public accountability.

Each kind of accountability can be simply defined. Fiscal accountability refers to the audit of public expenditure by government departments. Usually done on an annual basis, it is conducted by a public auditor and his staff who necessarily are independent of the administration. As departments have expanded their scope and budgets, the auditors have found it increasingly difficult to fulfil their task, and not infrequently large government departments do their own auditing – the Pentagon does, for example – leaving the audit office to inquire more into specific items of expenditure, such as major weapons projects and broader management issues.

The trend in recent years has been for the audit office to become more concerned with departmental management problems than with purely financial matters. Fiscal accountability determines – or should at least establish – that public money appropriated by legislatures is spent according to prescribed procedures in the manner defined in legally and openly approved public budgets in Parliament, and on authorized items. It is fundamental to democratic government, as E. Leslie Normanton has argued persuasively in his study of the *Accountability and Audit of Governments*. It stipulates proper accounting standards. Without it, there would be no check against the use of public money for private gain, or, more simply, corruption. Careful accounting, however, can reveal gross abuse of public money, such as the famed $500 toilet seats charged by an American defence contractor, and the 'massaging' of accounts that gave the Ferranti Company massive profits during the 1960s on its Bloodhound missile contract with the British government.

Process accountability is closely linked to fiscal inasmuch as it is only through the latter that defence contractors can be held accountable for the former. Process accountability refers to the general procedures and manner in which a government or defence programme (or contract) is conducted. Process, therefore, has much to do with notions of efficiency and good management. Private defence contractors who execute government funded weapons programmes in a sloppy and inefficient manner should hardly expect to be compensated or re-compensed for poor management. Nor should defence contractors deliberately underestimate costs in order to win contracts on the assumption that, being defence and essential to national security, compensation would be forthcoming at a later stage. But what consti-tutes good or bad management is hard to determine: even minor errors of the order of 0.001 per cent on a $5 billion defence contract – a total not uncommon nowadays – leaves either the government or the contractor facing a gain or loss on the total project of $5 million! Ameliorative procedures have been introduced in most large defence manufacturing states whereby both parties, government and contractor, can renegotiate their contracts *ex post facto*, in order that a fair adjustment might be made. Nonetheless, the sensitive problem of the right of the government to monitor the efficiency of contractors remains, especially when issues such as confidentiality, proprietorial information, patents, expertise, and commercial secrets are raised.

Programme accountability operates at a higher level of analysis. It has to do with the question of whether or not the government, in this case the defence department, is actually getting what it thought it was paying for from a contract with a supplier. This seemingly illogical situation is not as bizarre as it appears. Little is bought 'off the shelf'. Often it is not always clear what the armed services are looking for from a contract, despite rigorous contract clauses and tight specifications; this is especially true of research and development contracts for new weapons, or production contracts for weapons that are intended to perform multiple roles. Not infrequently, specifications change during the lifetime of contracts, often with disruption to the programme in question and increases in cost. In consequence, programme account-ability has two elements to it: one is the accountability of government and relevant departments for programme choice, and the other is the accountability of private contractors to government for producing to specification, at the quality required and on time, the goods and services for which they were contracted.

The last area of public accountability is that of policy. It represents the highest level of accountability in that it refers exclusively to the government itself, and not to agencies employed by, or contracted to, it. It concerns choice. Whereas programme accountability started from the point where the programme choice had been made, policy account-ability is concerned with the procedure leading to choice, and the assurance to the public that proper and serious consideration of all alternatives, and their short-term and long-term implications, had been given. In the secret world of government, these debates are seldom aired in public; if they are, they tend to be more a justification of the government's decision than an open affair with wide public participation. The British governments' public 'debate' on the Polaris nuclear deterrent replacement between 1979 and 1981 was more cosmetic than real, since the negotiations with the Americans over the Trident C4/D5 missile had been opened well before the 'public' debate had begun. It is also worth noting that this sort of information is most likely to be acquired from American sources, where the attitude to information and official policy is more open and flexible than in France or Britain.

There is an irony and a 'catch 22' situation, here. Where policy accountability is concerned, the more that legislatures – and by inference the general public – become involved in the formulation of defence and security policy and in matters of policy choice, the more they become party to the decision. Yet the principle of accountability is that government and its agencies should be accountable to the legislature and the public at large; the legislature in these circumstances would find it difficult to be accountable to itself, and the necessary distance and objectivity for effective scrutiny would be compromised. However, the trend in the West has been for greater involvement of legislative committees in the process of defence policy making and there has been constant pressure for more information about armed services, details of weapons and threat assessments to be made available for public debate and participation.

Information is the prerequisite of public accountability, irrespective of category. The amount, quality and type of information differs according to what the government is being held accountable for, and to whom. Fiscal/audit accountability requires, *ex post facto,* masses of accurate, hard data; it needs exact details of expenditure, set against authorized votes. Process accountability operates in a wider framework and demands information on current practices within the context of government and industry expenditure patterns and compared with accepted management practices and techniques. Whilst the former is, usually in law, easy to acquire, practice has demonstrated that there is ample scope for 'camouflaging' expenditure, for swamping legislature with mountains of undigested data, and obfuscating what has gone on, bearing in mind that there is always a time-lag of at least a year before evidence of any impropriety would be made evident.

Information on programme accountability is on a different level of analysis, and relates to current progress and projection about the outcome. Here the subjective and interpretive element enters, and accountability centres on the assessment of a programme by the government, and the relevant departments, and by the legislature. Finally, policy accountability addresses the highest level of policy making, concerning issues of strategy, broad choices of future commitments and judgments about the future (in the security context) of defence and the armed services. Given the long lead times involved in such choices (the 'Star Wars' (SDI) initiative is a good example) and the long-term implications of such choices for future public expenditure, it is proper that governments should be accountable for the serious, detailed analysis they have put into their final conclusions and policy choice.

Such policy commitments are of enormous public significance and should not be the product of whim, or the outcome of the attitude, which seemed to prevail after 1945, that 'it seemed a good thing at the time'. Without suggesting that those concerned with the decision to develop, deploy and then improve nuclear weaponry did not act responsibly, given their circumstances and the security situation they faced, available evidence would suggest nonetheless that the highly closed, secretive, and subjective way in which these decisions were taken in the late 1940s was not, perhaps, the most prudent. Greater policy accountability within, and indeed among, the major powers, even if it were in the realms of projection and subjective preferences about futures, might have had some effect on the earnest search for security in the world at that time; at worst it might have delayed, or even halted, the international arms race which followed and which is still a dominant feature today. It could also have helped the ambition of an effective United Nations Security Council to be realized. History has shown that secrecy and suspicion prevailed, and these wishful projections went unfulfilled.

Although the type and quality of information differs, in respect of different processes of public accountability, it is in the arena of national security and military secrets, that information is most difficult to acquire. The rule of thumb that generally operates is that of 'the right' or 'the need' to know. Depending on legislation defining what are and are not official secrets, and how governments choose to interpret that legislation, so information on defence and security is, or is not, accessible to those to whom governments should be accountable. As military technology continues to gather pace, intelligence becomes increasingly crucial in military planning and to avoid a surprise pre-emptive attack, weapons are progressively more destructive, political and military crises prove ever difficult to manage and are quicker to erupt, and costs in material and resources rise exponentially, the public's need, therefore, for relevant information has increased; but this requirement has been matched by an apparent corresponding need for governments not to provide it. There is no obvious way of resolving this critical problem; in the first instance, the problem has to be acknowledged by both the public and by governments. The prerequisite is to establish mutual trust, so that both needs, at least from a minimalist's perspective, might be satisfied.

Public accountability is fundamentally a matter of determining who is accountable to whom, and for what. Often it is not clear which government minister, administrative department or public official should be accountable for policies or action taken in the public's name; nor is it always clear at which level within the government machine responsibility should be assumed. The problems become all the more difficult when responsibilities for public policies and programmes are widely delegated among public and private organizations. Likewise, the question of for what government should be accountable is never entirely clear. Such matters of concern as errors of judgment, incompetent management, or fiscal impropriety are often committed well before their discovery, by which time the individuals who were in office and therefore responsible can well have moved on to another post. It is equally possible, with the rapid turnover of jobs among the armed services and government bureaucracies, that many will be required to assume a responsibility for which they had no, or inadequate, preparation. Despite all these complications, one principle is clear: government alone is ultimately accountable for its policies and the raising and expenditure of money in the public's name; it is first and foremost to the public and its elected representatives that it must account.

All political systems have mechanisms established in constitutional or statute law, or by convention, which enable citizens to have some way of finding out what their government is doing, and how it can be held to explain why. The most prominent, yet in some way the bluntest, instrument is that of a general election; a government that does not have the confidence of the electorate can find itself voted out of office. In the conduct of the election, the public has the opportunity to challenge members of the government and to ask for explanation of its policies and record while in authority. If either the record, or the answers, are unsatisfactory, the public can register disapproval by withdrawing its support, and vote into office other candidates or parties. In the past, defence has generally tended not to be a major issue area at elections; in recent years, however, as defence expenditures have inexorably risen relative to other sectors of government spending, and controversies have arisen over such policy areas as nuclear weapons, international arms sales, alliances and foreign forces stationed in one's own territory, command and control over armed services, rules of engagement, priority choices in defence science and technology research, state-sponsored terrorism, and scandals over cost escalation ('gold plating') on the services' weapons programmes, the subject of defence and national security has moved onto centre stage of the political arena, nowhere more so than in most of the advanced industrial states. There is certainly not the consensus among competing political parties in the West that characterized the post-Second World War period up to 1970.

The traditional mechanisms for defence accountability are elections, legislative debate, questions tabled in legislatures and directed at the government, political party conferences, independent audit of government departmental spending, investigatory journalism and media exposure, and judicial review. The effectiveness of these mechanisms collectively and separately is questionable, partly because the tactics that can be, and are, frequently employed by governments and officials to evade having to respond have proved eminently successful.

Samuel Huntington in his book on American defence, *The Common Defense*, differentiated between two areas within which governments have to take defence decisions: strategy and structure. The former is concerned with strategic doctrine, force contingency plans, deployment of the nation's available armed services and other resources at its disposal, and defence priorities; the latter addresses more practical and detailed questions of weapons acquisition and availability, defence budgetary matters, armed services' morale and personnel considerations, and service units and organization. Taken together, these two areas form the whole spectrum of defence accountability; security accountability would also have to include an even wider spectrum to take account of public perceptions of security and agencies other than armed services, those that are concerned with law and order, intelligence and public protection, including fire, ambulance, and customs services.

In public debate, relatively little information tends to be available. It is usually insufficient for any significant challenge to be made to government policy or action in either sphere. In the former, opinion is much more easy to voice; but without the detail, it lacks substance. The latter requires substantial amounts of data to be effective, but these tend to be protected under legislation and are unavailable. Despite the mounting importance of defence issues, the quality, rather than the volume of debate in the public domain, or within legislatures, is generally superficial and poor. To some extent this reflects, in part, a public attitude that defence, as with foreign policy, comes within the realm of 'high politics' – that of which the population at large has no real appreciation and which by dint of its elevated significance for other policies, should be left to their political 'masters' – and, in part, to the dearth of information at their disposal, both in quantity and quality. Generally speaking, relatively few politicians anywhere choose to make defence and armed services matters their area of expertise, since experience suggests that there are no votes to be gained from it. Even within legislatures, participants in debates on defence policy have tended to be proportionately small in number, but since defence expenditure has increasingly had a significant impact on the economies of regions and constituencies, considerably more politicians have registered interest, but usually only become exercised over matters of local impact, such as defence contracts and service locations.

The size of the defence budget has undoubtedly had a major influence on legislative interest in defence. For this reason the structure and procedures of legislatures have witnessed an increase in the number and authority of specialized committees charged with the oversight of defence matters. These committees have the power – in some cases subpoena – to call government witnesses to testify. The United States Congress, for example, has operated a specialist committee system almost since its inception, though even here the importance of those committees concerned with defence and the armed services is very much a post-1945 phenomenon.

In Britain and the rest of Europe this development is only relatively recent, and the emphasis is still more on scrutiny of expenditure by departments than on future policy options and overall spending estimates. Nevertheless, this development has helped build up a reservoir of expertise in defence matters, though its importance should not be overestimated. There remains the vexed issue of these committees' right to know and, if they meet *in camera*, their right to bring information into the open, the public domain. An alternative, more parliamentary and immediate way of holding governments accountable is through the procedural convention of asking written and oral questions of ministers and government representatives. The capacity of this mechanism to elicit more than the evasive, general, or partial response is limited. As a last resort, legislative assemblies can instigate commissions of inquiry, as in the instance of the French Assemblée Nationale over the Marcel Dassault defence contract scandal, or call for judicial review where there are defence irregularities before the law.

The mass media, and television in particular, is a powerful political force and can be an important ally. Defence is not a topic that commands the amount of media attention it deserves, perhaps because the newsworthiness of the journalists' revelations is not commensurate with the effort involved in getting it, or that serious matters of national security and integrity simply do not sell copies. Here again official secrets are an important consideration, and governments can, and do, put restraints on the media and either stop, or render anodyne, stories or revelations which it considers prejudicial to national security – or governmental interests. Nonetheless, the media, by articulating and guiding public concern, can put pressure on governments to account for their policies. They can also give weight to politicians' and others' demands for accountability in defence, and security issues, or any other sphere of government activity for that matter. Likewise, political parties within their own organization and structures can demand explanation. Where a party forms a government, such pressure is likely to take the form of routine support rather than of criticism; but divisions within a party, such as in the case of the British Labour Party, can generate marked differences on defence matters, and force the party leadership to account for, and defend, its position.

All of the above discussion, however, begs the major problem raised earlier: how does the public hold accountable those organizations that are working under contract to central government departments – when commercial and industrial secrecy is added to the problem of defence secrecy? The problem is a very serious one. Without adequate mechanisms of accountability there is no public safeguard against defence contractors overcharging, 'feathering their own nests', giving scant regard for value for money, and, to use the American term, engage in 'boondoggling'. From the experience of the performance of defence contractors in the US, Britain and the industrial world at large, and the many scandals of waste and corruption that have been exposed over the past 40 years, all publics have good grounds to be very suspicious.

In theory, there should not be a problem. Defence contractors, after all, when working on a government contract are, in a manner of speaking, an extension of the public sector. This applies even when they are private companies. It has been assumed by government agencies that private companies in receipt of public money to produce, under contract, products and services for the public benefit, would do so with the same integrity and efficiency that is expected of all government agencies. Corruption, defined as the use of public office for private gain, is strongly condemned. In practice, however, this expectation of honesty has seldom been fulfilled. The attitude of private contractors has tended to be the opposite: since public funds seem to have no proprietorial interest, they therefore become fair game for whatever tactic or device that the contractor can use to advantage.

The relevant government defence contracting agencies that work on behalf of defence departments and armed services usually insist on the right to have technical cost officers, system programme officers and/or quality control officers on site to monitor the conduct of the contractors. But the task before them is complex and the solution almost unsolvable: few defence contractors work solely on defence contracts; their businesses are intertwined with civil work; and they often work in conjunction with other companies. Few of these monitoring officers have time to discover what is going on; and if they do stay long enough they tend to become too company-oriented, thereby losing their detachment. Many of those appointed are servicemen on short-term tours of duty; often they display only passing interest in the job, and can claim only modest expertise. Frequently, these serving officers duplicate the procurement agency personnel, and fail to communicate with them on such matters as changes to specifications, quality control or costings. This is largely because they have differing priorities; the former concerned with performance and delivery, and the latter with costs, specifications and fiscal propriety.

Defence contracting has proved an almost intractable problem; the record of cost control, delivery times and performance to specification has not been good anywhere. Consequently, various expedients have been tried which have put questions of defence accountability into cold storage. One such expedient was to place all the emphasis on the terms of the defence contract, giving the contractor virtually total responsibility for the conduct of the programme. Called the total package procurement programme, the idea was to agree a global contract price and leave the contractor alone to produce to time and specification. If by skill, industry, or sheer acumen the contractor delivered on time and to specification, but below the agreed contract price, the profit was his; but so too would be any loss. Having tried the system over the C-5A strategic transport plane and bankrupted the country's largest defence contractor, Lockheed, in the process, the Pentagon abandoned the idea. It returned to a system of contracts largely employed in all the other defence manufacturing states, one that endeavoured to balance incentives for efficiency against a guaranteed reimbursement for work in a field which traditionally displayed a low elasticity of substitution: that is to say, one in which they would find it hard to find civilian markets for their products.

Although services' procurement agencies have all grappled with the problem, the conclusion would appear, in a defence non-market situation with, usually, a monopsony–monopoly relationship between government and contractor – one producer and one purchaser – that there is little that can be done, other than to ensure close scrutiny where possible and promote an improved spirit of integrity and public commitment on the part of the contractors. There remains vast room for improvement, even though the system of private renegotiation of government defence contracts has eliminated the worst excesses.

On the wider issues of public accountability, however, it may well be that the populations in the advanced industrial states have to accept that defence is one area of government activity that necessarily comes under the label of 'high politics'. If nothing else, the veil of secrecy that has more and more come to surround security and defence matters, and the activities of armed services, has determined that it should increasingly, even subconsciously, be seen that way. But herein lies the irony: defence has more than ever permeated the lives of the populations in all societies and influenced the direction those societies have developed, yet without serious challenge. At a time when there should be more openness and accountability than ever if democracy and democratic institutions are to be properly preserved, there is actually less. And this should give us all, and the armed services themselves, cause for reflection and deep concern.

8

Armed Services and Society: Military–Industrial Complexes and Central Organizations of Defence

Conscientious objection and public accountability are concerned with the rights of the individual in a democracy. They pose what is essentially a philosophical problem; whilst they can, and have, raised practical difficulties for governments and armed services, they are generally debates of a theoretical nature. This is not the case with two further issues arising from the relationship between armed services and society, which are more practical and matter-of-fact in character: the first is the emergence within advanced societies of a new power nexus, called a 'military–industrial complex', the dimensions, power and composition of which are not always easy to ascertain; the second is the crucial problem of the most appropriate structure and decision making process for central organizations of defence. Both subjects have commanded much attention in recent years, and therefore require a chapter devoted to them.

The military–industrial complex is not a reality; it is a concept which is useful as a shorthand way of referring to an interdependence in advanced industrial states between armed services, government departments and industry. Today, this confluence of powerful institutions has emerged as a consequence of the coincidence of a technological revolution in modern weapons, and a period of prolonged international confrontation between two ideological blocs. But it is more than an interdependence: a suspicion has arisen that this three-cornered relationship is also symbiotic, with each party benefiting in one way or another from its association with the others. In other words, there is within the relationships a coalescence of interest that not only binds the parties together, but also as a consequence, gives them, when acting in

161

concert, immense political and economic influence and power both within society and the state.

This phenomenon, however, is not new. It has many theoretical antecedents, many of which have been identified and discussed in an article by Charles Moskos included in *The Military Industrial Complex* edited by Sam Sarkesian. Indeed, the close relationship between the feudal Lord and his armourer, the seventeenth-century gunmaker and the regimental colonel, the eighteenth-century monarch and the state arsenals and, finally, the nineteenth-century arms manufacturer and his national clients demonstrate that the producers of arms always have had influence. These last were identified in A. C. Engelbrecht and F. Hanighan's *Merchants of Death*, and Philip Noel-Baker's *The Private Manufacture of Arms*, evoking past names of immensely powerful men and companies like Maxim, DuPont, Krupp, Vickers, Colt, Schneider-Creusot, Zaharoff and Remington. Their influence on the course and nature of war in the late nineteenth and early twentieth centuries was enormous, and epitomized in the character of Andrew Undershaft, in George Bernard Shaw's *Major Barbara*. But for all their influence and commercial power, they pale in comparison with the huge high-technology arms producing corporations of today, massive enterprises that mushroomed and consolidated during the period of the armed peace that has characterized the world after the Second World War.

The phenomenon has long existed, but its significance and growth had not fully captured public attention until President Eisenhower's farewell address to the American people in 1961. Before then there might have been adequate grounds for thinking that the amount of American public money and national resources devoted to defence was justified, since the post-Second World War period had been one of massive adjustment in which the two major powers (the Soviet Union and the United States), had been obliged to fill the power vacuum left by the weaker, or defeated, European and Axis powers. To the two new superpowers this obligation necessitated sustained high military expenditure. It was a period of acute competition and hostility between the two, one that manifested itself in open conflict (as in the Korean War) and in a symbolic arms race which, over time, emphasized technical superiority in nuclear warheads, missiles, supersonic aircraft, carrier battlefleets, nuclear submarines and, ultimately, space.

The striving for technological advantage has continued unabated since Eisenhower's warning of a 'disastrous rise of misplaced power', with implications for American political culture and national life, and is now moving inexorably into yet more esoteric scientific fields such as space-based systems, particle beams, lasers, electronics and artificial

162

intelligence. The long-term future, which some claim will hold better prospects for the peace and security of the world, but which also carries a multi-trillion dollar price tag, is the American Strategic Defence Initiative (SDI) programme and its Soviet equivalent. First outlined in rather simplistic terms by President Reagan in March 1983, and more popularly known as 'Star Wars', it is a complex system of space-based, emerging technologies, designed to provide the United States with full protection against nuclear missile attack.

The weapons systems of the 1950s, though crude in contrast with those of the 1980s, and the effect of high annual defence spending to meet the needs of the American armed services, created a large and secure market which American industry was quick to recognize and capitalize on. In a relatively short space of time an indigenous arms industry, which had once been characterized by numerous manufacturers competing for armed service contracts, became dominated by a relatively small number of huge corporations, producing highly specialized and technical weapons systems in a closed market, each with a turnover in excess of the GDP of the majority of the world's states. So extensive was the range of work and the products of these industrial corporations, and so huge were their annual revenues, that by the mid 1960s over half the states of the United States had come to depend on federal defence spending to balance their budgets.

President Eisenhower was not, of course, the first to recognize what was happening; as our earlier chapter on elites discussed, C. Wright Mills was acutely aware that large defence-oriented industries were becoming immensely influential and in 1956, in his book *The Power Elite*, he pointed to their overlapping interests with American government, and the armed services. But Mills's message was not one that Americans wished to hear at that time: the country had never been stronger or richer, it was the world's major power, and its confidence had reached its zenith. The last thing anybody wanted to be told was that a country that had an idealistic, representative democracy, with checks and balances against the abuse of power, was becoming one ruled over by a closed, unrepresentative elite of 'commanders of power unequalled in human history, (who) have succeeded within the American system of organized irresponsibility'. Eisenhower did not go quite so far, but at least he drew public attention to the emergence of a military–industrial complex which, if only by implication, he felt had the potential for exercising undue, or 'improper' influence over the political and economic affairs of the nation. The obvious inference to be drawn from his address was that such potential was inimical to America's cherished beliefs in democracy and the rectitude of the American Constitution, and, of course, antithetical to long-standing traditions of civil–military relations.

What might have been an almost subconscious awareness of what was happening politically in America in the 1950s became a subject for speculation and increasing concern in liberal circles after Eisenhower's warning. To generalize a little, the address stimulated a variety of responses, each spurred on by the possibility that underlying the American political system there was indeed a conspiracy working to the advantage of an unrepresentative few. Two interpretations broadly emerged of the military–industrial complex assertion: the first tended to follow Mills, believing that there was indeed a conspiracy afoot working to the benefit of a nexus of powerful people. The second suggested that the military industrial complex was a form of sub-government, but one whose influence was confined to its own sphere of professional concerns, namely the defence and security of the United States. There was no suggestion, in this second view, that this sub-group had any interest in extending its influence into other areas of American economic, political or social life. It is within this context that the studies of Huntington and Janowitz in 1962 discussed earlier should be seen. Whatever might have been the response to Eisenhower's warning, had all things been equal, is hard to gauge; but soon after his speech the United States found itself (or deliberately became, depending on one's point of view) drawn into and embroiled in a war in South-East Asia. This war subsequently expanded to become the largest in American history in terms of duration, cost and loss of life.

Vietnam was a war that steadily escalated in commitment and intensity throughout the 1960s, moving from one that enjoyed popular support and endorsement under President Kennedy, to one that became characterized by disillusionment and open hostility under Presidents Johnson and Nixon. It was during this ten-year period that American defence spending reached its height, its arms industries were overextended with full order books and financially booming, and the armed services received almost anything they asked for. The seemingly endless source of funding for defence had the added stimulus of an awareness (though more myth than reality) that the major rival, the Soviet Union, had caught up qualitatively with the USA in many areas of military technology, and in some had even surpassed it, especially in missiles and the military uses of space.

As the war in Vietnam escalated and a favourable outcome seemed more distant than ever, popular opinion turned from tacit support to mounting opposition and, eventually, to overt hostility. Questions were asked why, for all the American superiority in men and equipment, victory was no nearer; why there was no clear statement of the purposes for which American forces were fighting in Vietnam; why the American military command appeared incapable of conducting operations efficiently and effectively; and why the war seemed to generate so much waste in financial, material, and human resources. To exacerbate the situation, the public found the answers to these questions less and less satisfactory and took increasing dislike to the tactics adopted by their forces. People began to look more and more for an alternative explanation; for a population accustomed to victory, to fighting for clearly defined and articulated ideals, and to industrial and technological superiority, the Vietnam War proved a traumatic experience for the nation as a whole. Pressures were immense to find some explanation for a general sense of disequilibrium, and to provide the American public with some catharsis.

To some extent, the spectre of a military–industrial complex provided that explanation. What better than a conspiracy thesis, one which focused on material gain, greed and personal advancement when honest, brave and innocent young Americans were dying unnecessarily for no good cause on the field of battle in some distant, alien, foreign land? In this context, it is hardly surprising that independent commentators, academics, and journalists directed their attention on the American military–industrial complex, promoting the view that those who formed it were the beneficiaries of the Vietnam War, and, moreover, were an unrepresentative, secretive, wasteful, irresponsible, rich, and unprincipled group of people. The fear was also voiced at the time that the complex was also sufficiently powerful to ensure that there was little that could be done to curb its influence.

The conviction grew at that time that the political system had become so distorted that the principles of democracy which the framers of the Constitution had so carefully worked out were compromised beyond redemption. Further, the dependence of so many states, constituencies, regions and organizations on the military–industrial complex had become so extensive that it was thought to be too well protected to be changed by the normal political process. Those fears are no less prevalent today as the United States accelerates its high spending Star Wars policies for the twenty-first century, with the added knowledge that when there have been attempts to curb military spending, as during the Carter Administration, not only was the resistance from the military–industrial complex extremely powerful, but the same people were able to generate a majority perception of American weakness in the face of further Soviet military technological advances.

Writings on the American military–industrial complex during the

1960s and early 1970s tended to focus on one of its three component elements, whilst recognizing a symbiosis with the other two. Those who wrote mainly about the military hierarchy as a determinant of the complex, and by inference, of the Vietnam War, high defence spending and anti-Soviet attitudes tended to stress the extent to which armed service generals had permeated the political institutions of Washington. Truman, whilst he was President, may have thought that the American armed services (in the form of Admiral Leahy, at least) belonged politically to the Middle Ages; but during the Eisenhower years, senior serving officers became very adept at politics, and successful in projecting and promoting service interests within the government.

This was hardly surprising; Eisenhower had a number of military officers on his White House staff; the new post-War Department of Defense gave them a stronger presence in Washington than the previous small service departments; new institutions like the National Security Council brought a new political–military responsibility; many retired senior officers had had political experience running occupied territories after the Second World War and had taken up political careers as ambassadors or politicians; and, above all, congressional post-War attitudes to senior officers changed dramatically from the traditional one of scepticism, if not hostility, to one based, first, on respect and trust, and, second, on mutual interest. Not least important in this politicization of the American military was the 'buddy system' of shared experience during the Second World War between politicians, top industrialists and military personnel.

Throughout the late 1950s, the political awareness and political skills of the American armed services increased, but no more so than during the 1960s when they had to be seen in the political arena during the debates over the Vietnam War. These took them into Congress, both before Senate and House Committees and behind the scenes, into the country to lecture and put over the administration's policy in South-East Asia, and frequently before the television cameras. In customary military style, their response was thorough and disciplined, not only in training and preparation of these non-military skills, but also in establishing and refining a Pentagon public relations and propaganda machine of considerable expertise. It was this last phenomenon that attracted Senator Fulbright's attention in his work *Pentagon Propaganda Machine*, a subject touched also on by J. Swomley in his broader study of *The Military Establishment*, published in 1964, and by Clark Mollenhoff in *The Pentagon*.

Given that the military hierarchy element of the power triad has acquired influence and the political skills to go with it, how has that influence been exercised? According to Colin Gray in his study of the 'Organisational nexus' in R. Beaumont and M. Edmonds's *War in the Next Decade*, it is first and foremost exercised at the formulation stage in the planning of national defence and security policy. Assisted with analyses, prepared and paid for by them by independent, private 'think tanks' to support their position, the armed services have presented a formidable influence within Washington, regarding not merely defence, but also foreign policy, science policy and economic and industrial affairs. For example, when industrial corporations with defence interests are in financial difficulty, be they airlines, railroads, aircraft manufacturers, or automobile companies, national security and military strategic arguments have always been used to effect a 'bail-out' with public money. On matters of American relations with the Soviet Union, and perceptions of the communist threat, the Pentagon's influence has been dominant, the more so since President Reagan took office and his first Secretary of Defense, Caspar Weinberger, was encouraged to assume so much personal policy authority and spending power. Even the public relations euphoria over the American-Soviet arms control agreements over INF disarmament and START negotiations to reduce strategic arsenals by 50 per cent does not fundamentally reduce the deep-rooted mistrust in which the Soviet Union, and its leadership is held, particularly in American military circles.

The second element in the triad, the administrative bureaucracy, has attracted the least attention. One possible explanation is that it is hard to isolate encompassing as it does the administrative and legislative branches of the American government. Whilst it is recognized that Congressmen have used their association with the military and industry to help secure defence contracts for their constituents, and have ensured that their constituencies received a share of available defence spending, there is a reluctance to acknowledge that they themselves benefit materially. To do so would suggest bribery or misuse of public money. Nonetheless, they gain indirectly, partly from the patronage that accompanies large federal spending programmes, and partly of course from the electoral popularity that follows from being associated with bringing in work and additional sources of income to their area.

No person better exemplified this than Mendel Rivers, Chairman of the influential House Armed Services Committee during the 1960s. He used his position, as a conservative Democratic Party Representative, to ensure that his constituency of Charleston, South Carolina was a regular recipient of Navy spending. During his tenure he was directly responsible for bringing an array of service installations and defence industrial plants, including a naval shipyard, a Polaris submarine base, an Air Force base, a Marine recruiting depot, a Marine Air Corps station, an Army supply depot and two Naval hospitals. Among defence industrial companies he attracted to Charleston within four years of becoming House Armed Services Committee Chairman were the AVCO Corporation, J. P. Stevens, General Electric, McDonnell-Douglas, Lockheed and United Aircraft. As if to confirm the fact, he campaigned for re-election on the slogan 'Rivers delivers', and since 55 per cent of his constituents' payroll ($317 million a year in 1968) was derived from defence sources, his was considered a 'safe seat'. Indeed, as Representative James Whetten of Mississippi said of the military–industrial complex in 1963, 'We have reached a point where tenure of office of a Congressman . . . to a great degree is controlled on how many defense contracts they may get in their own area.' This point was given emphasis by James Donovan in his *Militarism, USA*, with his comment, 'the military are smart enough to exploit a [this] political advantage'. There is little to suggest that the situation has changed significantly in the past 20 years, other than that different Congressmen and other constituencies have been beneficiaries, with California becoming the leader.

A severe critic of the military–industrial complex phenomenon, and one who focused on the administrative bureaucracy was Seymour Melman. In a lengthy analysis, *Pentagon Capitalism*, he expressed concern about the extent to which the state – by which he meant the central administrative machine – had encroached into the free market economy and American industry through defence and armed service spending. He saw this as being detrimental to proper operation of free market forces and private enterprise, and an insidious form of state intervention and control, harmful to the basic tenets of the American capitalist politico-economic system. The consequence he considered was harmful to industrial enterprise and business acumen, and interfered with management efficiency. His analysis had much in common with Galbraith's technostructure, except inasmuch as the central government administration had joined forces with the new breed of top industrial managers to 'direct' in an indicative and corporatist way, the policies and priorities of industry and the economy.

What most offended Melman, though, was the removal from the defence industries of the spur of competition, and the incentive for profit and efficiency. Defence contracts were becoming sinecures; profits were guaranteed; inefficiencies were covered up; and penalties for incompetent management, or, even, dishonest business conduct, were non-existent. Conversely, poor management was often rewarded, cost over-runs excused and paid in full, and no-one held accountable for mistakes. Advances in technology were creating a defence industry of many monopolies with one monopsonist (single purchaser), the government; open and proper competition had all but evaporated; and all interest in improving efficiency and performance eradicated. Attempts to counter this trend by Robert Charles, David Packard, Charles Hitch and Roland McLean from the Office of the Secretary of Defense in the Pentagon lacked support, or were treated cosmetically. The military–industrial complex, Melman concluded, had fallen into the hands of state managers, few of whom, if any, were accountable, either to an electorate or to shareholders. The result was 'state capitalism', manifest through the Pentagon and independent of established political processes. To Melman this was an insidious form of socialism in which the central bureaucracy had become the industrial managers and decision makers. He deplored this development, and advocated a return to open competition using different forms of defence contracts, and imposing the severest penalties on those who failed to produce defence equipment on time, to specification, and to contract price.

The third and last party to the military–industrial triad is the defence industry itself. This is the world of corporate wealth, and encompasses those enterprises that are the main beneficiaries of massive military spending. Critics of the complex who focus on industry tend to have done so from a Marxist perspective, stressing that such an arrangement furthers class interests. There have been only a few studies of the link between industry and the military, but among them Adam Yarmolinsky's *The Military Establishment* must be one of the most detailed. It is clear that the two are constantly in touch regarding technological developments, weapons research and development, and the production of service equipment. The defence industries have made a policy of employing retired service officers, but whether or not this is proof of a class conspiracy or sheer prudence to help them understand the huge complex bureaucratic structure within the Pentagon is debatable. Defence manufacturers, however, ensure that their interests are well protected, not only through their personnel policies and extravagant lobbying by wining and dining officers and politicians, but also by being generous sponsors of congressional, secretarial and presidential candidates.

The Marxists' attack on the American military–industrial complex, however, was not confined to the more obvious personal links between industrial executives, top service officers, politicians, and senior bureaucrats. Their approach was much broader, contending that it is a by-product of compensating for the inherent weaknesses and contradictions in capitalism. This argument was spearheaded by P. Baron and

P. Sweezey in their book *Monopoly Capitalism* in which they contended that the Cold War and high American defence spending to counter a perceived (or projected) Soviet, or socialist, threat served the capitalist purpose in peacetime of stimulating economic growth, promoting prosperity at home, expanding economic and political interests externally, and providing an ever-present rationale for the maintenance in power of a political and economic oligarchy. Michael Kidron in his *Western Capitalism since the War* enlarged on these points, recognizing that high defence spending afforded all capitalist governments of the day fiscal and economic tools with which to manipulate their economies, thereby ameliorating the worst consequences and compensating for the inbuilt failures of their capitalist, free enterprise systems.

Returning to the very first point made in this discussion of military–industrial complexes, that it is no more than a concept to encapsulate, or organize, ideas about a state of affairs in which there is evidence to suggest a coalescence of interest between three powerful groupings in society (and not just that of the United States) the additional point should be made that its principal characteristics will alter over time as people, policies and circumstances change. However, relatively little analysis has been done or written up on military–industrial complexes outside the United States. Essentially it is an American phenomenon, and appeared at a particular point in time and in a particular way. It emerged when it did, according to J. K. Galbraith in his *How to Control the Military*, as a consequence of six separate developments that happened, by coincidence, to come together during the late 1940s and early 1950s. These are worth recalling, since they add emphasis to the fact that it is uniquely American in origin and, indeed, form.

The first development was the increased bureaucratization of American life, and, with it, the expansion in the scope and power of government organizations. Before 1939 the US State Department shared the same office block in Washington, DC as the Navy and the War Departments; today, that building houses only a section of the Executive Office of the President. The State and Defense Departments operate from their own massive administrative building complexes. This is something of what Ralph Lapp referred to as the 'weapons culture' in his book of the same name. Second, there were changes in the circumstances and images of post-War American foreign policy, particlarly with regard to the communist world. Next, as a concomitant of the first two, came a perceived need for secrecy, particularly about new weapons, intelligence about Soviet policies and American plans. Fourth, Galbraith identified a sense of personal fear about communism among ordinary Americans, a fear stimulated and heightened by McCarthyism and the House Un-American Activities Committee. The experience was novel inasmuch as the American public had never had to address the possibility of attack or invasion, or sedition from within. Fifth, the United States had never been a country where social welfare had figured high on the political agenda; expectations of state support were correspondngly low, even after the recession of the 1930s. It was an innocent age, according to Galbraith, in which taxation was low, and any increases in military spending were not considered detrimental to other priorities. Finally, there was no ideological objection to military–industrial power either from the more conservative element, who welcomed increases in defence spending, or from liberals who 'accepted a lesser threat to liberty to forestall a greater one'. And so it was that the conditions were right for the military–industrial bureaucracy to emerge, expand and become established.

Although the concept originated in, and properly only refers to, the United States, it has been used sufficiently freely to suggest there are comparable coalescences of interest in Britain, France and other advanced industrial states. The idea in most general terms is the same; but the realities are very different. Basically, the concept refers to a locus of power within a state, and also to the exercise of power. Unfortunately, in the transfer of the concept from the United States, pejorative connotations, most evident during the Vietnam period of the abuse of power and influence for sectional gain, have also been carried over. The greatest danger arising from the almost cavalier way in which the concept has been adopted by students and others, is that it is taken to be a reality, with the assumption that no analysis or proof of its existence is necessary. It should never be forgotten, however, that there is no such thing as a military–industrial complex, any more than there is a medical–industrial, or a construction–industrial complex. The term is a concept and refers only to a set of relationships that, given certain circumstances, exist in a state at a particular point in time.

Discussion of the military–industrial bureaucracy immediately leads on to the last core issue of concern to students of armed services and society considered in this volume: that of central organizations of defence in different states. The issue is a fundamental one since it is within the structure of government that armed services and the political authorities come directly into contact. They have the combined, rather than the joint, responsibility to take decisions regarding the defence and security of the state. Armed services do not live in isolation, independent of governments, and whilst much responsibility in defence matters is delegated to them as professionals, decision making about the direction and content of security, and defence is not one of them.

At the beginning of Chapter 1, reference was made to the relevance of the study of the relationship between armed services (forces) and war, and the greater propensity of some societies to pursue aggressive policies towards their neighbours and the outside world. Decisions about going to war, the use of physical means to protect and defend the state and society, or the promotion of their interests abroad is an internal matter and the responsibility of governments. Armed services are essentially the executive means of implementing those policy ends. Nevertheless, the two are not independent of one another. Armed services' capabilities and their perceptions of the outside world have proved a strong influence on the policies of governments. Policy planning about defence, or indeed offence, is undertaken within the context of government and government departments; it is here that top political and service planners meet, confer and decide on policy.

This function was identified in the model of the national security system outlined in Chapter 6, but did not elaborate how the various functional elements in the system, the central bureaucracy, the armed services, the government decision makers, the advisers and the intelligence agencies in different states interacted. It is this problem that the remainder of this chapter addresses. The assumption underlying the analysis is that the structure of central organizations of defence, and the processes of decision making that are employed not only have an immediate bearing on the content of policy, but also give some insight into the relative influence of the organizations involved. Not least among these organizations are the armed services themselves.

It is in central organizations of defence that the contrast between the advanced industrial states and the Third World is most evident. This is largely due to the magnitude of defence matters in the former which increases exponentially in complexity with increases in size and diversity. One factor which assumes almost an imperative as size and complexity increase is the extra bureaucracy that is also generated. In advanced industrial states, for example, it is not unusual to find as many civilian bureaucrats being paid under the defence budget as those serving in the uniformed branches of the armed services.

Central organizations of defence are important today as a direct consequence of the highly technological nature of modern weapons, the global reach of modern warfare, and the combined nature of military operations. But more important than any other reason is the character of modern defence and security planning which recognizes that the first necessity is to maintain forces in being since past assumptions about mobilization and the redirection of industrial capacity are no longer valid. It is not simply a matter of sustaining forces on an annual basis, either; the effect of modern technology has certainly increased the accuracy, range, fire power and response time of modern weapons, but it has also extended their cost and lead time – the time it takes to conceive, research, develop, produce and introduce into the inventory of the armed services. Defence planning, therefore, has taken on a whole new complexion and has gone far beyond the need to stockpile weapons in arsenals. Such policies are far too expensive a luxury. Defence plans have progressed far beyond the requirement to maintain a sufficient capability at all times; they have developed into projections of up to 20 years into the future, not just about who presents the most likely serious threat to the state, but, equally importantly, what sorts of esoteric technologies are likely to be available, affordable and applicable to both one's own and the enemy's forces. Defence planning has become a difficult exercise in deciding about futures, while simultaneously mantaining a credible capability for the present.

Earlier studies of civil–military relations were restricted to central defence decision making, and focused, as in the case of Michael Howard's *Soldiers and Governments* and Harold Stein's *American Civil–Military Decisions*, on the dialogue between politicians and senior officers regarding such momentous issues as wartime strategy, rearmament, colonial expansion, and responses to international crises. Only in the 1980s did the study assume a wider, sociological dimension; but this should not diminish the relevance of where the apex of civil–military relations really lies, in the central organizations of defence. In the introduction to my *Central Organizations of Defence* the relevance of the subject was highlighted, alluding to the constitutional, cultural and political contexts within which these organizations had to operate. Since these contexts have already been discussed in previous chapters, the emphasis here will be on the organizations themselves and, in particular, the significance of their structures and processes.

The first thing to remember with central organizations of defence is that they are a relatively new phenomenon in the experience of modern government. Indeed none effectively existed before the second World War. Before then, there were various departments and ministries responsible for looking after each branch of the armed services, and to prosecute its interests within government. When the British entered into the Second World War in 1939, there was the War Office, the Admiralty and the Air Ministry; the USA did not then even have a department responsible for its Air Force. Planning for defence in both countries was done largely on the basis of agreement between the relevant services and government departments when the occasion dictated, and very much in a reactive way. Very little was done by way of forward planning, in a coordinated, logical manner; each service planned and operated along separate lines, looking first to satisfy its own immediate organizational, equipment and operational needs. The approach was predominantly of a war being fought in the air, or in a maritime or land context, but never all three simultaneously. Amphibious operations, air support of land operations, maritime reconnaissance, all clearly evident from the First World War experiences, were given lower priority than immediate service needs. When there was any obvious defence operational requirement, each service preferred to respond using its own resources.

It was neither an efficient nor a logical way to plan defence. Its shortcomings in war were soon exposed, and quickly seen in contrast with the German *Wehrmacht* approach of a centralized planning body coordinating the plans and preparations of the three armed services. With his customary insight, Churchill recognized this shortcoming in British defence planning, and wrote a note on 6 June 1936 to the effect that the arrangements for the supply of equipment to the armed services through the Office of the Minister for Coordination of Defence were ill-conceived and comprised 'unreflected and wrongly-grouped functions'. He advocated instead a functional separation of strategic planning and material supply, and proposed four separate departments, Army, Navy, Air Force and Supply, with 'the Coordinating Minister at the summit of the four having the final voice upon priorities'.

He was later able to implement this proposal during the Second World War through the formation of the Defence Committee of the War Cabinet, which he chaired both as Prime Minister and as Minister of Defence. Not only was this in itself a significant constitutional development, since no such ministerial post had existed before, but it also established Churchill's personal authority for central defence planning over the service Chiefs of Staff Committee. When combined with his authority as Prime Minister, Churchill not only consolidated his control over the conduct of the war and the armed services, but also introduced the first vestiges of a centralized organization of defence outside Nazi Germany. The United States finally introduced its central Defense Department, the Pentagon, after the *National Security Act* of 1947; such an arrangement was first established in the Soviet Union only in 1953. In Europe, Italy introduced a ministry of Defence in 1947; France never really could decide on who should be ultimately responsible, the President, the Prime Minister or a Minister for Armed Forces, but finally settled on a formal central defence machinery under a Minister for Defence in 1959, following the formation of the Fifth Republic, though the influence of the President remained dominant. Despite Churchill's wartime initiative, the UK did not finally move to a central Ministry of Defence until 1946, and not until 1963 did it effectively become one with service departments no longer independent entities.

Each central organization of defence has its own history, depending *inter alia* on: past military experiences – Japan and West Germany have quite separate defence problems from the other advanced industrial nations consequent upon their defeat in the Second World War; ideological background – China and the Soviet Union both require party involvement in defence decision making and management; political experience – Spain only recently replaced a military dictatorship with a democratic system of government, and France changed constitutional course in 1958 when de Gaulle's Fifth Republic replaced that of the post-Vichy 1946 Fourth Republic; and tradition – Britain and the United States, victors in the Second World War, inherited a situation of constitutionally well-established armed service departments whose power and influence took a long time to dissipate. Time and space does not allow for any elaboration of these complex and sometimes colourful stories of power struggles for authority over policy and command over armed forces; they are, anyway, well covered in numerous books including my own *Central Organisations of Defence; F.* Johnson's *Defence by Ministry;* S. Huntington's *The Common Defense;* G. G. Walpuski's and D. Wolf's *Einführung in die Sichefheitspolitik;* V. Ilari's *Le forze armate era politica e potere;* and D. Chantebout's *L'Organisation générale de la défense nationale en France.* What can be done, generalizing from their various experiences, is to identify the common problems that each faces, particlarly with regard to the relationship between the armed services and civilian authority.

In *The Common Defense,* Huntington differentiated between decisions concerning strategy and structure, the former being concerned with defence policy, priorities and disposition; the latter with armed service organizations, equipment, resources and training. In peacetime, this analytical distinction is satisfactory, but in war an additional area has to be included. This is the overall conduct, control and command of fighting units about to be engaged, or engaged, in combat. Of particular pertinence here is the sensitive issue of rules of engagement in time of crisis, and the degree of discretion that service units may exercise in an emergency, or when under threat of attack. The complex characteristics of modern warfare and the technologies – especially nuclear – now employed has made this area, once a responsibility that devolved largely onto the armed services, one that political leadership has increasingly assumed the authority to control.

For purposes of analysis, these three elements of central defence decision making are considered separately. Strategy is that sphere which, given scarce resources, has to determine priorities between defence needs and all other social requirements. This question has already been alluded to earlier with regard to the definition of 'security', and is concerned with the problem of whether or not the concept should be confined to the roles of the armed services or widened to encompass Lord Beveridge's approach. Ultimately, it is a decision of the government as a whole, taken in the light of available national resources, projected economic growth, political mandate, perceptions of domestic and international threats, existing commitments and other competing claims. The practice in recent years, almost everywhere, has been to hold defence spending at a ceiling figure, expressed in terms of a percentage of the country's GDP and to put pressure on the armed services to plan within that upper limit.

In some states – France, for instance – the problem of defence planning within a global figure is made easier by calculating the total for a five-year period, thus enabling annual fluctuations to meet the peaks and troughs of spending programmes without exceeding the final figure for the period as a whole. The UK attempts to plan over a long term, and costs programmes accordingly; but the budgetary ceiling is usually given for one year only and this usually means the Secretary of State asking Parliament for supplementary funding to meet overspending towards the end of the financial year.

Armed services can only influence, but not participate in, these high government policy debates. Nonetheless, their influence either within central organizations of defence acting on defence ministers and secretaries of state, or outside, putting pressure on government members and members of legislatures, should not be underestimated. In the battle for resources within the central administration, the armed forces everywhere behave like any other interest group. Generally, the outcome is a compromise; depending on the status and power of the relevant defence minister and the strength of the case with which the armed services have equipped him, so the outcome is more or less favourable to the armed services. Within inner government and Cabinet circles, defence tends not to have the same standing, politically, as foreign, financial and home affairs, unless the party in power and/or its leader happens to have a personal interest in defence and security. This was certainly the case with President Reagan who had in Caspar Weinberger a singularly tough and demanding Secretary of Defense.

But this can work the other way, also; Francis Pym, British Defence Secretary from 1979 to 1981, proved too tough and too successful in arguing the armed services' and defence case for Margaret Thatcher's liking, and was relieved of his post in a Cabinet mid-session reshuffle. Whilst Denis Healey was unquestioningly a strong, knowledgeable, and long-serving Secretary of Defence in the Harold Wilson administration, his attention was focused more on the direction of defence policy and restructuring the services than in prosecuting service interests within Cabinet circles.

Defence policy itself is not always easy to define. Before central organizations of defence began to address the problem of security and defence differently in the 1960s, defence policy was expressed in terms, quite simply, of what the armed services did. It was no more problematical than that, except inasmuch as what the armed services did was largely determined by what they perceived the enemy to be doing. Defence planning and weapons choices were, and still are, fundamentally, 'threat-driven', no matter how much they might subsequently be dressed up in terms of strategic theory and laudable sentiments about peace-keeping and international stability. To this 'bottom line' determinant of defence policy planning have also to be added various declaratory policy commitments through international treaty or custom; for example, to come to the defence of, or join in, an alliance with other states. In the case of the latter commitment, there is a strong likelihood that the process of national defence policy making and, moreover, national resource allocation would have to accommodate additional alliance obligations.

The simplest model of defence decision making allows the government, as political masters, to decide and the armed services to ask for the men, the equipment and other necessary resources to fulfil these policy directives. Before the early 1960s, this tended to happen: defence policy was laid down in terms of who the enemy was, and resources were allocated to the armed services, separately, to prepare what they judged to be necessary to counter the threat. In terms of the overall defence posture, what any state had at any one time was the aggregate of the contributions of the armed services. Since force planning, therefore, tended to be based more on the basis of service priorities than on defence criteria, the outcome was always less than satisfactory. The sum of defence was, and is, not the sum of its parts, particularly when the degree of combined-joint contingency planning was minimal, duplication of functions frequent and wasteful, and standardization and interoperability, essential ingredients in combined operations, for the most part absent.

177

In pressing governments for the necessary equipment as they saw it, the armed services of the advanced industrial states before 1960 not only engaged in inter-service rivalries to take on new defence functions, but also independently developed new weapons that not infrequently performed the same role as those in service with the other two branches. This not only made for waste, but meant that governments, and ultimately the public, had little or no chance of being able to assess, outside a purely service context, what the overall cost of defence was to the nation, and what precisely was being acquired for the resources being expended. The problem was further exacerbated by the extent to which armed services, operating largely independently, not only had access to their own sources of information, but also had their own political representation. Furthermore, in many instances the Chiefs of Staff meeting in committee, ostensibly to advise the government on policy and feasibility as well as the execution of policy and coordination of their different contributions to the defence effort, had privileged access to political leaders or heads of state. This frequently afforded them political initiative and clout over their own immediate political defence ministerial masters. In other words, the formal structures of central organizations of defence which present line charts of authority culminating in the political authority of a Minister of Defence, tended to belie the reality of competing and semi-autonomous armed services, a multitude of functional agencies supporting them, and a huge central bureaucracy, creating what one analyst has described in the American context as 'organized anarchy'.

But these armed services in the 20 or so years after the Second World War were, to a degree, their own worst enemies. First, they failed to anticipate the growth of the welfare state and the concomitant rise in public preference and expectations for social welfare as a higher priority than defence and security; second, outside the United States, they did not anticipate the slow economic growth of the world's economy after the end of the war and the pressures for economic restructuring and renovation; third, they anticipated neither the Cold War and its associated technological arms race nor the exponential rise in the cost of modern weapons, which nevertheless have made no relative advances in ensuring international security; fourth, they did not recognize that the development of nuclear weaponry and the policy of deterrence would have the benefit of both forcing an adversary to think twice before attacking and of being able to do so for less cost – the so-called 'bigger bang for the buck' – but would also increase domestic opposition towards consistently high defence and security expenditure, and stimulate anti-nuclear resistance groups; and finally, they failed to learn the lessons of the Second World War, in which joint operations also required joint preparation and planning. Time and time again since 1945 the armed services of the industrial nations have found themselves in conflict, sometimes against modest Third World opponents, and discovered that they had inadequately prepared to plan and fight effectively alongside one another, that their equipment was not always relevant to the task, and that basic logistics were inadequate.

It was only a matter of time before some degree of rationalization was introduced. The United States led the way, though in Britain some structural changes had been taken in 1958 consequent upon the poor performance of the armed services during the Suez Crisis of 1956. These changes coordinated a number of armed service functions, the most important of which was the creation of a Chief of Defence Staff (CDS) immediately responsible to the Minister of Defence for 'the formulation and application of a unified policy relating to the armed forces as a whole and their requirements'. The anticipated demise of the Service and Supply Ministries did not happen, and the proposed integration of functions, such as medical services, disappeared in the face of the services' opposition.

The post of CDS itself was little more than cosmetic for as long as the service Chiefs of Staff had virtual autonomy within their services and separately enjoyed political ministerial support and a separate budget. This state of affairs could not last if the Minister responsible for defence was to exercise any influence over policy, control over defence spending or operational coordination, a problem earlier recognized by Prime Minister Harold Macmillan in the mid 1950s and, from a Command perspective, by Lord Mountbatten in the early 1960s. Mountbatten, as CDS, promoted the idea of greater functional coordination between the services, drawing on his experience when, as a theatre commander in the Far East during the Second World War, he had found it difficult, often impossible, to get the services to agree and coordinate their plans and their lines of command in the face of the enemy. It is worth noting also that Field Marshal Montgomery, himself a theatre commander, advocated in the early 1940s a similar course, fearful that 'the coordination between the Services and the relationship with central political leadership that had worked well in war would break down in peacetime as partisan service interests assumed higher priority'.

Mountbatten's pressure added to a realization that the Ministry of Defence 'had been superimposed on the Services and had not grown organically out of them'. After the demise of the War Cabinet and the dual role of Churchill as Prime Minister and Defence Minister, the Defence Ministry had exercised little real authority over either strategic, structural or operational decisions. By the early 1960s, there had been a radical change in Soviet capabilities, along with poor British national economic performance, rising defence costs and shifting priorities following the dismantling of the Empire, for which a radical structural change to the Ministry was considered necessary. In what was labelled 'one of the most important constitutional changes' in the post-war era, a central Ministry of Defence was created in 1963 out of the old ministry plus the three service departments. At the apex there was a Defence Council with the new Secretary of State – a sort of superminister – as chairman. The long saga of the battle for power and influence within the central defence organization was, however, not resolved even then; a full account up to the late 1960s is given in F. Johnson's *Defence by Ministry*.

The real change, however, in the shift of influence and power happened only after the Thatcher administration took over in 1979. First, after a succession of defence reviews, and a clash between the government and the services Chiefs on defence cuts, the armed services finally lost their senior political ministerial representation. Second, the emphasis placed on management and efficiency in government bureaucracy, as a matter of policy, led to the Chief of Defence Staff and the Central Administrative Staff gaining influence and authority at the expense of the service chiefs whose role became residual. From providing major input into defence policy debates, they were left with the executive responsibility for the training, morale and state of readiness of their respective services in preparing them to meet the directives of the central planning staffs.

The experience of the central organization of defence in Britain over 40 years illustrates the basic dilemma surrounding defence policy planning and the relationship between the armed service chiefs and their political masters. This is the dilemma of authority and responsibility. It is the opinion of servicemen that in time of war it is their exclusive responsibility to defend the nation, without consideration of personal sacrifice. They contend, therefore, that they should have some significant say, perhaps a determining voice, in the equipment, operational plans and preparations that go into that policy, and even, some say, in the policy itself. No policy is worth the paper it is written on if it cannot be fulfilled. As the professionals, their conviction is that they are better placed to judge what is necessary, and what is not; what is possible, and what is not. When economic constraints are stringent and defence commitments are not moderated, the services regularly complain of 'overstretch', a euphemism for being asked to do more than they have the capability to accomplish.

A government, conversely, is the elected authority; decisions regarding such critical issues as peace and war, the transition from one to the other, resource allocation and defence priorities, targeting strategy and so on, must be theirs. And the government alone has the mandate for policy. The higher the level of decision, and the more political and strategic it becomes, the more the government and its administrative machine is both responsible and accountable. The ideal would be some mechanism whereby the two 'sides' could be enabled to work in collaboration and accord, but both have organizational, institutional, and even philosophical interests to satisfy; these have not always been compatible, even, on occasion, in the face of the enemy.

Although Britain and France were engaged in structural reforms during the late 1950s, the United States pioneered the most radical change in defence decision making procedure, changes that, in partial and amended ways, all other advanced states emulated. Concerned with the extent of duplication and waste that had characterized the US Department of Defense during the 1950s, a pattern of behaviour that was spiced with overt and quite uncompromising inter-service rivalry (as Michael Armacost's study of the *Politics of Weapons Innovation* demonstrated), President Kennedy charged his new Secretary of Defense, Robert McNamara, with the task of bringing efficiency to the Pentagon. Aided by a team of economists and management experts, McNamara shifted the focus of planning from one concerned with service inputs, costed annually, to one based on defence outputs, expressed in terms of a series of defence programmes and costed over a five-year or ten-year period. Programme outputs, when combined, made up the defence posture of the United States. Their costs could also be aggregated. This meant that collectively and separately they could be set immediately against US declaratory policy and spending, something that could not be done under the previous service input system. Predictably, the services were strongly opposed to the idea.

This new managerial approach to defence decision making became manifest in the procedure known as the Planning, Programme and Budgeting System (PPBS). Its effect was to heighten the conflict of interest and the struggle for influence between the armed services and the central political and administrative hierarchy. As with the Europeans' structural changes to their defence departments and services, the American armed services also proved to be their own worst enemy, especially as their record in the 1950s of pursuing wasteful projects gave them little ground upon which to object to new procedures that promoted efficiency. The new system worked to the extent that each programme was identified and related to policy objectives; it was a

181

change that Congress welcomed, since it meant that, for the first time in an intelligible way, costs could be attached to each defence programme, each programme element, and the total defence outlay. Comparisons could therefore be made relatively easily, long-term projections made with some degree of realism, and, at a lower level of analysis, programmes could be broken down into elements, and alternative systems with which to fulfil those programmes analysed, measured and compared.

By directing attention to defence programmes and breaking those programmes down into their component elements, and then conducting cost-effective analyses on alternative systems, the initiative tended to become transferred to the central defence administration and their analysis staff. The more subjective approach of the armed services to their requirements, based on claims of professional knowledge, expertise and experience, was replaced with objective systematic analysis, executed with close attention to total and long-term costings. The effect was to further the trend towards the centralization of defence decision making, and to concentrate power of decision in the Office of the Secretary of Defense (OSD). Within a short period of time, however, the balance had swung back towards the armed services, partly because the outcomes of decisions based on systems and cost effective analysis were not as successful as had been projected, and partly because the armed services themselves quickly adapted and began doing their own similar cost-effectiveness studies to back their recommendations on equipment and policies.

The relationship between the services and the central defence bureaucracy in the USA was strained for some time. To ameliorate the situation, and in recognition of the valid contribution that the armed services could make to defence policy making, President Nixon and his Secretary of Defense, Melvin Laird, restored some influence to the services and the Joint Chiefs of Staff within the PPB system. Nevertheless, the OSD has gained power significantly at the expense of the service departments (as William Lucas and Raymond Dawson have shown in their book, *The Organizational Politics of Defense*). They have not done so, however, as much as the formal structure or the decision making process would indicate. The explanation lies to some degree in the enormous size of the Pentagon, and its complexity.

Equally relevant, however, is the tendency of the US Defense Department to be concerned with micromanagement at the expense of the need to establish a unified joint military participation in OSD policy formulation. Also there is inadequate attention given to such measures as joint operational planning and readiness capabilities in resource allocation, and a clear delineation of authority between OSD and service departments. Because of his involvement as Commander in Chief of all national armed services the American President is in a position to influence defence policy directly, but not all have taken that interest. His position, however, compromises that of the Chairman of the Joint Chiefs of Staff (JCS) in that it tends to have political overtones. This can get in the way of the JCS Chairman offering independent military advice. Further, the JCS Committee with a voting chairman who is also subordinate to the Secretary of Defense, has generally found it difficult to agree within itself on either structural or strategic issues, with less than satisfactory results (such as the invasion of Grenada, an operation that revealed both the absence of any clear unity on a civilian-prepared defence policy, and no clear consensus on inter-service standardization and equipment). More seriously, the JCS, whilst being responsible for the conduct of war in wartime, is denied that role on a day-to-day peacetime basis.

The situation within the Department of Defense has been such that, in recent years, there have been calls for further structural reform, rather than procedural. These have been discussed at length in A. Barrett's *Reappraising Defense Organization*, A. R. Millett's *Reorganization of the Joint Chiefs of Staff*, A. Clark *et al.*'s *The Defense Reform Debate* and the volume on *Reorganizing America's Defense*, edited by Robert Art, Vincent Davis and Samuel Huntington. Appreciating that the situation had to be confronted, President Reagan appointed a Presidential Blue Ribbon Panel in 1985 under the chairmanship of David Packard, a former Deputy Secretary of Defense, to inquire into ways of sharpening the Pentagon's decision making processes. It concluded that strengthening of the JCS was necessary and particularly the authority of its president, and that much more could be done, especially in the choice and procurement of future weapons systems.

Nowhere, yet, have the problems of central defence decision making been finally resolved: strengthening the decision making authority of the armed services themselves and of their collective Chiefs of Staff in Committee, may enhance and strengthen (i.e. sub-optimize) the capabilities of the armed services; increasing the power of a single Chief of Defence Staff may help to optimize the overall defence posture of the nation; but neither is necessarily compatible with pressures for economy, efficient management of defence resources, civil political control, or wider public accountability. Meanwhile, the 'wars within' continue. Sometimes the balance of power swings towards the political leadership; at others, the armed services, when they can put aside their own rivalries, gain the initiative. Whatever the outcome – and it changes all the time with the arrival and departure of different personalities – systems muddle through, not least because they have a momentum and a robustness of their own.

Radical structural or strategic decisions are not easy to implement; when the political masters have endeavoured to take such initiatives – such as the Duncan Sandys 1957 White Paper in Britain, President Eisenhower's attempt to strengthen the Office of the Joint Chief of Staff under the 1958 *Defense Reorganization Act,* and the French Ordinance in 1959 which tried to locate the legal responsibility for defence in the office of the Prime Minister and the Minister for Armed Forces – each system proved that it had the capacity to neutralize what was disruptive and to continue, largely, with the customary and more traditional methods of going about defence planning and preparation.

Before closing this discussion of issues in armed services and society in advanced industrial states, a brief mention must be made of a relatively recent phenomenon, the importance of which has still to be assessed. It can be no more than mentioned here, but should stimulate further research and inquiry. The old assumption of defence and armed services matters as falling within the realms of 'high' politics is seriously under challenge: defence issues tended in the past not to be newsworthy or of great public interest; today, the populations of the advanced industrial states are better informed on security and defence, in part because government departments are providing more information about policy and the background to defence decisions, and in part because the people generally are more concerned about defence matters, both strategic and structural.

On strategy, public attitudes have been mostly influenced by nuclear weaponry, superpower and regional arms races, the international arms trade, and attempts to introduce arms control and disarmament measures. When placed alongside other world problems, such as famine, pollution and poverty, defence, nuclear and strategic issues have aroused public passion and, on occasion, have polarized opinion. Of paramount concern, of course, is the question of the future of the world itself, now that the number of nuclear weapons, and the states that possess them, have increased, thereby raising anxieties about accidental war and nuclear thresholds. Knock-on effects include such issues as the public's right to know more details about defence, defence censorship and freedom of the press; on occasion, even more funda-mental questions are raised about national sovereignty and alliance commitments. Feelings have often been intense, as the rash of 'nuclear free zones' in cities and towns around Europe, the United States and elsewhere, and anti-nuclear and peace demonstrations testify.

At the structural level, the issues and public interest are more specific, but no less important to defence. Opinion in Europe has been voiced quite vociferously over conscription, for example; in Britain women's groups have been active in raising questions not only about role discrimination against women in the services but also about the rights of women married to servicemen; a recent problem in the USA would seem to centre on whether or not service trade unions should be permitted. And, of course, close public interest is focused on major weapons programmes and the procurement budget.

How much of this public interest is stimulated by the new genre of investigatory and committed journalism, both in the press and other parts of the media, and how much it is an *appearance* of interest because it also happens to be a preoccupation of the media itself, is a question for which no answer has yet been provided. The evidence is there, but the analysis has yet to be done and judgment made. Whatever the outcome, greater public awareness of defence and security issues is the very substance of the study of armed services and society.

9

Armed Services
and
Third World
States

Chapters 7 and 8 have focused on issues that at first sight seem to be of concern only to the advanced industrial states, not least because Third World and emerging states do not have large armed forces or burgeoning military industrial complexes. But this does not mean that these other, Third World, states do not have *some* industrial capacity with which to develop and produce military equipment for their own use, nor that issues of accountability, conscientious objection or central defence management are of no concern to them. It is really a matter of degree rather than kind – the relative importance of these issues to the governments and populations concerned. Objections to military service on grounds of conscience do occur in Third World states, but as an issue of philosophical or practical relevance they do not command much attention. Likewise, military industrial considerations are relatively minor, inasmuch as the level of weapons production in Third World states is low, on a small scale and rudimentary. Furthermore, such nations do not have the economic strength to sustain a weapons production industry, even if allowance is made for the purchase of sophisticated equipment – often with direct external financial aid – from abroad. Questions about the central organizations of defence rise to some prominence only if there is a threat of military intervention, or, as in the case of Central and South American states, the armed services exceed their constitutional authority.

The issues regarding Third World and developing states' relationships between armed services and society are of a different order from those of advanced industrial states. This is not surprising since the absolute sums of money devoted to defence and armed services in Third World states is invariably miniscule compared with those of advanced industrial societies. There is also a relative point: the difference between 5 per cent GNP in a poor, Third World state with problems of development and needing to expand growth, and 5 per cent GNP in a wealthy industrial state even with no growth at all, is immense. It is the difference between having armed services that are well-equipped, highly paid, full-time professional and distanced from society, and ones that are proportionately small in number, simply equipped and housed, conscripted for the most part, and closely identified with groups within the community. These marked differences, once identified and understood, should go some way towards explaining why advanced industrial states tend to become involved in foreign wars, and offer resistance to other industrial states which are perceived to be enemies; and conversely, why there are relatively few inter-state wars among the Third World countries, and their armed services' preoccupations are predominantly with domestic matters.

So far, states have been referred to either as 'advanced industrial' or as 'Third World' and 'less developed', as if there were some measure of consensus about what these terms mean. There is no such consensus; for the purposes of discussion about armed services and society relationships, 'advanced industrial states' has been used in a general way to refer to the Western states, plus China and the Soviet Union, and those which have an economy and level of education sufficient to sustain an indigenous arms manufacturing capability and maintain a high level of defence spending in absolute terms. In a rather unsophisticated way, 'Third World' has so far been used as a shorthand term to denote nothing more than all those other states that do not satisfy these 'advanced industrial' criteria. Some anomalies remain, for there are many states that are customarily referred to as being 'Third World' or with some other term that generally denotes similar characteristics, like 'less developed countries' (LDCs), 'emerging nations', 'underdeveloped countries', or 'developing states', which also have relatively successful and competitive indigenous arms industries and large professional standing armed forces: Argentina, Brazil, India, Pakistan, Vietnam and Egypt would fall into this group. Whether they should properly be called 'advanced', 'emerging' or 'less developed' is a matter of opinion; the terminological confusion demonstrates, first, the difficulty of generalization and, second, the wisdom of treating each country *sui generis*.

This latter course is not possible in this chapter; an alternative, therefore, is to attempt to generalize about what are the dominant characteristics of 'non advanced industrial states' and explore how these particular features affect the armed services and society relationship. Before taking the problem further, a warning must be borne in mind: the different areas of the world where 'Third World' states tend to be concentrated – namely the Middle East, Asia, Latin America, the Far

East and Africa – have their own individual geography, climate, topography, resources etc., and a distinctive and separate history and cultural tradition.

Even though all these states bear the same Third World label, comparisons between them (either within one area or across area boundaries) are fraught with difficulties and conceptual dangers. For example, consider briefly the recent histories of East and West Africa: their respective experience with differing colonial administrations, and the post-independence problems states in each region faced, show that straight comparisons, even within the same continent, are difficult. Then contrast these two African regions with, say, the Middle East and, to a degree, North Africa, where the cultural influence of Islam has to be considered a dominant factor, not least in its effect on the relationship between armed services and society. And although the states of Central and Latin America may appear superficially a more homogeneous group, their diversity and contrasting political histories over the past 70 years clearly demonstrate that even here no simple generalization or accurate comparison is possible.

It might be more prudent at this juncture to capitulate and say that no adequate general discussion of 'non-Western', Third World states is possible, and concede that an overview of general economic, political and cultural characteristics they may or may not have in common is not sufficient, not even for the most superficial of analyses. But the risk must be taken. In any event, all Third World states are concerned, after their own fashion, with security, and all have armed services. Providing that this narrow focus is kept, and the above warnings borne in mind, there is some prospect of the outcome being reasonably constructive and persuasive.

Scholars concerned with the Third World have generally been economists: their attention has mostly been concentrated on the economic issues that the poorer states confront. The terms they use – 'underdeveloped', 'backward', 'modernizing' – are terms that tend to reflect economic conditions. Certainly these Third World states are poor, when their wealth is expressed in terms of per capita income (leaving aside for the moment some oil-rich Third World states like Kuwait, which has the highest per capita income in the world). They are also states that tend to have a low ratio of population to area, largely because they are in areas of the world where climate and geography make human habitation difficult, if not sometimes impossible; consider the deserts of Central Africa, the tropical rainforests of the Amazon basin, and the Himalayan region for example. Continuing this economic approach, there is also a scarcity of capital in these countries, making many of them not so much underdeveloped, but, more accurately, undeveloped, for want of the necessary resources, technological know-how, and investment.

Scarcity of capital and, often, of natural resources, would seem to be a perennial problem facing Third World states. First, they have little capital of their own, and because they represent high political and economic risk, aid from the wealthier states – international organizations do not have large independent sums at their disposal – is either tied to the latter's interests or carries high interest charges. Second, there is a low ratio of capital supply to other factors of production necessary for economic growth. Another frequent characteristic of these states is the low ratio of industrial output to total production. Such industrial output as there is tends to be owned by, or dependent in some way on, private Western multinational industrial corporations. Non-industrial production tends to be in raw materials or on agricultural products; often there is a concentration on a few staple crops, which, in turn, tends to lead to a low-cost labour-intensive work-force with the further effects of a low standard of living for the majority of the population, a minimum level of urbanization, a rudimentary economic infrastructure, an inexperienced administrative network, and overall a low per capita income.

The people of the Third World have had to contend with these problems for centuries, but have not done so as groupings of independent nation-states until recently. As new states, few have relevant traditions, other than the legacies of the old colonial powers. These colonial legacies or the contrived constitutional political forms they left behind them were not always the most useful or practical to meet pressing economic, social and security needs. As 'young' countries, they had little experience that their new leaders could call on. Often the ex-colonial powers abandoned them at relatively short notice, and on departure removed much of the economic and administrative infrastructure they had brought in as colonists. To exacerbate matters many ethnic groups, introduced by the colonists for economic, commerical or administrative reasons, left with the departing colonial powers, leaving a further void in the economic, administrative and political structures of these new states.

On independence, these new states displayed many of the characteristics which S. E. Finer identified in his concept of a 'low' or 'minimal' political culture, not so much because they lacked a well-rooted culture of their own, but because they were left with very little after the colonial powers moved out. They lacked, in other words, the political traditions and an established, working infrastructure suited to the introduction and successful execution of new national policies of economic growth, and social and political development. Moreover, they were also faced with the preliminary task of creating some semblance of national cohesion within, usually, a heterogeneous population, and of fostering a common sense of identity and nationhood. These were two tasks for which armed services were particularly suited.

The problems of the Third World were, and still largely are, the alleviation of poverty, the establishment of social and political stability, the construction of relevant economic and political infrastructures for their short-term and long-term needs, and the introduction of the right combination of economic factors to bring about steady economic growth and sure social progress. But it is one thing to recognize what is needed and another to identify what has to be done (and in what order of priority) to lift Third World states to a level of development where life expectancy, a minimum standard of living, and the basic needs of a dignified human existence are at least within some level of comparability with the advanced nations.

Meanwhile, the advanced world gets progressively wealthier, both in absolute and relative terms. The disparities are not only widening, but are doing so at an accelerated pace. Economists have repeatedly addressed the question of what might be done, both by the Third World countries themselves, and by way of assistance from the wealthier nations, and have concentrated on a variety of different strategies. Some proposals have been manifestly more practical than others, but none can satisfactorily allay the sense of frustration, injustice and impatience that many poorer states feel. As has been demonstrated often enough, frustrated rising expectations has proved a strong motivating force for aggression and violence, two forms of behaviour that are least likely to promote the ends that Third World countries strive to achieve.

Under the generic term of 'development', some writers, like Bauer and Yamey in their *Economics of Underdeveloped Countries*, have emphasized *inter alia* the need for improvement in education; building the necessary infrastructure upon which future industrial investment can depend; eliminating past cultural practices that would hinder social, economic and commercial progress; investing in sectors of industry and commerce where Third World states enjoy comparative economic advantage; and establishing an environment of political and social stability within which development can take place simultaneously on all fronts – social, political, economic, financial and cultural. This prescription was summed up by G. Hunter in his study, *Modernizing Peasant Societies*, as follows: 'Unless politics can provide a framework within which development can take place without constant uncertainty and even violence, all other aspects of development policy fall to the ground. There has to be a stable political base for administration to operate, and for the political will to create a development situation to come forward.'

In his introduction to *Third World Politics*, Christopher Clapham notes in this context that the state is of central importance. It is the state, he contends, that provides a 'central synthesis of domestic and external elements through which politics is conducted. It is this state that makes Third World politics a kind of activity which is distinctive, related to, but none the less different from, politics elsewhere'. He also goes on to note, 'armed services operate of necessity from within the state itself. The maintenance of the state apparatus and the creation of conditions of domestic stability, external security and maintenance of the rule of law, is a primary concern of armed services in Third World states. On this premise it is therefore paradoxical that armed services are so often most responsible for frequently usurping the collapse of the state administrative machinery and the constitutional framework in Third World states.'

Whatever precise definition is used, it becomes immediately clear that there is a wide disparity between the armed services of one Third World state and another, in terms of their size, composition, equipment and training. Over a number of years, several of the advanced industrial states have competed for contracts, or even the invitation, to train Third World serving officers, partly for the opportunities that often follow for arms sales and commercial trade. Where a Third World state is ruled by a military junta, or a military dictatorship, or in instances where the reins of political power are in the hands of the armed services, the attraction is even greater. The early pattern was for new officers to be trained in the military academies of their previous colonial masters, or, in the case of members of the Organization of American States (OAS), as a consequence of treaty agreements.

The emergence, however, of the Soviet Union as a major military power after the Second World War, seeking global influence, and, during the period of the Sino–Soviet ideological dispute between 1963 until the mid 1980s, the readiness of China to act as a substitute, introduced an ideological alternative to these traditional Western, liberal democratic sources of professional military help. Many Third World states, wary of Western motives or wishing to divest themselves of past colonial associations, or having themselves become committed to Marxist prescriptions as the most relevant and practical guide to their economic and political development during their immediate post-colonial period (as in the cases of Tanzania, Vietnam, North Korea, Somalia, Syria and Cuba) turned to the Soviet Union as their principal source of political, economic and military help and instruction.

To this ideological rapport should be added the incentive of heavily subsidized and often highly advanced military equipment offered by the Soviet Union in its bid to widen its influence beyond its Eastern European satellites. These initiatives did much to fuel the qualitative competition in the arms trade, and was largely responsible for breaking the British and American policies in the 1950s of making available to Third World countries only old, secondhand and obsolete military equipment. Within the OAS, for example, the United States held back the availability of jet-powered fighter aircraft to other OAS members until France acted as an alternative supplier. The first real change, however, came in 1955, when the Soviet Union, through Czechoslovakia, sold advanced military equipment to Egypt, equipment that hithertofore had been continuously denied to Israel by Western suppliers. The acceleration in qualitatively superior equipment started in the 1960s when France, eager to use arms exports as a means of offsetting the costs of its own arms industry and in pursuit of independent foreign and defence policies, sold the latest equipment in its own military inventory to virtually any non-communist state that was able to pay.

Third World armies vary widely in size: figures taken from *The Military Balance*, the International Institute for Strategic Studies' annual survey of the world's armed services, reveal for example, that Egypt has a total of 445,000 men (and 380,000 reserves) of whom 250,000 are conscripts, in its armed services. Nigeria has a total military establishment (all services) of 94,000 men, all volunteers, and represents a military establishment twice as large as the next largest sub-Saharan Third World State, with the one exception of Ethiopia, whose military establishment is over twice that of Nigeria, but which uses conscripts. Twenty-five newly independent states of sub-Saharan Africa have fewer than 17,000 men in their armed forces, and 18 have fewer than 7,500; 20 of these 25 operate volunteer systems. Latin America, however, tends to support much larger military establishments: Five states have over 40,000 men, and six over 100,000. Almost all, however, operate conscription, suggesting that Third World States can sustain large military establishments only if men are required to perform a period of national service in the armed services.

When these global figures are set alongside other considerations (such as land area, topography, total population and demography) and geostrategic considerations, one general conclusion is almost unavoidable: without their being able to gain compensation from operating more sophisticated modern weaponry and highly destructive systems, there is little in a purely military sense that the armed services of Third World states can effectively do against well, or even reasonably, armed opponents, unless there are massive numerical odds in their favour. In only a few states are armed services of any size, other than an army, to be found; cost and complexity virtually prohibits them.

Nowhere is this more graphically illustrated than in Indonesia. This is a country of over 160 million inhabitants drawn from many different ethnic and cultural groups, scattered over 3000 or more islands. Many of these islands are almost inaccessible, though the majority of the population lives on the largest five. The total land area covers 735,000 square miles (Britain is 94,000 square miles) and is spread over a distance of 3,600 miles, east to west. The Indonesian armed services total 278,000 men, or 0.16 per cent of the population. Geographically isolated except from Malaysia, the Philippines and Papua New Guinea, Indonesia has little militarily to fear externally, for which reason the size and purpose of her armed services might reasonably be questioned. It certainly was during the so-called 'confrontation' with Malaysia during the 1960s. The Indonesian armed services, once the agents of repression of President Sukharno, and the instrument of an attempted coup in 1966, have primarily been employed in internal security roles and assisting in economic development.

The scale of the problems facing Third World states goes some way to providing an explanation why the incidence of wars between them is small and infrequent relative to those involving forces from advanced industrial states. Perhaps the best illustration of this is in Central and Latin America where armed conflict between states is still a rare phenomenon. This relatively lengthy period of international tranquillity has been bolstered by the 1943 Treaty of Chapultepec, a regional security agreement guaranteeing mutual support in the event of aggression. The success of the region in avoiding inter-state conflict is all the more surprising when it is borne in mind that there are still many unresolved boundary disputes and competing territorial claims; for example, there is the Chilean–Argentinian dispute over the Beagle Channel between Cape Horn and Tierra del Fuego, not to mention the Falkland (Malvinas) Islands, the highly publicized 'football war' between Guatemala and El Salvador, and Guatemalan claims on certain areas of Belize. A high proportion of the states in that region of the world (16 out of 26) are governed by a military dictatorship or have 'restricted parliamentary systems', meaning that they are states in which democratic processes are severely limited. In fact, Central and Latin America accounted for over half the world's military coups between 1946 and 1970, recording 136 out of a world total of 274. The curious phenomenon of a high incidence of military governments in the world and a low incidence of inter-state wars, though strongly influenced by the Latin American experience, led Stanislav Andreski once to suggest that military dictatorships, statistically at least, were the best guarantor of international peace! Then, again, the argument has been put that the incidence of wars between liberal democracies is also low; the problem seems to arise when democracies and totalitarian systems coexist. Then the incidence of international conflict and war becomes high. Whilst these are propositions to be used with extreme caution, they nonetheless highlight one fundamental characteristic of armed services in Third World states: as rulers, or as servants of the state, they are not used for quite the same purposes as those in advanced states.

In *Modernizing Peasant Societies*, G. Hunter has suggested that Third World states might usefully be compared with eighteenth century Britain, before the Industrial Revolution began to gain momentum and when no such institution as the Police existed. It was a country in which the provision of law and order was largely delegated to a standing army, in contradistinction to the county militias. Nothing like the French Marechaussée or its post-revolutionary Gendarmerie Nationale existed. The objectives of Third World states have been to stimulate economic growth, social development and individual prosperity – goals, according to Hunter, which would be impossible 'unless politics can provide a framework within which development can take place without constant uncertainty and even violence . . . There has to be a stable political base for administration to operate, and for the political will to create a development situation to come forward. Not infrequently uncertainty and violence occurs when the traditional interests of old social elites clash with the emergent political will to seek growth, advancement and development.'

Unlike Britain in the eighteenth and nineteenth centuries, today's Third World states do not have an overseas empire through which to prosecute these development and growth objectives; nevertheless, the requirement of a secure administrative framework is no less necessary. Armed services have the primary function of ensuring in the first instance internal law and order and stability, and then by assisting in providing that secure framework – even to the point, out of necessity as they see it, of assuming responsibility for taking over government and administration as well.

Armed services are principally a tool to assist the economic, political and social development of Third World States. The traditional advanced industrial state role of armed services, that of territorial defence and support of foreign policy objectives, has to take second place in a practical sense, though formally it is their cardinal function. This was made abundantly clear in an article by W. Folz in an edited book by V. McKay entitled *African Diplomacy*, concluding that the external significance of armed services in African states was minimal, Folz stressed the geographical and topographical problems they faced, the smallness of their armed services with, by and large, inadequate or inappropriate equipment, the small number of properly trained servicemen at their disposal, and a general lack of preparation and contingency planning. Indeed, he went so far as to suggest that were Third World states to venture as far as mobilizing their armed services, and then have the temerity to use them in support of diplomatic or foreign policy initiatives, such a move would be more a manifestation of weakness than either a demonstration of strength or the articulation of a credible threat.

Nonetheless, Third World states have at times engaged their armed services in conflicts with other states of similar standing. However, these occasions (other than when conducted in conjunction with advanced industrial states) are not only infrequent but also tend to be confined to restricted engagements with modest, short-term objectives, and last for a limited period of time. Tanzania, for example, intervened in Uganda to assist in bringing down the regime of President Idi Amin. The borders between Kenya, Somalia, Ethiopia, and the Sudan have caused constant friction between them all, and each has sent its armed services to the region at one time or another. Whilst there have been sharp military exchanges, the disputes have yet to break out into full-scale wars. For the most part the disputes have been carried on as an almost permanent day-to-day occurrence in their relations, exacerbated mainly by the constant movement of traditional nomadic tribesmen across the political divides.

Where there have been serious conflicts between Third World states, they have usually been over disputed sovereignty and conflicting definitions of territorial sovereignty. One major problem in this respect has been the boundaries of new Third World states, which were defined originally by the colonial powers, either for administrative purposes, or as the outcome of diplomatic agreement and expedient in the carving out of spheres of colonial influence or control. They were not drawn to correspond with traditional tribal boundaries of the indigenous populations. These problems were, and still are, most evident in Africa, though there is ample evidence of similar problems in the Middle East, Asia and Central and South America. Many of the secessionary movements with which Third World states are confronted today, emanate from poorly defined sovereign boundaries of the late nineteenth and early twentieth centuries. Examples include the struggle of the Kurds against Iraq, the Nagas against India, the Zaydi in the Yemen and the Anzaniens in Southern Sudan.

Even when there are conflicts between Third World states over sovereignty, the probability is that the situation would be unlikely to develop into overt war unless three conditions applied: first, one party would have to be manifestly superior in military strength to contemplate resort to armed force; second, an advanced industrial state, probably with commercial, political or strategic interests in the region, would provide one or other party financial and military assistance; and third, there would likely be internal problems, and resort to external conflict and war would serve as a way of generating internal cohesion and backing for the government and distracting popular attention from more pressing domestic issues. There are many examples of Third World conflicts where these conditions, sometimes separately, sometimes together, have applied. The Libyan encroachment into Chad was originally an instance of the first condition, at least until France came to the latter's aid with both aid and men and equipment. Morocco also felt sufficiently militarily superior to confront Mauretania and Algeria in the Saharawi Arab Democratic Republic over what were the disputed territories of the previous Spanish Sahara.

One major concern in the world has been the increasing trade in arms and military equipment from advanced industrial states to the Third World. Suggestions have been made (for example, by Mary Kaldor and Asbjorn Eide in *The World Military Order*) that this has been a premeditated policy to serve the industrial states' economic and political interests. They have also intimated that these rich states have wanted to draw Third World states into their own disputes and to use them as proxies. Their contention is that such policies should be resisted at all costs, since they do not serve Third World states individually, or the poorer states as a whole. In this context, the question has yet to be answered whether or not Third World states initiate the demand for weapons or whether they are pressured into taking them in return for advanced industrial states' economic assistance, political and moral support or other favours.

Poorer states equipped with modern weaponry from the advanced states can entertain using armed force in the more traditional role of support of foreign policy, as many of the wars that have punctuated the turbulent history of the Middle East have demonstrated. For example, the seven year war between Iran and Iraq over the disputed boundaries in the Khurramshar and Shatt al-Arab regions could not have been maintained at the level, the duration, or the intensity it has, had not either side been first armed and then resupplied from outside states; or, second, had not both sides been so totally committed. Bitter though this dispute has been, it is debatable whether or not Iraq would have taken the initiative to attack in the first place had its leaders not calculated a weakness in Iran consequent upon the deposition of the Shah and the revolutionary turmoil that followed in the wake of the Khomeini regime. It is equally debatable whether it would have acted had not it had some reassurance that it would be well supplied with modern equipment from France and the Soviet Union. The reliability of weapons supply from the United States after the deposition of the Shah was, in contrast, significantly less sure. It is important to note that prior to the Gulf War, as it is now known, neither Iraq nor Iran had ever been engaged in a full-scale war, though some Iraqi troops had participated on the Arab side in the 1973 Arab–Israeli conflict.

The picture that emerges of armed services in Third World states is essentially one of internal orientation, with limited external roles, mostly of symbolic relevance. Close examination of the structure of Third World armed services reveals a predominance of armies, with relatively modest, or non-existent, navies or air forces. Most have very limited defence budgets, which is reflected in the types and numbers of equipment in service with their armed forces. Although most have isolated examples of sophisticated military equipment, as the IISS *The Military Balance* and the SIPRI *Yearbook* reveal, they are not in sufficient numbers or at a state of readiness to constitute a significant war-waging capability. The purpose of these advanced items of equipment must be open to some speculation, but the need for image and prestige, of keeping up with one's neighbours, must rank high on the list of priorities. The classic example of image building through the symbols of military prowess was the purchase of a new frigate from Britain by the then President Nkrumah of Ghana. Impressive though it may have been at anchor off Accra, it had no obvious naval purpose whatsoever. The layout inside was perhaps more revealing: sumptuously fitted with luxury cabins, gold-plated bathrooms and dining suites, it was clearly intended for personal presidential indulgence rather than as a fighting ship. Nkrumah was deposed before he could enjoy its facilities, and the ship returned to the manufacturers!

As Michael Lee demonstrated in his sympathetic study of post-independence Africa, *African Armies and Civil Order*, most African countries started with the legacy of a colonial past. Their political systems and armed services were invariably modelled on their colonial masters, even in instances where independence was gained as a consequence of guerrilla war and colonial battle, and not through a negotiated transfer of authority. Not in every case was the previous colonial administration responsive to the needs of the new, fledgeling state; some provided no preparation before, or assistance after, their departure. The problems in Zaire after the Belgians left might have been avoided, or at least minimized, had their leaders not simply been abandoned at short notice and left ill-prepared to take up the responsibilities of government and administration. Even where some care was taken over the transfer of power, the sort of political regime, and the structure and function of the new armed services were not always appropriate or relevant. One particular shortcoming was the absence of an officer corps with suitable training or experience to lead effectively the forces under their command.

Many newly independent states engaged the services of ex-colonial or experienced military advisers and consultants to help them through the early stages of independence. Even here, the experience for either side was less than satisfactory. H. T. Alexander recounted his experience as adviser to the new Ghanaian armed services in *African Tightrope*, and concluded that, 'mixed training, mixed arms, mixed equipment, mixed transport and mixed techniques made for military nonsense'. His advice, which he judged was to train and equip the Ghanaian army for largely internal duties, went unheeded. The Ghanaian experience was often repeated elsewhere, and later compounded when other, and different, sources of advice were sought and received. The advanced industrial states competed with one another to provide whatever help was asked, almost without regard for the political complexion of the government in power.

The irony of this variable experience, however, is that despite the many modern items of equipment that were acquired, and the training the troops received, many Third World states still had to hire mercenaries or engage foreign forces on secondment from friendly nations either to operate them, or to provide the necessary maintenance. There are many examples of sophisticated weapons systems bought by Third World states which have been left unused because their owners cannot afford to operate them nor do they have the technological know-how to maintain them. Instead, they have been left in prominent places for symbolic purposes, but, in reality, they are no more than a museum exhibit.

Another influence on the armed services in Third World states is their prevailing political and social culture. A colonial past is one thing, but in many Third World states, as Cynthia Enloe has graphically demonstrated in her book, *Ethnic Soldiers,* armed services have tended to recruit their forces from particular ethnic, or tribal, groups. The colonial powers recognized the potential of this cultural diversity, and used it both to strengthen their control over the country and to build from it by selecting for their own armies men from particular ethnic groups and by being highly discriminative where promotions were concerned. In Nigeria, this happened particularly with the Ibo who, on independence, formed a disproportionate proportion of the new Nigerian officer corps. In India, where a caste system was deeply rooted, the Sikhs formed a majority in the armed forces under British command.

After independence, when the new Third World states were striving to find a sense of identity, cohesion and national unity, these ex-colonial armed forces were often found to be unrepresentative of the population as a whole and were not considered the most secure foundation upon which to depend, or to build the nation's future. The dominance of one tribe within the armed services contributed significantly to the outbreak of the Nigerian civil war, in which the Ibo ended up attempting to establish their own independent state of Biafra in 1967. They were ultimately defeated in their ambitions, but only after a most bloody and destructive civil war.

Despite all the difficulties with which the Third World states have had to contend, they nonetheless have expected particular functions to be performed by their armed services, even if these invariably have had little to do with external defence or support of foreign policy. During the early stages of independence, which for most of them was little more than quarter of a century ago (the first military coup in Africa, Togo in fact, happened in 1960), the emphasis was on national identity and cohesion. (This was given particular attention by William Gutteridge in his *Military Institutions and Power in the New States* written in the early 1960s.) With independence also came the requirement to be seen to be operating like a sovereign state, for which reason the armed services were immediately drawn into imitations of established states, such as performing ceremonial duties on state occasions. But these peripheral functions also had other benefits, such as helping to generate both a public and an external perception of statehood and nationality. With sovereignty, however, also came the problems of territoriality. An early function of armed services, according to Gutteridge, was to establish and mark out the political boundaries of the state, hithertofore delineated only on colonists' maps. A third function was that of internal security, particularly with respect to what Gutteridge defined as cross border 'tribal overspill' from surrounding states. He cited as examples the patrolling of boundaries between Somalia and Kenya, Togo and Ghana, and Burma and Thailand.

The internal security role of armed services is examined by both Gutteridge and Lee; but whereas Gutteridge emphasizes its practical relevance, Lee notes that its importance was more closely related to prevailing domestic political circumstances, particularly those of states like Kenya, Algeria or, later, Zimbabwe, where independence in each case had been gained only after a revolutionary (guerrilla) military struggle. In these states, the political background of the armed services has to be taken into account, especially in the light of possible counter-revolutionary developments.

Internal security is a necessary task of armed services in Third World states and is executed in conjunction with Police and other security organizations. Their role, however, has less to do with the maintenance of law and order, and more to do with monitoring, and indeed containing, the political ambitions and power struggles that were inherent at first in the immediate post-colonial situation, and later when regional, ethnic or class antagonisms began to break down the first optimistic perceptions of national unity and homogeneity. Lee concluded that intelligence and a firm security hold on the population were the hallmarks of armed service operations in newly independent Third World states. The political realities of the time demanded of the armed services the requirement to impose some form of internal stability which mere assertions of the rule of law alone could not provide. To this extent, Thomas Hobbes's sentiments about seventeenth-century Britain could apply equally to the new states in the 1960s. Samuel Huntington referred to much the same requirement in his *Political Order in Changing Societies*, noting also that the more prominent this role became, the more politicized the armed services grew in the process; as a consequence, the weaker the civilian political leaders appeared. From this he drew the conclusion that, unlike in advanced industrial states, armed services in Third World societies reflected the political and institutional structure of society, and were inextricably involved from the start in the mêlée of domestic politics.

There are many reasons why this should have happened and, moreover, why it remains the case today. The most obvious reason was the organizational strength and discipline of the armed services relative to the institutional strength of civilian political and administrative bodies. Lacking a political culture which lent support to civil institutions of government, Third World states easily fell prey to *force majeure*, and the power and influence of the strongest and most cohesive organizations. Not to be overlooked, either, was the coalescence of interest between Third World military leaders and traditional ethnic groups and ruling classes, in the sense of social standing and personal authority, people who encouraged the armed services to assume not just a political role but increasingly a praetorian one as well.

Another reason for armed services' permeation of civil political institutions was the range of secondary roles beyond the immediate requirements of internal security and symbolic sovereignty. These encompassed economic and social functions, and are included as part and parcel of the development goals of Third World states, namely nation-building and modernization. It is, therefore, to be expected that armed services should be utilized in any number of ways beyond the immediate requirements of security. With limited resources at their disposal, all available skills and assets have to be utilized. Armed services are one such asset and examples abound where they have been put to any number of uses for the general benefit of society.

They have provided, for example, for those who join, or have to join (in many states there is compulsory national service) a training and education that very often could not be given within the civil sector. Military service also provides young men and, quite often, women also, generally drawn from a heterogeneous society with many regional, ethnic and cultural variations, a sharper sense of unity and citizenship. A period serving with the military away from their home region at a time in their lives when they are most likely to be politically active and volatile also serves to reduce political internal security problems. These attributes of conscription were identified in the cases of Indonesia and South-East Asia by Guy Parker in J. Johnson's book, *The Role of the Military in Underdeveloped Countries* and in Latin America by Johnson himself in *The Military and Society in Latin America*.

According to Lucien Pye in his study 'Armies in the process of modernization' these roles and functions should not be underestimated. They do much to create the necessary climate for modernization. In a more practical way, armed services have contributed much towards building the infrastructure without which economic growth and social development would be extremely difficult. As the US Army Corps of Engineers had done much towards moving the frontier West in the nineteenth century by building bridges, clearing wildernesses and laying down roads, so the armies of Latin America (according to J. Johnson in *The Military and Society in Latin America)* have performed much the same service. Lucien Pye also cites similar work by the armies of Malaysia and the Philippines.

The whole subject of the political and economic development of Third World states, or, to put it another way, their 'modernization', became a topic of consuming interest among academics and idealists during the 1960s. Motivated by a genuine wish to be of help, a plethora of studies offered prescriptions on how these goals, might be achieved. Among the more important were M. Levy's *Modernization and the Structure of Societies*, G. Almond and R. Coleman's *The Politics of the Developing Areas*, E. Shils's 'Political development in the new states', and S. Huntington's *Political Order in Changing Societies*. Whilst each adopted a different approach, and there was no clear consensus among them of what 'modernization' or 'development' really meant, there was at least some agreement that meaningful progress had to be seen to have been made on all fronts, political, economic and social.

It is no coincidence that many of these authors were also interested in armed forces, and several came to the study of development via the military, not the other way round. Most recognized that Third World armed services were not just a state institution or a disciplined coercive organization, but more significantly were the most likely modernizing agent immediately available to these states. Compared with most other institutions, armed services stood out as the most organized, efficient, trained, technologically able and reliable. In a word, they were the most 'modern'.

It was on this supposition that Morris Janowitz wrote his *Military in the Political Development of New Nations*, concentrating his analysis on the backgrounds of the officer elite and civilian administrative groups. His emphasis on the advanced capabilities of the military was also shared by Levy, who concluded that the armed services of Third World states were 'the most efficient vehicle for the maximization of modernization with the minimization of the uncontrolled spread of side-effects'. What neither author anticipated at the time was the behaviour of those armed services, confidently expected to be obedient, committed and disinterested agents of modernization, they became aggressive political actors, intervening frequently with violence in the affairs of government and assuming total power within the state themselves.

Out of this comes the most fundamental dilemma for armed services in Third World states: on the one hand they are a (or perhaps *the*) principal agent of modernity, with all the necessary organizational skills; on the other, they symbolize those features which, in Western eyes, are indicative of political backwardness. For instance, they tend to secure for themselves the best talent; they promote military priorities over civilian; they display antagonism towards things 'political' and often ban or constrain political parties of which they disapprove; they impose a tight security system, and thereby restrict the development of those political institutions and processes that are the hallmark of politically developed societies; and they prefer not to delegate responsibility to non-military organizations. Above all, they have an unhealthy inclination towards imposing a degree of stability within society with the objective of reducing the levels of conflict and violence; but whilst this gives a semblence of order and control, it does not by any acceptable criteria constitute a politically developed, or mature, political regime.

Whether or not armed services act as agents of civil government, or as the government itself, their influence in Third World domestic politics is undeniable. The incidence of military coups since these early post-independence studies were carried out suggests that under civilian rule the goals of modernization and development were not achieved, and that armed services on many occasions in many states elected instead to take the initiative. The various reasons behind military coups have already been discussed and will not be repeated here, except to make the point that (as E. Be'eri states in his *Army Officers in Arab Politics and Society*, and which R. McKinlay and A. Cohan endorse in their study 'Military coups, military regimes and social change') military coups are not uniform, and their outcomes are very varied and complex. As a generalization, however, they provide figures that show that two-thirds of the world's military coups lead to a replacement of a one civilian government with another one; only seldom do armed services replace a civilian government with a military one.

The significance of a military coup in Third World states varies in importance according to the culture of the society. Dankwart Rustow, for example, played down notions of political culture having much relevance in the Arab world. In his 'Military in the Middle East', he noted that 'the regime's traditional culture rests upon a religion that accords great prestige and legitimacy to the military ... It is clear that the prominent and decisive role of the military on the current Middle Eastern scene is not a momentary lapse from normal constitutional practice, but conforms to ample historical precedent.' A similar point was made about Latin America in Edwin Liewen's *Military and Politics in Latin America*, where the frequence of military coups by armed services 'at large' caused the introduction of a 'perpetual ricorso', one with its own vocabulary of military intervention.

The question of when armed services are likely to effect a coup has exercised many people, not least the leaders of states and international groups which consider investing in them. There are no hard and fast rules, though some indicators might be suggested. Probably the best of all is precedent: when states have experienced a military coup in the past, the likelihood of there being a repeat, all things being equal, increases. At least the statistics suggest that this is the case, though the figures are skewed heavily by the Latin American experience which accounts for most pre-war and almost half of all post-war coups. E. Luttwark in his *Coup d'Etat* places economic backwardness at the top of the scale. Political independence, and a domestic political vaccuum are also significant. C. Welch in *Soldier and State in Africa* enlarges on this list, and points to other considerations such as the declining prestige of politicians and political parties, schisms amongst government leaders, external interference, contagion from military coups in other states, economic malaise, social antagonisms, political corruption and inefficiency in the government and bureaucracy, and the personal political ambitions of senior armed servicemen.

Christopher Clapham's *Third World Politics* and Gavin Kennedy's *The Military in the Third World* both emphasize the concept of legitimacy as holding the clue to why military coups happen. To Clapham, legitimacy is linked to the centrality of the state; where the state is both legitimate and powerful, control over it by any external agency 'becomes extremely difficult, and a military coup represents the ultimate refinement of the process by which the state is taken over by its own servants'. Kennedy's approach is more direct: the less legitimate a government becomes, the higher the propensity for it to experience a military coup. 'Military intervention', he says, 'is a sign of elite incohesion'. In other words, where there is incompetence, weakness in government, or a political vacuum, there is likely to be instability and loss of popular support. This is followed by a military coup. What neither adequately explains is the distinction between the lack of legitimacy of the political system (to which Finer referred in his concept of political cultures) and the lack of popular support for a government because it is trying to force through unpopular policies.

Two issues remain: the first is the performance of military regimes; and the second is the process of demilitarization. It is generally assumed that a military coup in Third World states is an unwelcome and traumatic experience. Invariably the opposite is the case, except in those instances where the ethnic composition of the military leads to discrimination and persecution of other minority groups. For the most part, armed services take over government at a time of domestic crisis, internal instability or social breakdown. Often the circumstances that prompt military intervention are not caused by internal factors at all, but by a national economic decline and subsequent financial difficulty consequent upon major shifts in the world economy over which the country has no control or influence. Because of their low levels of technical expertise, few – if any – Third World states, by definition, have reserves. Dependent on a limited range of primary agricultural products, they are always extremely vulnerable, and their domestic economic equilibrium can be easily upset with disproportionately far-reaching consequences for the population as a whole. The circumstances, for example, that brought Flight Lieutenant Jerry Rawlings to power after a military coup had their origins in Ghana's economic vulnerability and dependence on one staple crop, cocoa. While his charisma and personality might be sufficient to carry internal popular support for some time after he took over the government, he had only a limited number of options open to persuade other world states to recognize the long-term economic viability of his country.

One common pattern of behaviour of almost all armed service leaders when they lead a coup, is to declare that their action was taken 'in the national interest'. This somewhat ill-defined motive is more often than not supplemented with some reference to an intention to 'return to barracks' at an early opportunity, as and when the situation that precipitated the coup in the first place is resolved to their own or the population's satisfaction. These assertions interested A. Bebler, and he put them to the test in four African states, Ghana, Dahomey, Sierra Leone and Mali, which he analysed in his *Military Rule in Africa*. His findings were what might have been expected: that the causes of the coups were clearly the deteriorating socio-economic and political conditions which necessitated drastic, decisive, and swift remedial action. From the evidence of the behaviour of the subsequent military regimes, however, the new military–political leaders could scarcely have been considered the 'selfless patriots and modernizers' they, by and large, considered themselves to be.

Nigeria is a particularly interesting case of the performance of a military regime. Since 1966 a succession of Nigerian military governments (Gowon, Ironsi, Muritala Muhammed, Muhammadu Buhari, and Ibrahim Babangida) have repeatedly asserted that their policy was to restore parliamentary democracy and civil government; Muritala Muhammed even went so far as to specify the date when this was to occur, only to rescind his decision on more than one occasion as the time drew nearer. A period of civil government, that of Alhaji Shagari between 1979 and 1983, only led to another military coup and further declaration of interest to restore civilian rule, a period optimistically analysed by Bayo Adekson in *Nigeria in Search of a Stable Civil–Military System*. To date, good intentions to restore civil rule and stable democratic institutions have not been translated into positive results. By and large, the performances of military regimes have fallen far short of their confident declarations upon assuming authority. Bebler

205

contended that this poor record arose because their own interests took precedence over their declared motives. A more charitable interpretation might be that coup leaders tended to be over-sanguine about their ability not only to run their country efficiently and effectively, but also simultaneously to accelerate the development and modernization process. More realism about the task they assumed for themselves might have been more appropriate; at least it would have reduced the tendency for them to be judged in the light of their own somewhat extravagant declared intentions. To be yet more charitable, the pressures on military leaders on intervening in government, first to curry favour with their population, and then with the international community – a much more difficult task – are immense. The search for legitimacy is a crucial one, for which expressions of patriotic and constructive 'good intent' are essential.

From the evidence of most African states, and Bebler's four in particular, the record of Third World military governments in solving fundamental economic, social and political problems has not been impressive. One explanation is that armed servicemen lack the political skills and necessary aptitude to complete their task. It is an explanation that carries considerable credibility, partly because armed services, no more than previous civilian governments, were not up to the task (as E. Feit explained in his study *Armed Bureaucrats*) and partly because of the enormity and intractibility of the problems with which they usually have had to contend. It should be remembered also that they have to start to govern with the double handicap of initial resistance to any *de facto* regime established by force, and of a state of internal crisis – possibly even social and economic breakdown. Armed services, on taking power in Third World states, are faced with a 'no win' situation. Nevertheless, it is surprising not only how often they do succeed, but also that they do sufficiently well compared with the record of civilian governments to draw the conclusion that military rule might be in many instances the most appropriate form of government for states seeking rapid development and modernization.

Samuel Finer considered the problem of military regimes 22 years after his examination of military intervention in a paper entitled 'The morphology of military regimes' included in R. Kolkowicz and A. Korbruski's *Soldiers, Peasants and Bureacracies,* and suggested that not all military regimes are necessarily what they seem. Indeed, he concluded that military regimes exhibit as much diversity among themselves as civilian regimes. Many, for example, were 'military supportive' regimes, others 'indirect military regimes', whilst the remainder, 29, according to Finer in 1982, could be classed *prima facie* as 'military regimes, proper'. Of this last category, 15 were African states, seven Latin American, five Middle Eastern and the remaining two were Asian. According to the composition of military governments, the extent to which civilian bureaucratic and legislatures become involved in the policy decision making process, and the degree to which the military have control over local and central bureaucracies, it is then possible to talk either of a military regime, a military government or a military dictatorship. Depending on the particular mixture of these variables, so the ease with which the military can be persuaded, or are likely to volunteer to, give up the reins of government and political power will differ.

To some extent the work of R. McKinlay and A. Cohan confirmed Finer's proposition but refuted Bebler's argument that military regimes prosecute their own interests when enjoying political authority. In their article 'Military coups, military regimes and social change', they demonstrated that according to such criteria as economic growth, social welfare spending, and defence spending, military governments fare very well. In fact they usually do better than civilian regimes. Furthermore, on average, 48 per cent of military regimes lasted less than two years, 31 per cent less than five, and only 21 per cent of military governments survived beyond five years. More significantly, they demonstrated that 82 per cent of all military regimes voluntarily terminated themselves, though what was meant by 'termination' was never made clear. Finer's classification could well be relevant here: by pointing out that what was a military dictatorship could be converted into an indirectly military supported regime, where the armed services continued to exercise power and influence without actually holding office.

The critical question, however, is the problem of 'demilitarization'; that is to say, the restoration of true civilian government and representative democracy. The issue was addressed by C. Clapham and G. Philip's edited volume, *The Political Dilemmas of Military Regimes*. They arrived at the overall conclusion that there is no simple solution between the options of institutionalizing the military regime or demilitarizing. Much, they considered, depended on the support the military and armed services received while in power, external considerations, and the degree to which the state administrative machinery held up under their governance. This largely conformed with the conventional wisdom first articulated in an Institute of Commonwealth Studies collection of papers on the *Politics of Demilitarization*, namely that the problems of getting the armed services out of politics, or the armed services getting themselves out, depended on the reasons why they became involved to the degree that they did in the first place.

There is no hard and fast prescription as to how this can be done; this points to the inevitable, but perhaps necessary methodological conclusion, that there are so many variables to consider that to make any sense, every case should be looked at *sui generis*. But one obvious point should be made: once the armed services have intervened, and have gained experience of government, the precedent has been established. In Latin America it has even become absorbed into the political process, with the whole gamut of comings and goings by quasi-military regimes, quasi-civilian regimes, indirect military regimes, and so on – via such tortuous procedures as: *derrocamiento; displazar de poder; inquilab; golpe de estado;* and *pronunciamento.*

In the final count, demilitarization, that is to say the disengagement of the armed services from exercising political authority, is achieved only when the successor regime 'neither needs the military, nor is needed by it', to use Samuel Finer's conclusion in his paper, 'Military disengagement from politics'. But herein lies yet another dilemma: as was demonstrated in Chapter 5, armed services are always involved in politics, and are more so in Third World states where their internal contribution to the development and modernizing process is crucial. To talk of 'disengagement', or even 'demilitarization', is misleading, except in so much as these terms reflect the passing over of the formal reins of authority to a civilian body.

Before handing over formal power, armed services officers with experience of government have to be satisfied that: the state of the country is stable; its prospects for continuing growth, development and modernization are good; the incoming civilian regime has the experience, the competence and popular support to govern effectively and efficiently; any new civilian regime is adequately protected against internal dysfunction or administrative breakdown; the country is adequately protected from external political, economic or military interference; their own conception of the 'national interest' is generally shared by the incoming regime; and their own material interests will be adequately met under the new administration. These are stringent conditions; but they go some way to explaining why many Third World states, after a military coup, have never subsequently been able to divest themselves of a significant degree of armed service participation in their central policy making process.

The most frequent course of action taken by military regimes is not to withdraw from politics and government and return totally to their barracks, their job done, but either to turn the nature of the regime into

208

a military-dependent one, or to 'civilianize' themselves, in much the way of Egypt's Colonel Nasser, Sudan's President Nimeri, Iraq's President Hussein, Libya's President Mu'ammar al-Qadhafi or Algeria's President Boumédienne. The extent to which military leaders have succeeded in divesting themselves of their military background, or, conversely, in assuming the mantle of a civilian leader convincingly, is highly debatable, not least because they have to recognize that even if they do not need the support of the armed services to implement their policies, they nonetheless cannot achieve anything if their armed services should choose to put up any opposition.

Returning to the warnings outlined at the beginning of this chapter, the cultural diversity and infinite variety of the Third World states of Africa, Latin America, Asia and the Middle East make it almost impossible to make any general statement or arrive at any wholly satisfactory overall conclusion. The exception will always disprove the rule. However, there are over 100 nation-states that fall within the general Third World category, each struggling, in a harsh and unsympathetic international environment, to develop and modernize. Their goal is that, in time, they might enjoy some of the standards of living which the First World has come to take for granted. In that struggle, their armed services have assumed an important, sometimes central role, largely by dint of the functional and organizational strengths they possess in contrast with other civil institutions and organizations. It is this contract that separates the two worlds; and it explains why, for the student of armed services and society, assumptions made about the advanced nations should not be carried over to studies of the Third World.

Postscript

If this book has achieved its purpose those who have read it will be persuaded first to address contemporary defence and security problems both in their own countries and in others, and then to look beyond them to the relationships between armed services and society. It has been the contention that it is in those relationships that strategic and defence problems originate, and it is only in these relationships that explanations and solutions are likely to be found. But to understand these relationships, some background to the salient variables that shape them must be acquired. This was the primary purpose of this book.

Without rehearsing the content of the book a second time, we might recall that technique of lecturing much recommended by the armed services themselves: say what you are going to do, do it, and then say what you have just done. With three attempts at doing the same thing, the message should, eventually, get across! After clarifying some of the terms used, this book has tried to look at the dominant, functional characteristics of armed services, and then at those aspects of society that impinge most on the character, style, role and nature of a nation's armed services. Both were examined independently, even though they are not mutually exclusive. Their interdependence was demonstrated in the number of theories of civil–military relations developed over the past 25 years, though it has been stressed that each of these theories tended to address a specific civil–military relations issue, rather than look at the nature of the civil–military relationship as a whole.

The most common issue to have exercised students of civil–military relations is that of military intervention in politics. Aside from the obvious point that intervention is more a matter of concern for liberal democratic societies than totalitarian ones, it has been an issue that has given a wrong perspective on civil–military relationships. More significant would be an acceptance of the constant involvement of armed services in government policy making; and although this influence has been exercised chiefly in defence and security matters, the complex and encompassing nature of modern warfare has determined that armed services' influence has spilled over into almost all other spheres of government concern. Chapter 5 considered the nature of this involvement, what motivates it, and the forms in which it becomes manifest. This, however, was only partial theory, addressing only one specific civil–military relations problem. An overarching theory is provided in the following chapter which uses as its organizing framework the concept of national security.

The remainder of the book looks at particular issues which affect relations between armed services and society, first in advanced industrial and then in Third World states. Chapter 7 considers public accountability and conscientious objection, chosen because they are concepts which lie at the very heart of liberal democracy – the latter because it is the ultimate assertion of freedom not to have to comply with state law if it runs contrary to one's conscience and fundamental beliefs, and the former because without it, especially in the security field, there is no protection against autocratic and arbitrary government. Chapter 8 considers the concept of the military–industrial complex, a term used to encapture the coalescence of interest and power exercised by a particular segment of advanced industrial societies which not only bears many hallmarks of undemocratic processes, but also may artificially stimulate defence expenditure and international tensions, motivated by reasons of self-interest. The chapter ends on a structural note, that of the central organization of defence, since it is here, within the structure of government, that armed services and their political masters meet face to face to determine policy, priority and prerequisites. The way they organize their business is the essence of civil–military relationships.

The final chapter is concerned with the specific civil–military problems of Third World states. Numerically these states form the largest group in the world, though not in terms of international military power and capability or economic capacity. Third World states come in many guises, and generalizations are difficult to sustain. However, some general observations are possible, the most important of which is the essentially domestic orientation of Third World armies – few have navies or airforces of any size or significance. This internal focus, coupled with the problem these states face – many only having gained independence in the past 25 years – to develop socially and economically, and 'modernize', has not only drawn their armed services deeply into domestic political and social affairs but also, frequently, left them with the responsibility of forming the government and the task of administering the state administrative machinery.

It is to be hoped that the chapters speak for themselves and furthermore, will then help to make the right connections between theory, method and analysis. But the content of the book is really offered as a possible way forward: it provides a means with which case studies, like that of the military–industrial complexes, or of a central defence administrative reform, can be subjected to rigorous analysis. The world of defence and security has never changed so rapidly as it has during the past quarter of a century, and evidence points to the trend accelerating. The student of armed services and society relationships is going to have a hard, but highly rewarding and immensely relevant, time ahead. The sorts of issues that will have to be dealt with in the advanced industrial states are those which will arise as a consequence of the technological revolution in modern weaponry, with its new products, new suppliers and extended military strategic and tactical performance.

As for the future, many new problems and issues are on the horizon; many are already with us. In the advanced societies, for example, the successful assertion of individual and civil rights has raised the expectations of women, not merely as servicemen's wives wishing for their own careers, but more especially in respect of their inalienable right to serve as full members of armed services with equal opportunity to all roles, combat or non-combat. Emerging technologies are making new demands on the skills and qualifications of servicemen, and armed services are having to compete with other occupations for suitable men and women in a labour market that itself is rapidly declining in size following demographic decreases. Attitudes are also changing to the conditions of service for servicemen and the more traditional approaches to discipline, not least among conscripts. But most interesting of all is the trend towards the internationalization of armed forces; here, the pendulum would have appeared to have swung back towards the time of the 1950s, when the European Defence Force was in full debate; and of the late 1960s, when there was talk of integrating certain units within the NATO alliance.

Glasnost and *Perestroika* are two terms about which we in the West still know very little; but from informed guesses of what they really mean, the Soviet and Warsaw Pact armed forces are likely to be affected significantly. As the process of arms control gathers momentum – assuming that the INF is the first of many such agreements – the forces of East and West will have to address a period of change in their respective armed services' composition and, moreover, their organization. If reports are correct that the American SDI programme has a Soviet equivalent, both superpowers will have to accommodate a new form of science–military–technological complex, far more influential and powerful than the old military–industrial complex.

Over the past 20 years, the armed services of industrial states have had to come to terms with an exponential increase in weapons costs. This has had the effect of reducing the numbers of professional armed servicemen, altering the ratio of combat forces to logistic support units, and forcing some states to review their defence and security policies. The knock-on effect of defence costs has now begun to reach the Third World States, suggesting that they, in turn, will have to consider seriously whether or not they should continue to procure expensive weapons. A market in secondhand, refurbished first generation equipment would appear to be emerging. Meanwhile, their task of political and economic modernization and development continues. As they fall further behind the advanced nations, relatively, and many of the immediate problems of poverty and unemployment continue, defence issues will likely assume a different perspective.

There was great hope in the 1950s that following the introduction of nuclear weapons and the completion of the process of decolonization, international wars would become fewer, and even cease altogether. Whilst a major war between the advanced nations seems to have been successfully deterred, their involvement in wars in the Third World has continued unabated. At the time of writing, massive fleets sail off the Iranian coast in the Persian Gulf, the USSR is still fighting and losing men in Afghanistan after five years, the USA is embroiled in Nicaragua, Cuba in Angola, and many states, by proxy, in the Iran–Iraq war. The demand for armed services and defence equipment does not seem to have diminished at all, despite those earlier hopes; no immediate prospect that the world is likely to be a safer place is in prospect. Indeed, as low-intensity operations, state-sponsored terrorism, and the 'fourth dimension of war' assume greater importance, the old 'security dilemma' seems as alive and intractable as ever.

The study of armed services and society relations has indeed much still to address: perhaps more than ever before. When a country like Fiji, which has epitomized all that is peaceful, benign and sensible about life, is confronted with a military coup, and drugs, the military and covert dealings are proving to be the norm in Central America, we know there is much more to be done, and still more to be properly understood.

Bibliography

Note: Places of publication are given only for works published outside the United Kingdom

1 Introduction: Questions and Assumptions

ANDRESKI, S., *Military Organisation and Society* (2nd edn, 1968)

Armed Forces and Society, Quarterly Journal of the Inter University Seminar on Armed Forces and Society

ENLOE, C., *Ethnic Soldiers* (Pelican Books edn, 1980)

FINER, S. E., *The Man on Horseback* (1962)

HUNTINGTON, S. P., *The Soldier and the State: The Theory and Politics of Civil–Military Relations* (Cambridge, Mass. and London, 1957)

JANOWITZ, M., *The Professional Soldier* (New York, 1960)

LANG, K., *Military Institutions and the Study of War* (Beverly Hills, 1966)

MILLS, C. W., *The Power Elite* (New York, 1956)

NISBET, R. A., *The Social Philosophers: Community and Conflict in Western Thought* (1976)

PRESTON, R. *et al.*, *Men in Arms* (1962)

2 Armed Services: the Organizational Dimension

ABRAHAMSSON, B., *Military Professionalization and Political Power* (Beverly Hills, 1972)

ETZIONI, A., *A Comparative Analysis of Complex Organizations* (New York, 1961)

FINER, S. E., *The Man on Horseback* (1962)

GREENWOOD, 'Attributes of a profession', *Social Work*, 2 (July 1967), 44–55.

HUNTINGTON, S. P., *The Soldier and the State: The Theory and Politics of Civil–Military Relations* (Cambridge, Mass. and London, 1957)

JANOWITZ, M., *The Professional Soldier* (New York, 1960)

3 The Societal Dimension

ABRAHAMSSON, B., *Military Professionalization and Political Power* (Beverly Hills, 1972)
ANDRESKI, S., *Military Organisation and Society* (2nd edn, 1968)
BARNETT, C., *Britain and Her Army* (1970)
BARON, P. AND SWEEZEY, F., *Monopoly Capitalism* (New York, 1966)
BRERETON, J. M., *The British Soldier* (1986)
BURNHAM, J., *The Managerial Revolution* (1942)
COOKE, F., *The Warfare State* (1963)
DJILAS, M., *The New Class and Society* (The Hague, 1967)
DOMHOFF, W., *Who Rules America?* (Englewood Cliffs, 1967)
ELLIS, J., *The Social History of the Machine Gun* (1975)
FULLER, J. F. C., *Armaments and History* (New York, 1945)
GALBRAITH, J. K., *The New Industrial State* (New York, 1971)
HACKETT, J., *The Profession of Arms* (1984)
JANOWITZ, M., *The New Military* (New York, 1964)
KAUFMAN, R., *War Profiteers* (New York, 1961)
KIDRON, M., *Western Capitalism since the War* (1972)
LEIBKNECHT, K., *Militarism, Anti-Militarism* (1917)
LUNDBERG, F., *The Rich and the Super Rich* (New York, 1968)
MARWICK, A., *The Deluge* (1981)
MELMAN, S., *Pentagon Capitalism* (New York, 1970)
MICHELS, R., *Political Parties* (Glencoe, Ill., 1958)
The Military Balance, International Institute for Strategic Studies (annual)
MILLS, C. W., *The Power Elite* (New York, 1956)
MOSCA, G., *The Ruling Class* (ed. Livingstone) (New York, 1939)
MUMFORD, L., *Technics and Civilization* (1934)
NEF, J., *War and Human Progress* (New York, 1963)
NISBET, R. A., *The Social Philosophers: Community and Conflict in Western Thought* (1976)
PARETO, V., *Sociological Writings*, selected and introduced by S. E. Finer (London and New York, 1966)
PEARTON, M., *The Knowledgeable State: Diplomacy, War and Technology since 1830* (1982)
PERLO, V., *Militarism and Industry* (New York, 1963)
TOYNBEE, A., *War and Civilization* (1951)
VAGTS, A., *A History of Militarism* (New York, 1959)

4 Approaches to the Study of Armed Services and Society

ABRAHAMSSON, B., *Military Professionalization and Political Power* (Beverly Hills, 1972)
ANDRESKI, S., *Military Organisation and Society* (2nd edn, 1968)
FELD, M., 'A typology of military organisations', *Public Policy*, 7, 3–40
FINER, S., *The Man on Horseback* (1962)

GERMANI, G. AND SILVERT, K., 'Politics, social structure and intervention in Latin America', in W. MacWilliams (ed.), *Garrisons and Governments* (San Francisco, 1967)

GOFFMAN, E., *Asylums* (1968)

HUNTINGTON, S., *The Soldier and the State: The Theory and Politics of Civil–Military Relations* (Cambridge, Mass. and London, 1957)

KOLKOWICZ, R. AND KORBOUSKY, A., *Soldiers, Peasants and Bureaucrats* (1982)

JANOWITZ, M., *The Professional Soldier* (New York, 1960)

LASSWELL, H., 'The garrison states', *American Journal of Sociology*, 46 (1941), 455–68

LASSWELL, H., *National Security and Individual Freedom* (New York, 1950)

LUCKHAM, A. R., 'A comparative typology of civil–military relations', *Government and Opposition* (Winter 1971), 5–35

MACWILLIAMS, W., *Garrisons and Governments* (San Francisco, 1967)

MARWICK, A., *Women at War* (1977)

MILLIS, W., *Arms and Men* (New York, 1958)

MILLS, C. W., *The Power Elite* (New York, 1956)

PERLMUTTER, A., *Military and Politics in Modern Times* (New Haven, 1977)

RAPPAPORT, D., 'Comparative civil–military types', in S. P. Huntington, *Changing Patterns of Military Politics* (New York, 1962)

WELCH, C. AND SMITH, A., *Military Role and Rule* (Belmont, 1974)

5 Military Involvement in Politics

DOORN, J. VAN AND HARRIES-JENKINS, G. (eds), *The Military and the Problem of Legitimacy* (1976)

ECKSTEIN, H., *Internal War* (New York, 1964)

ECKSTEIN, H. AND GURR, T., *Patterns of Authority* (1975)

FINER, S., *The Man on Horseback* (1962)

FORSYTH, F., *The Dogs of War* (1974)

LUTTWAK, E., *Coup d'État* (1968)

THOMPSON, W. R., *The Grievances of Coup Makers* (Beverly Hills, 1973)

6 Towards a Theory of Civil–Military Relations

ACKROYD, C., MARGOLIS, K., ROSENHEAD, J. AND SHALLIS, T., *The Technology of Political Control* (1972)

BEVERIDGE, LORD, *The Pillars of Security* (1943)

CAMPBELL, D., *The Secret Society* (forthcoming)

KAPLAN, M., *Systems Theory of International Relations* (New York, 1957)

WOLFERS, A., *Discord and Collaboration: Essays on International Politics* (Baltimore, 1962)

7 Issues in Civil–Military Relations

BLOCH, I., *The Future of War* (Boston, 1902)

FIELD, C., *Pacifism and Conscientious Objection* (1948)

216

Bibliography

FOOT, M. R. D., *Men in Uniform* (1961)

HOWARD, M., *Continental Commitment* (1978)

HUNTINGTON, S. P., *The Common Defense: Strategic Programs in National Politics* (New York, 1961)

KOLODZIEZ, E., *Making and Marketing Arms* (Princeton, NJ, 1987)

NATHAN, O. AND NORDEN, H. (eds), *Einstein on Peace* (New York, 1968)

NORMANTON, E. LESLIE, *Accountability and Audit of Governments* (1966)

PONTING, C., *The Right to Know* (1985)

SINGER, J., *Democracy and Disobedience* (1973)

SMITH, B. L. R. AND HAGUE, D. C. (eds), *The Dilemma of Accountability in Modern Government* (1971)

8 Armed Services and Society: Military–Industrial Complexes and Central Organizations of Defence

ARMACOST, M., *Politics of Weapons Innovation* (New York, 1969)

ART, R., DAVIS, V. AND HUNTINGTON, S., *Re-Organizing America's Defense* (Washington, 1985)

BARON, P. AND SWEEZEY, P., *Monopoly Capitalism* (New York, 1966)

BARRETT, A., *Re-Appraising Defense Organization* (Washington, 1983)

BEAUMONT, R. AND EDMONDS, M., *War in the Next Decade* (1974)

CHANTEBOUT, D., *L'Organisation générale de la défense nationale en France* (Paris, 1967)

CLARK, A. (ed.) *et al.*, *The Defense Reform Debate* (Baltimore, 1984)

DONOVAN, J., *Militarism, USA* (New York, 1970)

EDMONDS, M., *Central Organizations of Defence* (Boulder, Col., 1985)

ENGELBRECHT, A. C. AND HANIGHAN, F., *Merchants of Death* (New York, 1934)

FULBRIGHT, SENATOR W., *Pentagon Propaganda Machine* (New York, 1970)

GALBRAITH, J. K., *How to Control the Military* (New York, 1967)

GRAY, C., 'The organizational nexus', in Beaumont, R. and Edmonds, M. (eds), *War in the Next Decade* (1971)

HOWARD, M., *Soldiers and Governments* (1957)

HUNTINGTON, S. P., *The Common Defense: Strategic Programs in National Politics* (New York, 1961)

ILARI, V., *Le forze armante era politica e potere* (Florence, 1979)

JOHNSON, F., *Defence by Ministry* (1980)

KIDRON, M., *Western Capitalism since the War* (1972)

LAPP, R., *The Weapons Culture* (1974)

LUCAS, W. AND DAWSON, R., *The Organizational Politics of Defense* (Pittsburgh, 1974)

MELMAN, S., *Pentagon Capitalism* (New York, 1970)

MILLETT, A. R., *Re-Organization of the Joint Chiefs of Staff* (New York, 1987)

MILLS, C. W., *The Power Elite* (New York, 1956)

MOLLENHOFF, C., *The Pentagon* (New York, 1967)

MOSKOS, C., 'The theoretical antecedents of the military industrial complex, in Sarkesian, S. (ed.), *The Military Industrial Complex* (Beverly Hills, 1972)

Bibliography

NOEL-BAKER, P., *The Private Manufacture of Arms* (1938)
SHAW, G. B., *Major Barbara* (1905)
STEIN, H., *American Civil–Military Decisions* (Alabama, 1962)
SWOMLEY, J., *The Military Establishment* (Boston, 1964)
WALPUSKI, G. G. AND WOLF, D., *Einführung in die Sicherheitspolitik* (Munich, 1979)
YARMOLINSKY, A., *The Military Establishment* (New York, 1972)

9 Armed Services and Third World States

ADEKSON, B., *Nigeria in Search of a Stable Civil–Military System* (1981)
ALEXANDER, H. T., *African Tightrope* (1965)
ALMOND, G. AND COLEMAN, R., *The Politics of the Developing Areas* (Princeton, 1960)
Armament and Disarmament, Stockholm Institutional Peace Research Institute Yearbook (annual)
BAUER, P. T. AND YAMEY, B., *Economics of Underdeveloped Countries* (1957)
BEBLER, A., *Military Rule in Africa* (New York, 1973)
BE'ERI, E., *Army Officers in Arab Politics and Society* (1970)
CLAPHAM, C., *Third World Politics* (1985)
CLAPHAM, C. AND PHILIPS, G. (eds), *The Political Dilemmas of Military Regimes* (1984)
ENLOE, C., *Ethnic Soldiers* (1980)
FEIT, E., *Armed Bureaucrats* (Boston, 1973)
FINER, S., 'The morphology of military regimes', in Kolkowicz, R. and Korbruski, A. (eds), *Soldiers, Peasants and Bureaucracies* (1982)
GUTTERIDGE, W., *Military Institutions and Power in the New States* (1965)
HUNTER, G., *Modernizing Peasant Societies* (1969)
HUNTINGTON, S. P., *Political Order in Changing Societies* (New Haven, 1968)
JANOWITZ, M., *Military in the Political Development of New Nations* (Toronto, 1964)
JOHNSON, J., *The Military and Society in Latin America* (Stanford, 1964)
KALDOR, M. AND EIDE, A. (eds), *The World Military Order* (1979)
KENNEDY, G., *The Military in the Third World* (1974)
LEE, M., *African Armies and Civil Order* (1969)
LEVY, M., *Modernization and the Structure of Societies* (Princeton, 1963)
LIEWEN, E., *Military and Politics in Latin America* (New York, 1961)
LUTTWAK, E., *Coup d'État* (1968)
MCKAY, V., *African Diplomacy* (1966)
MCKINLAY, R. AND COHAN, A., 'Military coups, military regimes and social change', *American Political Science Review*, (1974)
The Military Balance, International Institute for Strategic Studies (annual)
PARKER, G., 'The role of the military in Indonesia', in Johnson, J. (ed.), *The Role of the Military in Underdeveloped Countries* (Princeton, 1962)
Politics of Demilitarization, Institute of Commonwealth Studies (1966)

PYE, L., 'Armies in the process of modernization', in Johnson, J. (ed.), *The Role of the Military in Underdeveloped Countries* (Princeton, 1962)

RUSTOW, D., 'Military in the Middle East', in Fisher, S., *Military in the Middle East* (Ohio, 1963)

SHILS, E., 'Political development in the New States', in Johnson, J. (ed.), *The Role of the Military in Underdeveloped Countries* (Princeton, 1962)

WELCH, C., *Soldier and State in Africa* (Evanston, 1970)

Index